MATERIAL WONDER

THE INTERIORS OF
FIONA LYNCH

MATERIAL

WONDER

THE INTERIORS OF
FIONA LYNCH

T&H

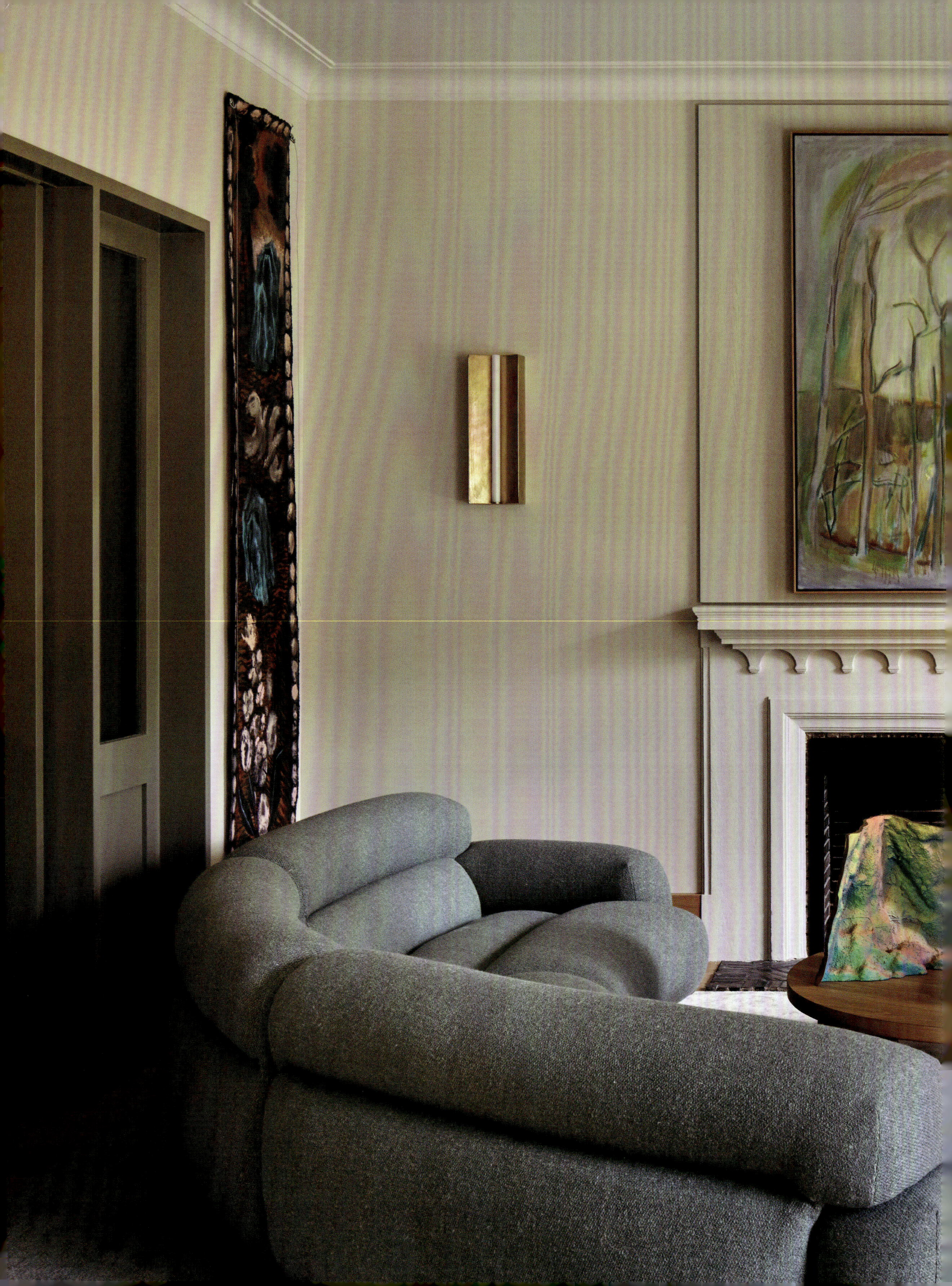

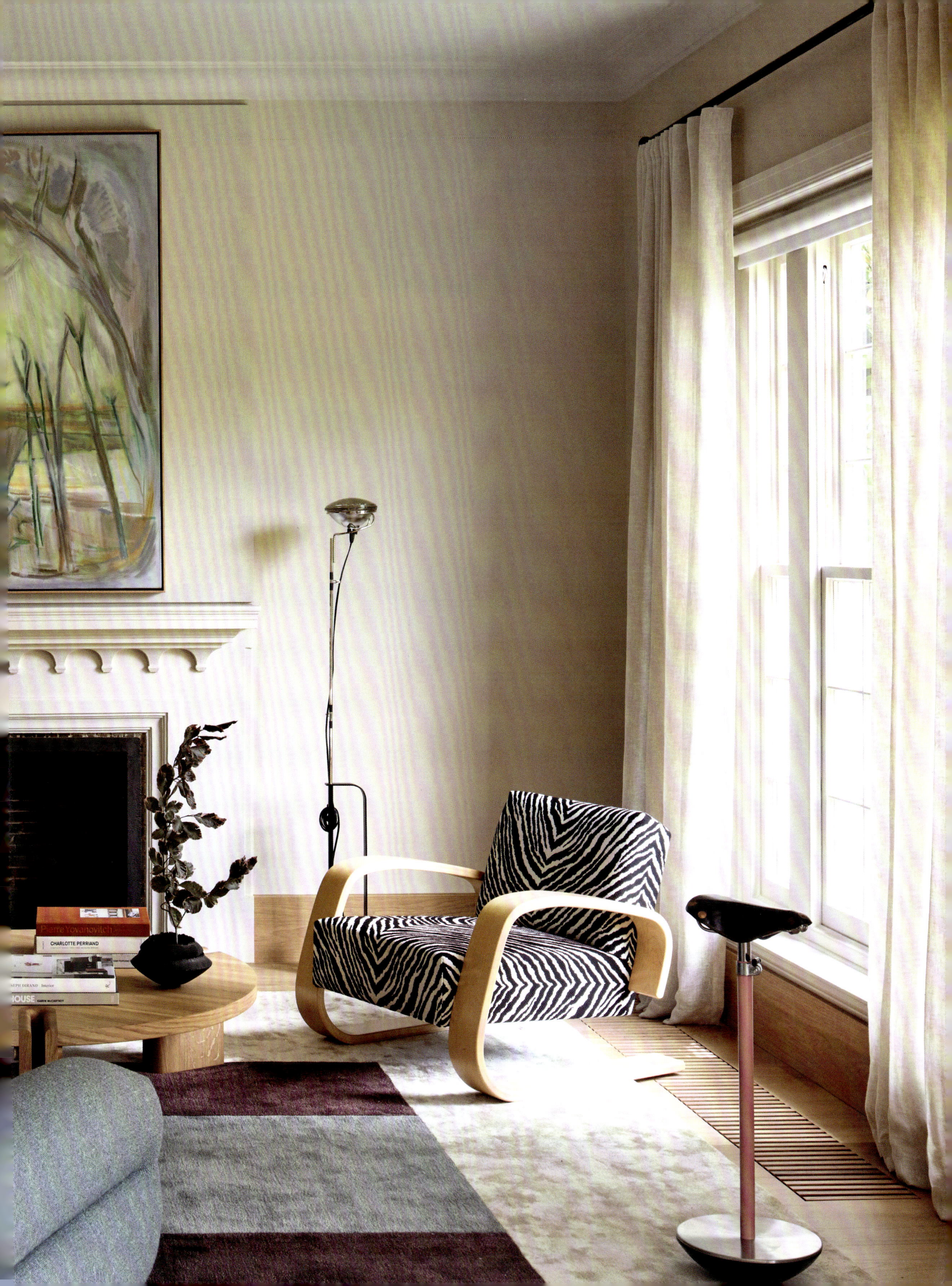

INTRODUCTION
11

STONE

25 Somerville House.
37 River House.
49 Auburn Residence.
61 Ottawa House.
75 Rose Bay House.
85 St Kilda Apartment.
95 GIANT STEPS

METAL

101 Melbourne Penthouse.
117 Fitzroy House.
131 Surry Hills House.
141 LEE MATHEWS

MATERIALS LIBRARY
234

PROJECT CREDITS
240

ACKNOWLEDGEMENTS
244

BIOGRAPHY
245

WOOD

- 147 Hill House.
- 161 South Yarra House.
- 169 Mosaic Garden House.
- 181 Elsternwick House.
- 189 ST. ALI & THE QUEEN
- 191 80 COLLINS

TEXTILE

- 197 Grace Park Residence.
- 207 Sorrento House.
- 217 Burnley House.
- 225 Paddington Terrace.
- 233 KILN, ACE HOTEL SYDNEY

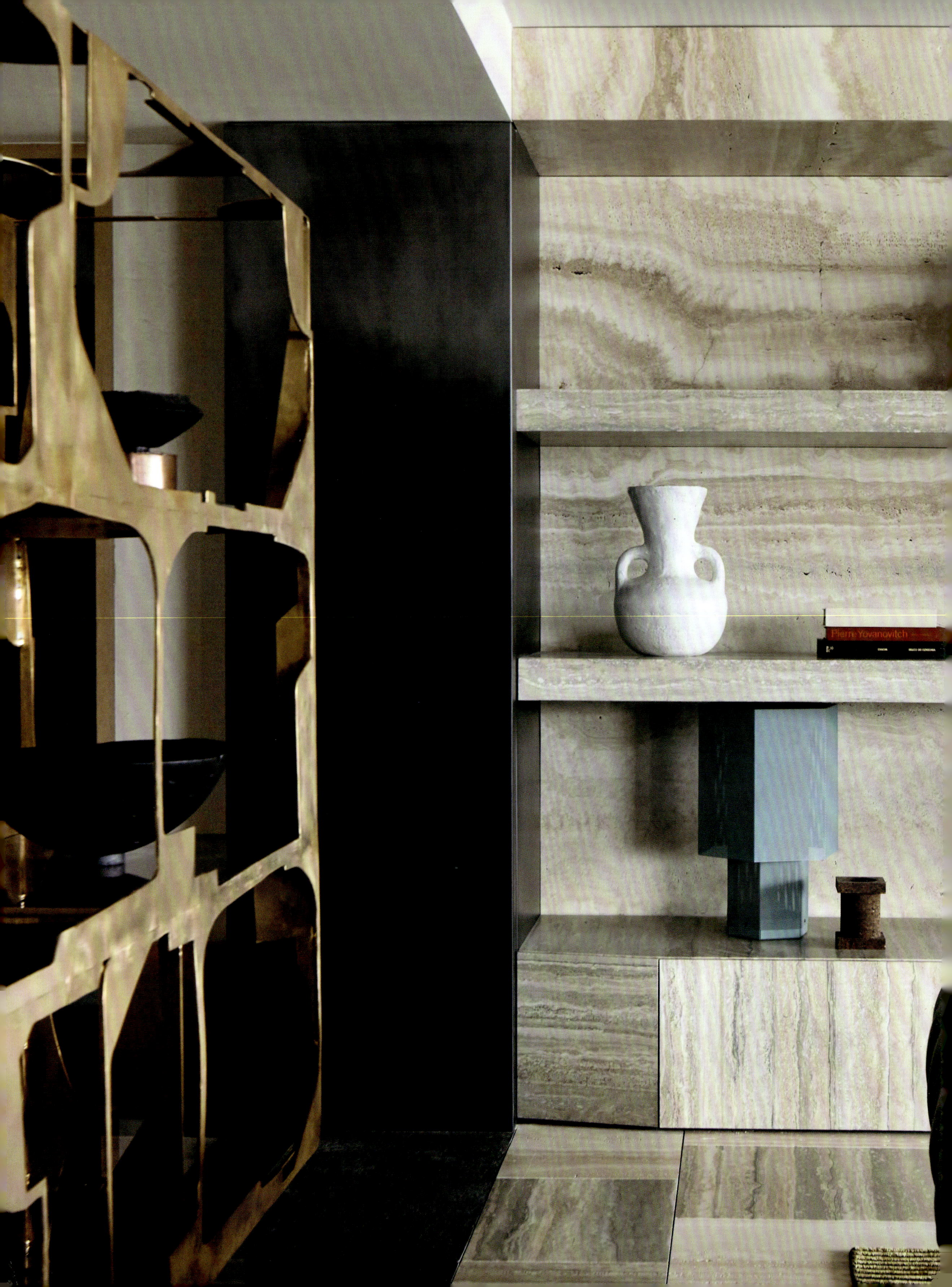
Pierre Yovanovitch

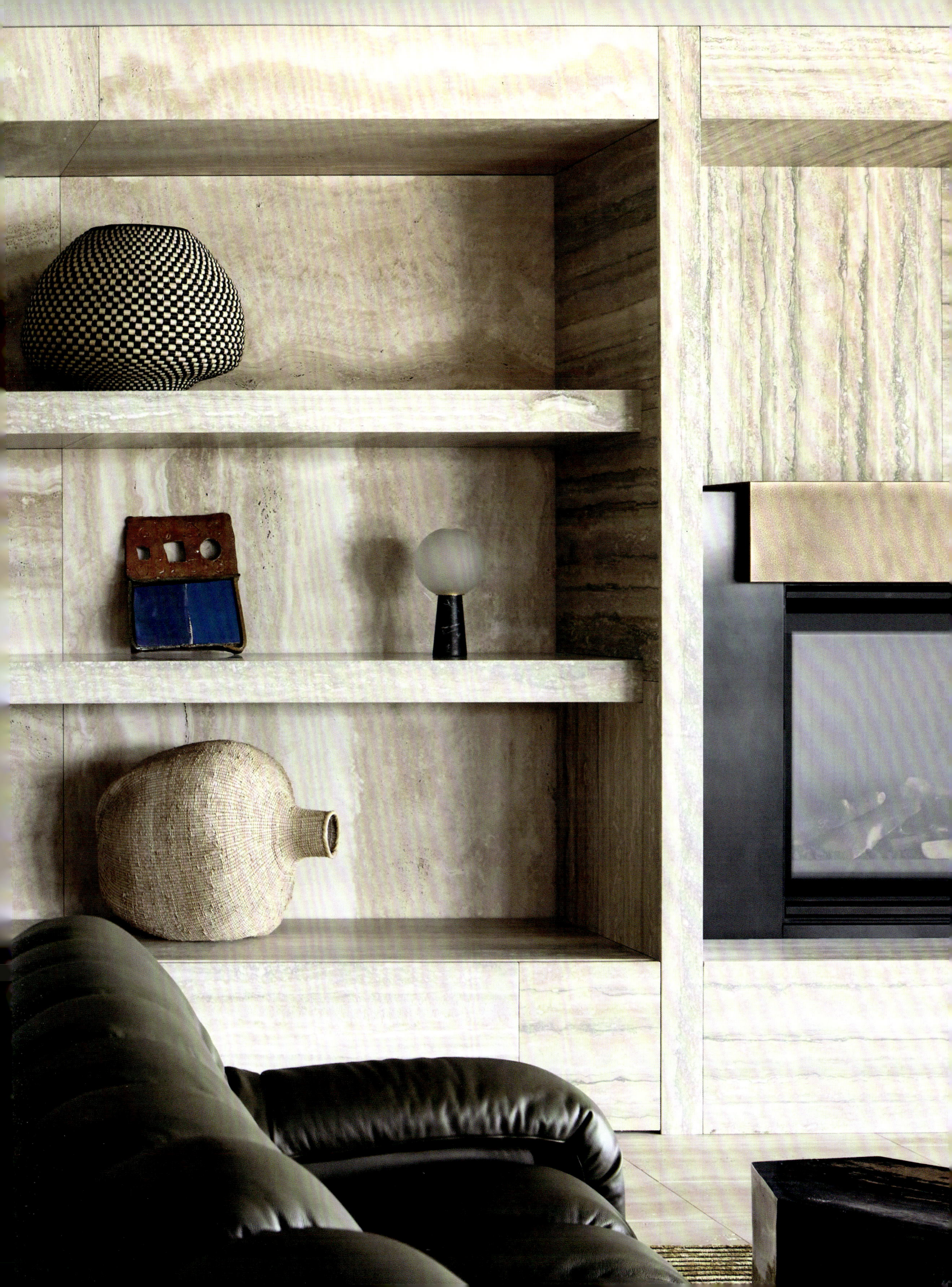

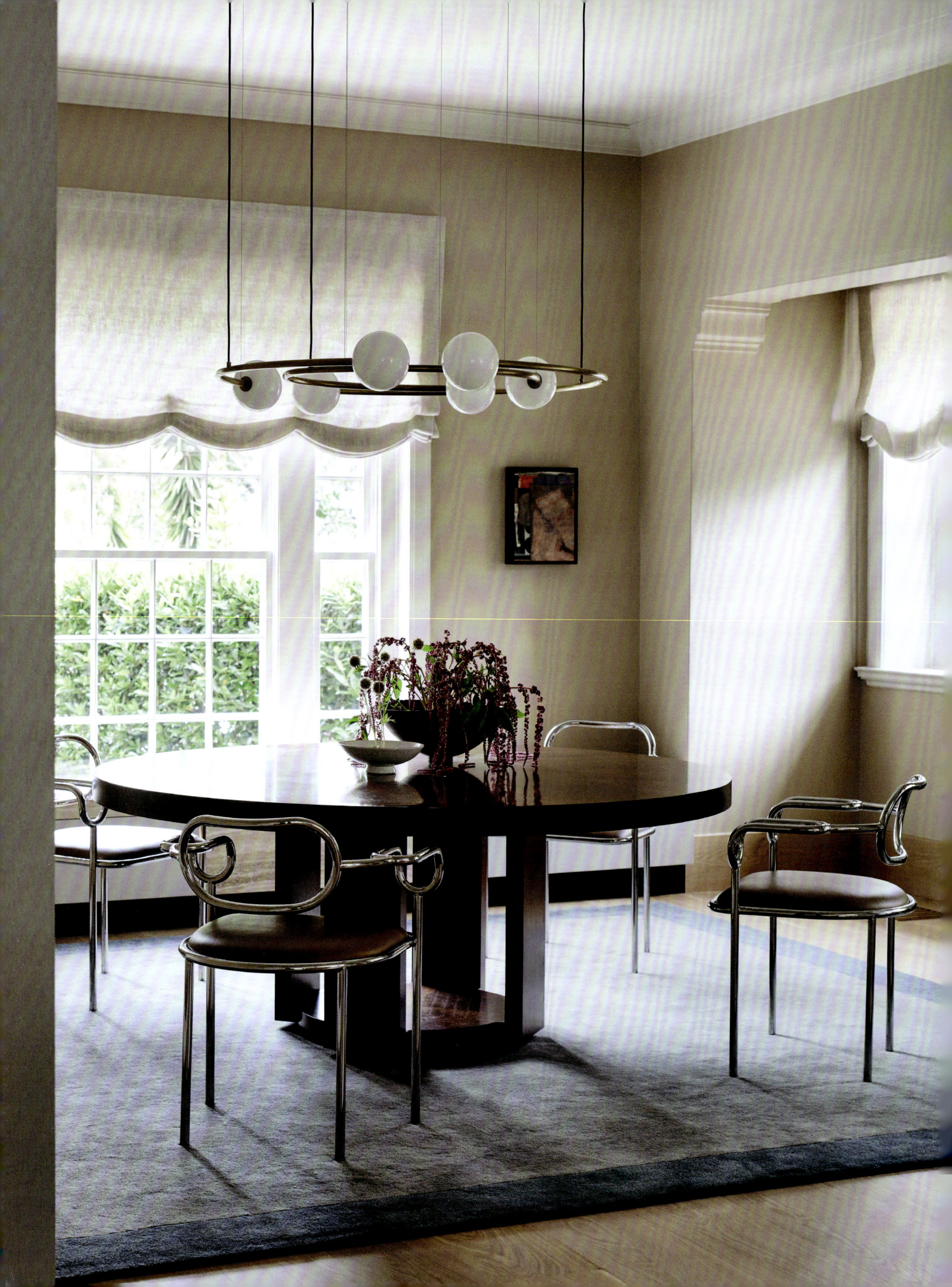

INTRODUCTION

From a young age I was acutely aware of materials and nature. I never imagined that this fascination would lead to a life exploring both in my design projects.

One of my earliest memories is sitting in the car as a kid looking out at the Australian landscape and being blown away by the changing terrain and kaleidoscope of colours. The characteristic hues and distinctive light have been etched into my memory, influencing the way I marry colours and textures.

1970s dreaming

My interest in materials and design really began with the homes I grew up in. We lived between two houses: one on the banks of the Yarra River near the city in Melbourne, and the other on a farm up in the mountains. The youngest of six kids, I didn't realise how privileged we were to spend time in both places.

I remember watching our farmhouse, an A-frame kit home, being assembled in one day. With two bedrooms, one bathroom and six children, the house was small and cosy – it felt like a tree house. I loved the exposed, chunky wooden rafters and the steeply pitched ceiling. My father expanded the house in the 1980s using recycled materials, wood panelling and amber-coloured glass salvaged from an old bank building. Looking back, he was incredibly inventive with the materials he found and transplanted into our home.

In contrast, my parents had renovated our Melbourne house in true 1970s style. There was white, red and green shag-pile carpet, textured woollen wallpaper, red felted walls, yellow laminate, stained olive-green oak joinery and beaten copper pendants. There was a warmth and richness to it, with layers of colour and texture.

My childhood and time spent in nature has shaped my design aesthetic and underpins my passion for natural materials and tones drawn from the colours of the landscape. On the farm, we were surrounded by scrappy bushland and scenic, mystical mountains. Big storms and winds would often sweep across the farm and at times it felt dangerous – especially when trying to sleep in our assembled-by-hand A-frame house. The farm machinery had patinaed metal and peeling paint from being out in the harsh summer sun and dramatic winter storms. The seasons felt intensified, but it was always picturesque, romantic and beautiful. →

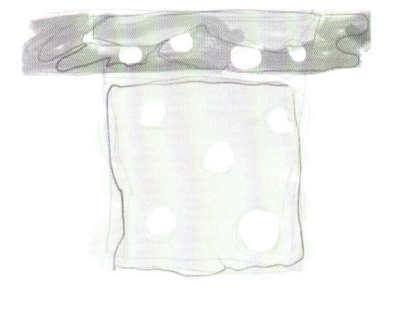

Cool culture

After finishing school, I studied fine art painting and later went on to study interior design. I spent eight years at university in the centre of Melbourne, when the city was undergoing a period of interesting change. (It was the free-spirited grunge era.) I would often walk the back streets, peeking into spaces where the roller door was up and discovering the most incredible things being made, from sculptures to paintings or ceramics.

Though I studied painting, there was nothing I loved more than exploring other artistic disciplines. I would visit the silversmiths, ceramicists and printmakers, then cross Swanston Street to see what was going on in the sculpture department. This budding creativity informed my love of materials.

Melbourne in the late 1990s was cool. A mood of change and reinvention was in the air. The times felt modern and forward-looking. Architecture, art and jewellery were minimal and considered, but, mostly, materials were being explored in totally new ways. In between lessons I would wander down to Flinders Lane, where the Adelphi Hotel had just been created from a converted warehouse, its traditional facade dressed in aluminium and steel blades painted in pale yellow. A glass-bottomed swimming pool jutted over the street. Anna Schwartz's eponymous gallery next door was wrapped in hand-finished aluminium. My attraction to aluminium was born out of these early experiences. There were cool fashion stores and cafes that resembled white cube art galleries. Crossley Street had Gallery Funaki, a place I loved to visit, and I would marvel at the intricacy and skill of contemporary jewellery makers. I still do.

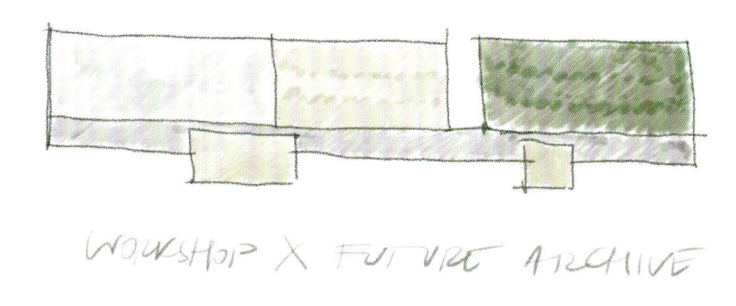

Left: Installation of folded papers and plastics during my final project studying fine art painting, 1995.

INTRODUCTION

Branching out

My first job in design was at a big commercial studio. I didn't always connect with the projects at this studio or the materials being used, which were slick, pressed and shiny. Even at that early stage, I imagined my future in design as being completely intertwined with art and the examination of alternative, less refined materials. However, I loved my time assisting Jenny Angel in the library where I created a catalogue of furniture and lighting to assist the designers on their projects. At this time, the internet was its early stages, and accessible websites were numbered.

Moving to Canberra to work with Romaldo 'Aldo' Giurgola really opened my mind to the possibilities of material exploration, especially as Aldo used a diversity of stones and timbers in his projects. Following this was time spent with John Wardle, a master craftsman of materials who is constantly challenging what is achievable. These experiences were deeply informative for my education and development. By the time I opened my own studio, my design aesthetic was forming and my practice direction was clear. It would encompass projects that combine art and elemental materials to create distinctive, refined spaces.

Travel also holds potent memories and possibilities for me. I have toured widely in the past fifteen years, often spending time in art galleries or the studios of much-admired makers gathering new ideas and challenging my understanding of materials. Two fundamental experiences I had were visiting the Noguchi Museum and their notable outdoor sculpture garden in New York, and seeing an exhibition of sculptor Rachel Whiteread's work in Rome. Both artists place great importance on materials in their work, whether stone, resin or paper. I try to bring the same uncompromising focus and passion to our studio practice: seeking innovative solutions that uphold the value of our work.

Discovering unfamiliar places and cultures, whether in Australia or overseas, opens the door to researching new materials. I find travel to be the best way to keep our work forward-looking; it helps me to understand our place in the global design world, and drives our practice to be resourceful and inventive. →

INTRODUCTION

The vessels above are made from locally sourced, reclaimed Monterey cypress wood. Following our 80 Collins commission project, I asked Makiko Ryujin (now a good friend and collaborator) to be a part of our first *Work Shop* exhibition in Collingwood. Hand-turned on a lathe and then burnt with a blow torch, Makiko's carefully crafted vessels are both tough and fragile at the same time.

The *Work Shop* exhibitions

In March 2019 I launched my inaugural exhibition *Work Shop* as part of the National Gallery of Victoria's (NGV) Melbourne Design Week. The exhibition is a showcase of experimental design, artworks and objects by Australian and international artists, artisans and designers that examines the dialogue between art and design. Informed by my fine art studies and background of artistic practice, it explores the creative dualism between artistic disciplines in response to a lack of public platforms, presenting them together in a non-hierarchical manner.

Given that so many of the interior projects I work on feature collaborations with artisans and artists for custom elements, the exhibition space (in our office annex) also embraces displays of early prototypes – the unfinished and undone – granting designers the opportunity to test ideas before proceeding into full production.

The 2019 exhibition showcased my original designs plus pieces by New York-based lighting designer Mary Wallis, Australian sculptor Makiko Ryujin, painter Jiaxin Nong and British porcelain artist Olivia Walker. The works investigated the tension between the constructed and deconstructed, the resolved and incomplete and the built and undone, encouraging viewers to discover beauty at all stages of creative evolution. →

Work Shop 4 was formed as part of the NGV's Melbourne Design Week 2020. I designed and curated an eclectic assemblage of artworks, objects and sculptural furnishings that reflected my studio's interest in technology and curiosity about the use of hand-crafted processes across multiple mediums and disciplines.

My interest in artistic collaboration – ever present in the studio's practice – underpinned the bespoke pieces I designed in collaboration with local craftspeople, including an aluminium cabinet handmade by Daniel Barbera – a functional meditation on consumption, given its single drawer and compact maple rail crafted by Ross Thompson. While aluminium is usually known for its slick machined veneer, here it was given a matte surface combined with Frank Stella-like chalk outlines for a hand-finished sensibility. I also co-designed a crumpled illuminated balloon of hand-sewn silk stiffened by acrylic paint in collaboration with archival seamstress Catherine Shannon. Tethered to both ceiling and floor, it was neither a lamp nor pendant light. Its sheer lunar force probed the precious and vernacular nature of materiality. The exhibition also included a curation of works by artists Rebecca Agnew and Jacopo Moschin, who explored photographic and digital mediums.

Since launching in 2019, each *Work Shop* exhibition has featured original designs and commissioned pieces, and included furnishings and ceramics. Some iterations have been co-created by myself and my team, while others have been guest curated by creatives. →

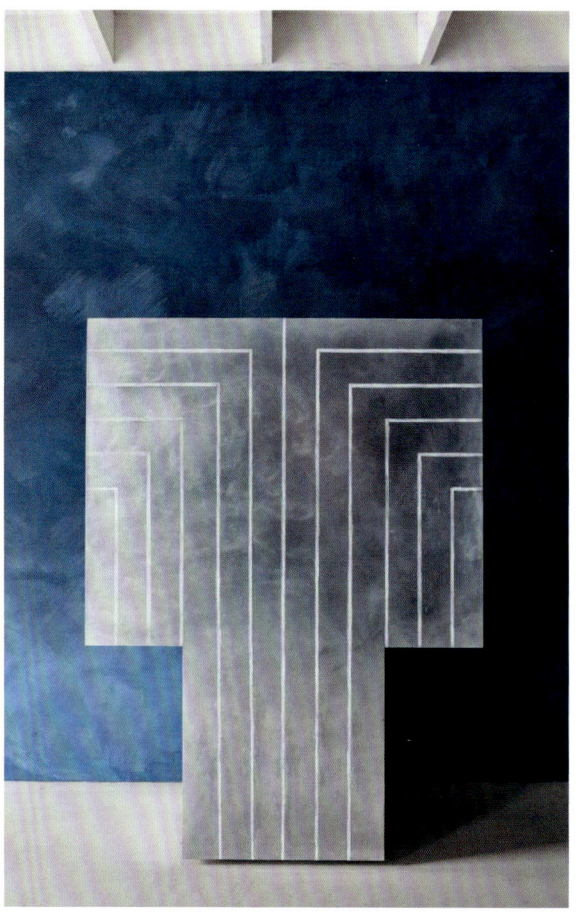

For *Work Shop 4* I had the idea to make a wardrobe out of hand-worked aluminium. Inspired by American painter Frank Stella, the line work on the back of the wardrobe is applied with a white crayon. Maple dowel with a finely turned end and chunky blocks line the base, and the overall shape took on the appearance of a kimono which was a lovely surprise. The Bauwerk blue painted wall was a deliberately vibrant and moody backdrop.

The power to transform

I have always been drawn to projects where there is an honesty and integrity to how the materials are expressed and assembled. Our projects are curated to explore materials and the ways in which they interact. It is always about the essential, and not overwhelming the dialogue between the materials.

My design approach is to focus initially on problem-solving and planning – researching an angle our studio can take for a project. Often I will go back through my image library to draw on places I have visited and seek out details or materials I have captured in photos. I create a collage of these images and then start sketching ideas for my team to explore.

I consider how we can investigate materiality and new techniques. For me this is an intuitive response to the site, my client and their brief. I will usually start with a broad approach to the inclusion of raw elements and then refine these to a few select materials.

Having worked through this process, it is then about feeling and connection: how will the client feel in the space? The mood that's created and the materials used influence the way a client responds to and connects with a space.

I find the most interesting use of materials transpires when they have been manipulated – usually by an artist or maker. The Lee Mathews store on James Street in Brisbane's Fortitude Valley was a pivotal project, in which the client and I were equally passionate about materials and art. The large-scale plaster work designed by Alana Wilson, which wraps around the change room, is an example of integrating art as part of the interior built form, rather than adding it later. This exemplifies the way I aspire to do all my projects, with art and design embedded.

The projects and case studies in these pages embody our practice's approach to design, using a palette of materials that are elemental and expressive. They demonstrate the way we respond to design challenges and collaborate with artists and makers to create mood and evoke feeling, whether for functional commercial installations or private residences.

Each of the key materials profiled – stone, metal, wood and textile – are used in each of our projects, usually in combination. I love the connection between these materials and how they relate to one another, coming together to create signature spaces that are luxurious, purposeful, innovative and pleasurable.

Understanding materials and how they affect our lives is a never-ending subject. As the design world focuses more closely on ways to source and repurpose materials, I feel we are on the brink of a new era where we will only be working with materials that are local or recycled. It's an exciting time to be on this journey.

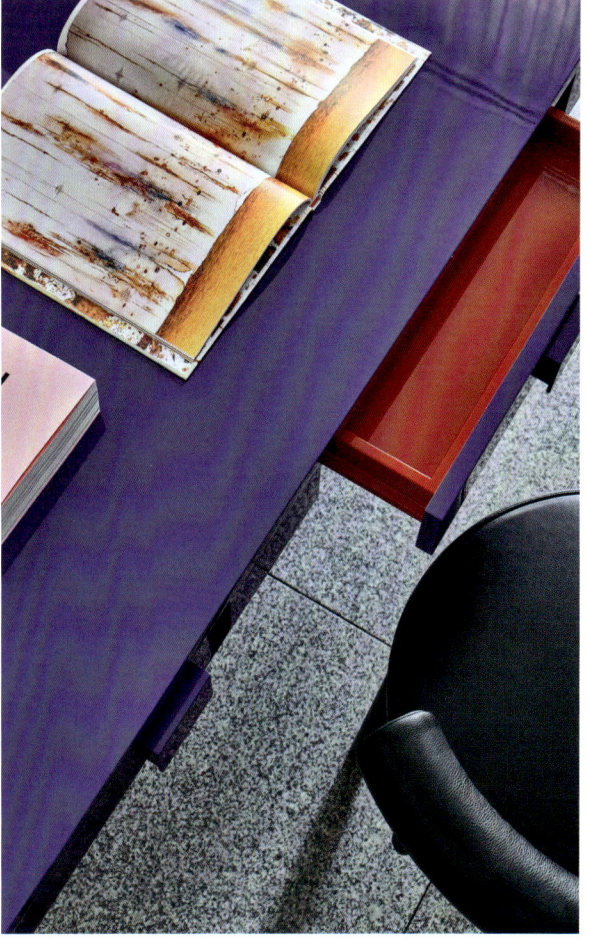

Natalie King, a leading curator and writer, asked me to design a desk for her new home. Natalie adores colour, so I created a desk painted in high-gloss purple paint and lined the pencil drawers in a vibrant red lacquer. She wanted her space to be an eclectic, stylish sanctuary for art, collectibles and inspiring pieces. We furnished the space with a ruby-coloured Le Bambole sofa by Mario Bellini and a red velvet Lady Armchair by Marco Zanuso.

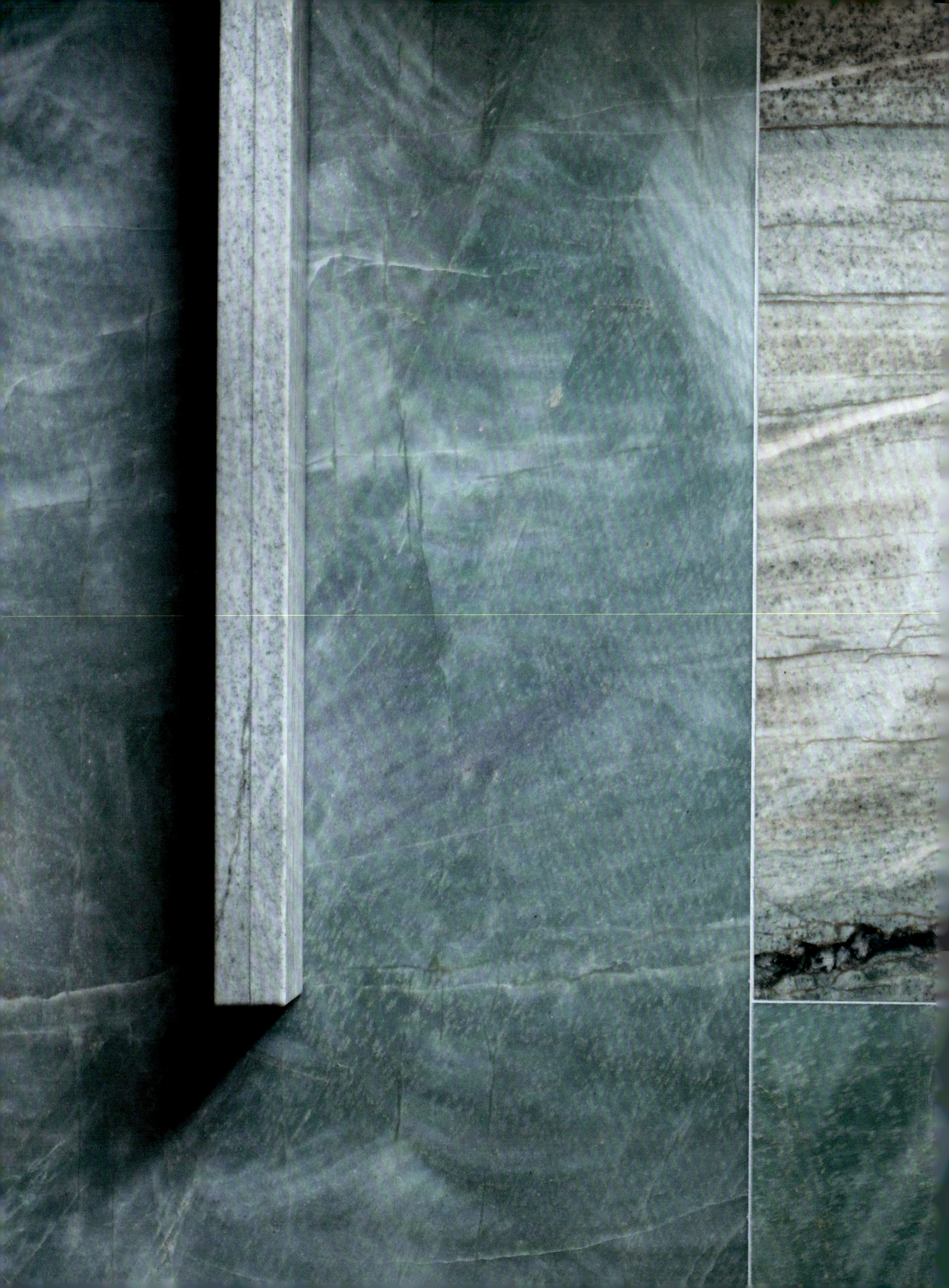

STONE

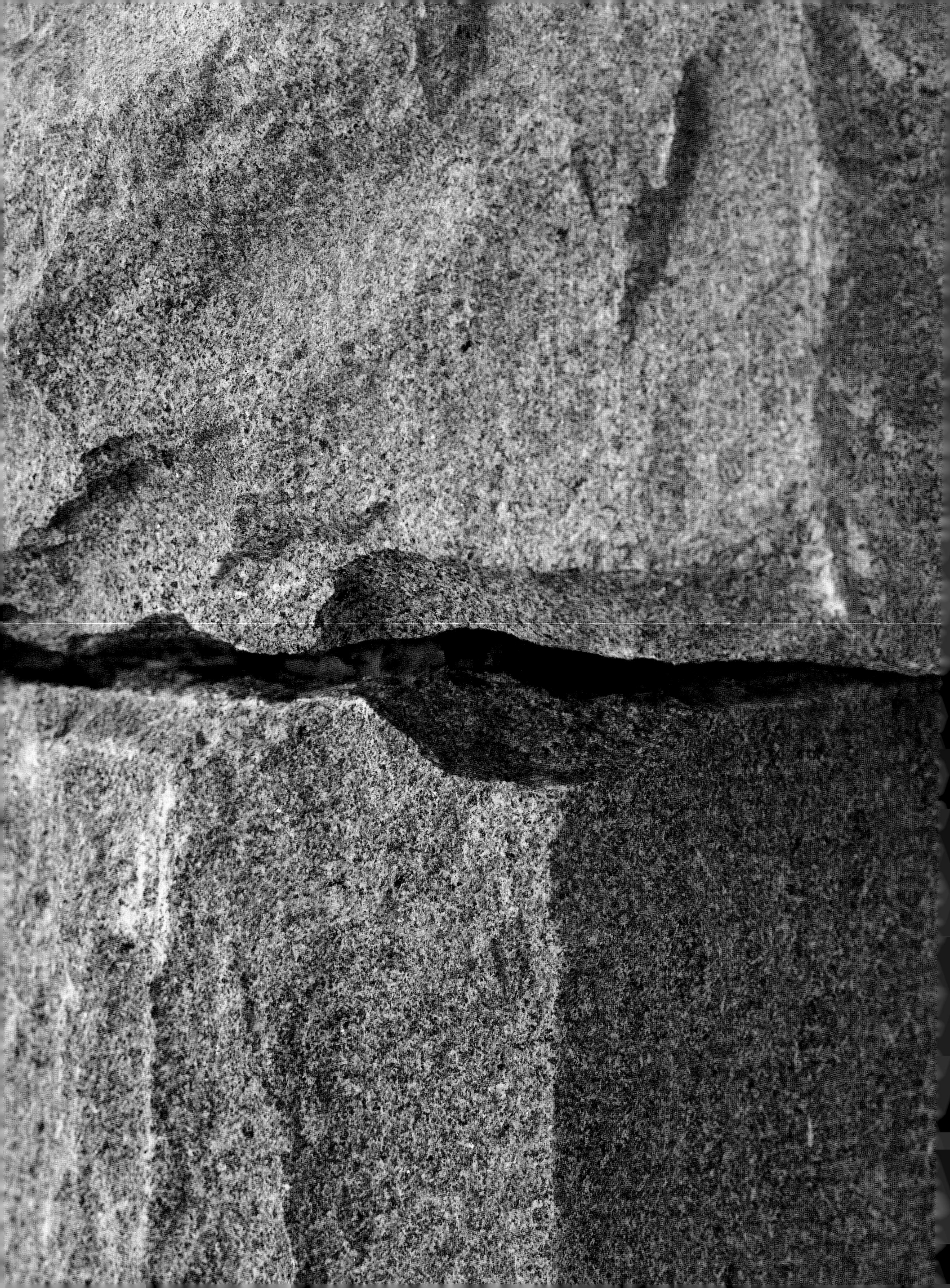

Walking into a church, especially one of great age, you may observe how the floor often shifts and morphs. New patterns emerge as the stones in the floor change, reflecting what was available at the time. For centuries, the Italians have been repairing surfaces like these in their churches and palazzos, occasionally making do by patching a floor with a different stone. This inventive form of 'recycling' is one of my favourite ways to use stone.

The Noguchi Museum in New York was a revelation for me. Until I visited it, I had no idea Isamu Noguchi worked with stone. He would polish or hone different parts of a single piece of stone using separate techniques or tools, with each yielding a distinct finish. I have since incorporated this technique into several projects. I love that this is a subtle change, and even more delightful when you notice it.

Our residential projects have become celebrations of stone. Our clients have become increasingly brave and daring, which is gratifying to see – collaborators in creativity. Our studio is passionate about finding local Australian stones, which have some incredible patterns and colours. Melding of different stones, as in Somerville House with its blend of richly hued marble and earthy sandstone and granite, can create a dramatic yet convivial effect.

These projects showcase stone for its natural beauty, its strength and its flexibility across settings, whether as a textural finish, in a functional built form or as art, or on surfaces, interiors and exteriors.

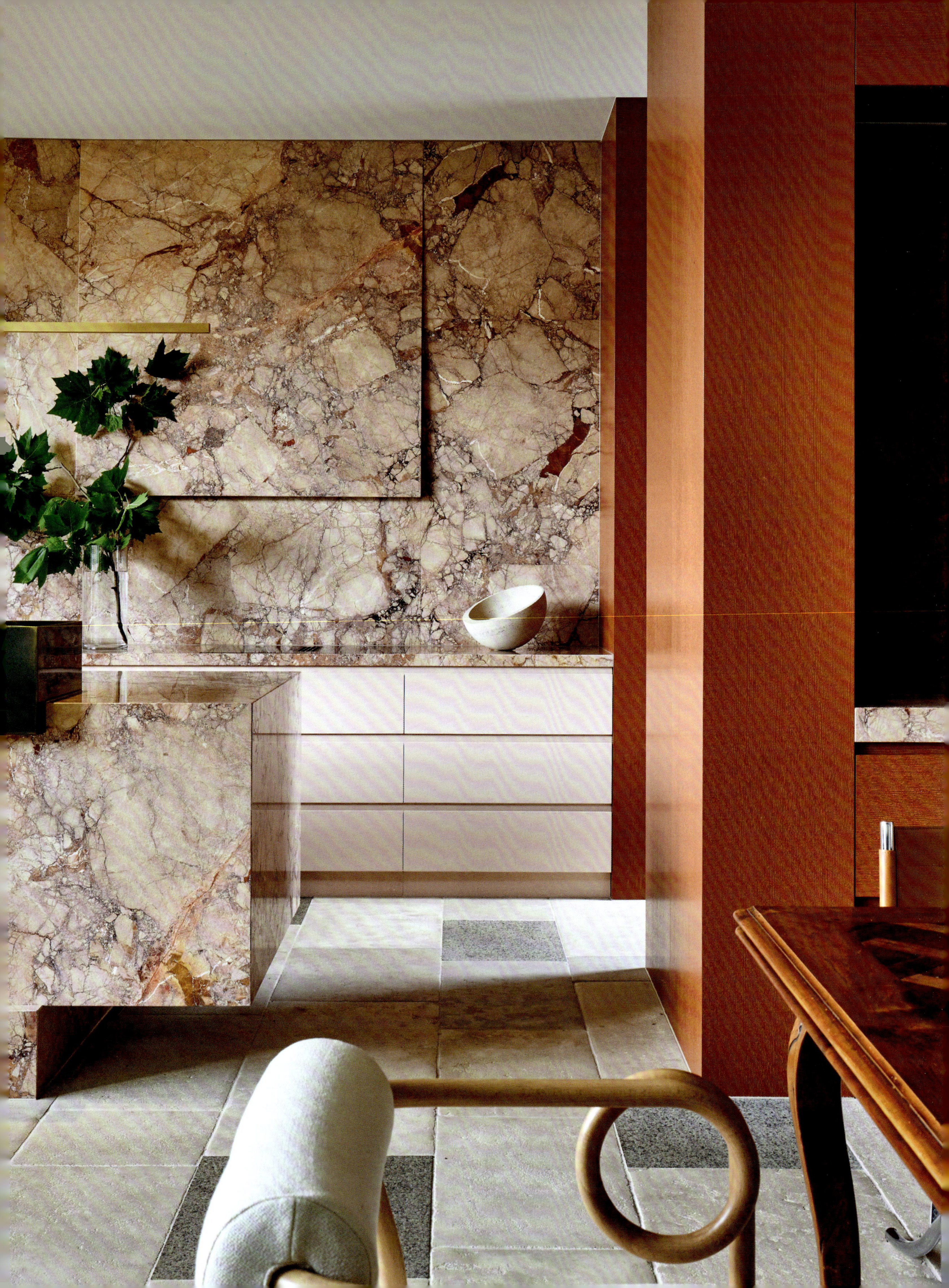

STONE

Somerville House.

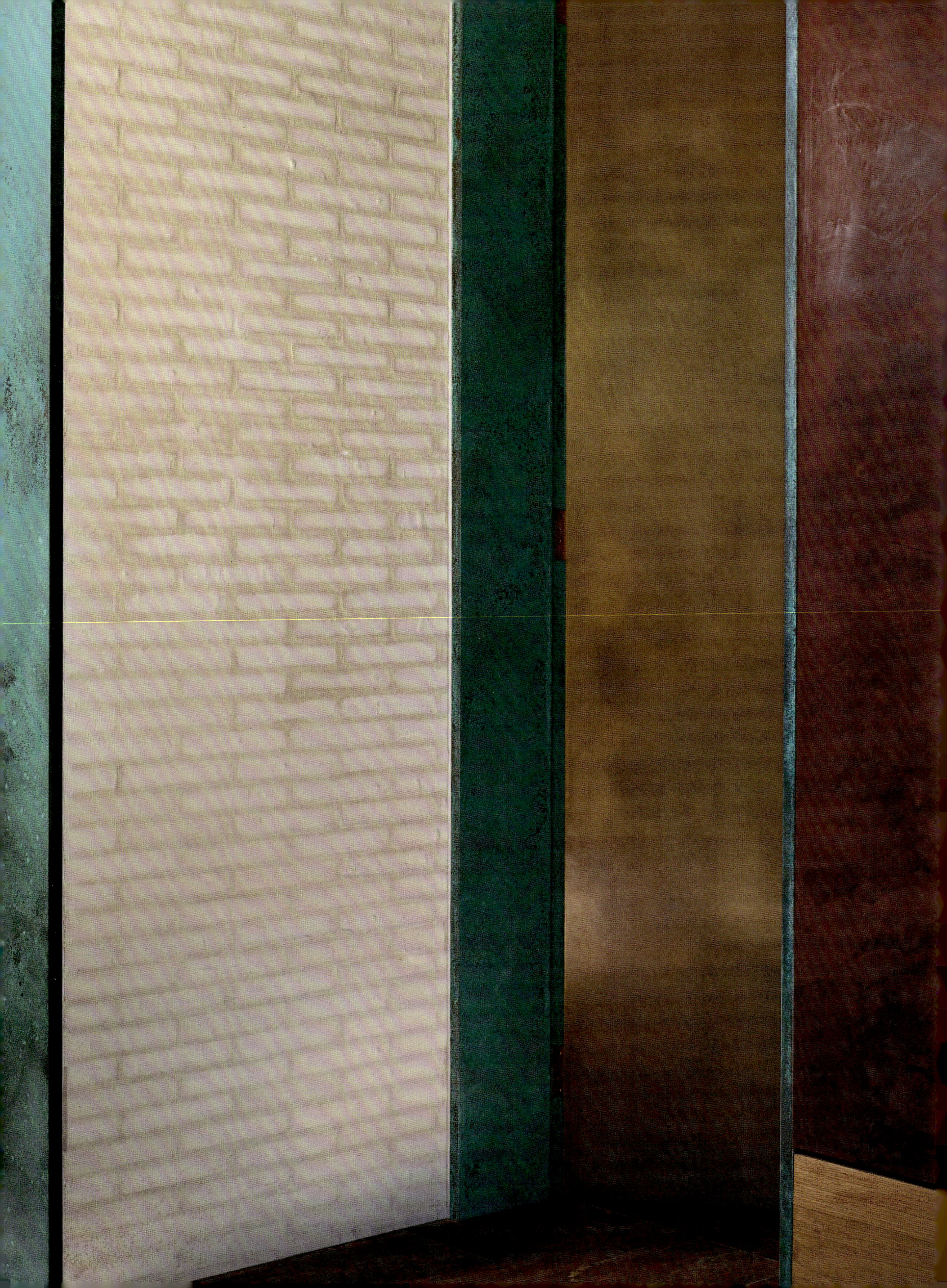

A passerby would never guess a sumptuous, sculpted stone interior lies within this Victorian weatherboard cottage. The single-fronted facade of the house gives nothing away as to the materials and level of finish behind it.

Our wonderful clients moved to the Victorian-era house from their family home next door. They engaged Pandolfini Architects to design a contemporary two-storey rear extension and asked us to do the interior design and decoration. The couple are very confident with colour and we began our design process by looking at stone. We were taken by an amazing Breccia Pernice marble from northern Italy. Drawing out the colours of the stone, we layered the interior with burgundy and blush tones and contrasting accents of green.

The kitchen showcases the expressive beauty of the marble. It is sculptural and monumental. However, the pink hue and tick-tacked tiles soften the scale to create a space that is alluring and approachable. A versatile metallic vessel nestled in the island benchtop can be used as an ice bucket or filled with flowers or fruit.

Resting the island on chunky stone blocks that deliberately protrude just beyond its base accentuates its sense of solidity and allows the flooring to flow beneath. We peppered this surface with hand-distressed Moroccan sandstone and Balmoral Green granite for variation in colour and visual interest. Evocative of outdoor paving, the flooring is durable and refined and has a satisfyingly tactile feel underfoot.

The rear wall of the kitchen is another dramatic expression of stone. Here, it's articulated in two and three dimensions with tick-tacked tiles and applied panels, one concealing the rangehood. Drawing from the hues in the Breccia marble, the oak drawers are painted soft pink and the pantry dark burnt red. We set the woodgrains at right angles to each other so the lower pink grain flows horizontally in contrast to the vertical of the burnt red.

For the living room fireplace, we picked up on the very subtle green in the stone to pair it with Tugela Apple Green marble, which has grass- and turquoise-coloured tones that capture the colours in the garden.

The colours deepen in the entry foyer and powder room, becoming more saturated and vivid. The new entry to the house sits to the side of the cottage and serves as a threshold between the living spaces in the extension, and the main bedroom and ensuite in the cottage. To harmonise both the cottage and extension, the foyer continues the burnt red, turquoise and metallic features via the use of Travertine Rosso flooring, brass panels and an aged-copper finish to frame openings. We enveloped the powder room with tonal colour. Red travertine wraps around the curved wall, with luminous polished plaster above, and the vanity sleeves over a limestone base.

We repeated the design language of the kitchen in the main ensuite to create an indulgent retreat. Breccia Pernice clads the vanity, integrated drawers and wall, with rotated tiles and applied panels adding even more dimension. Bronze tapware provides gentle golden highlights.

The pinks and greens in Somerville House remind me of the captivating marble foyer in Canberra's Parliament House, its pink and eucalyptus-coloured stones laid side by side. Here, perhaps, is an influence from my time working with architect Romaldo Giurgola and MGT.

STONE

SOMERVILLE HOUSE.

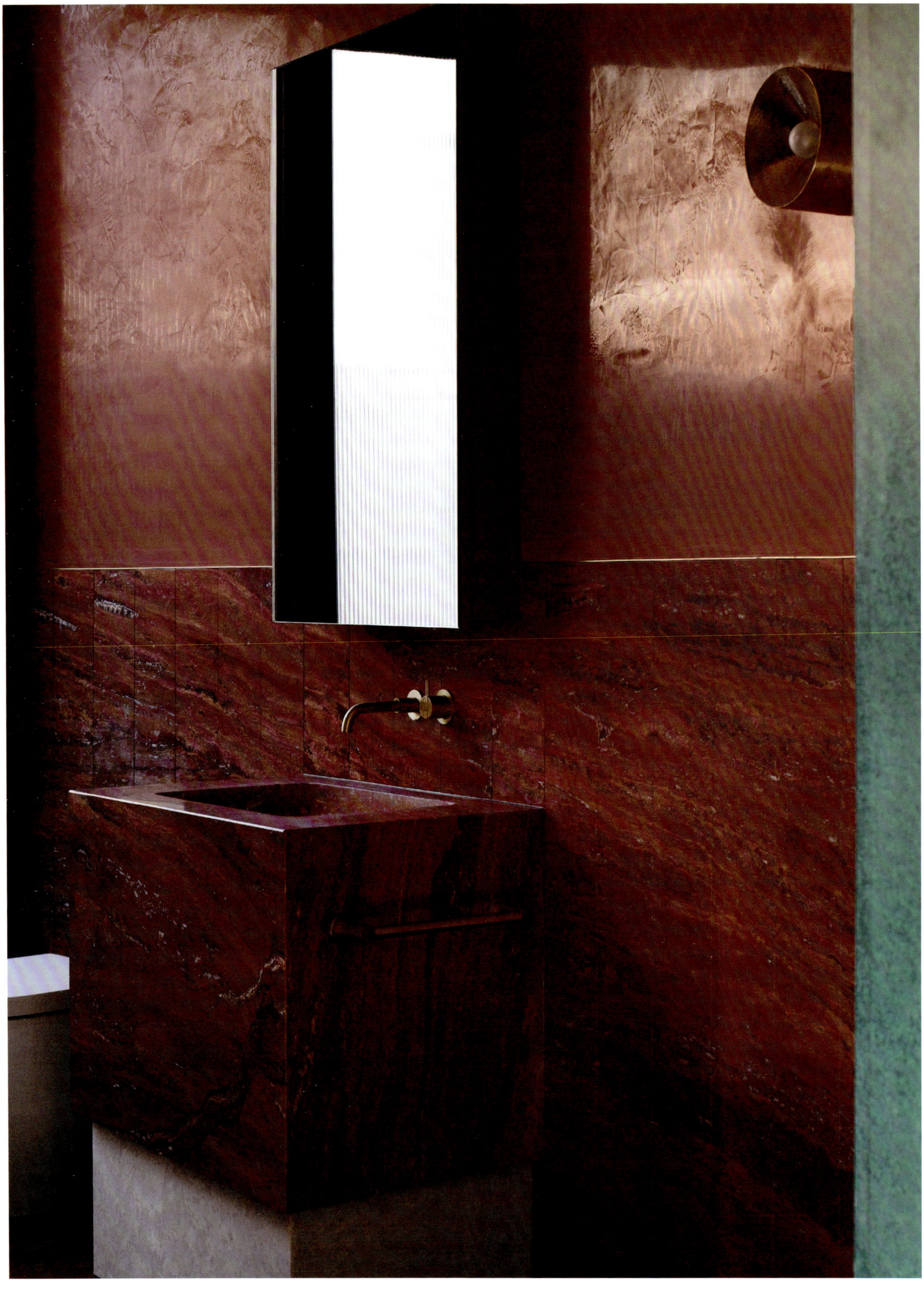

Opposite: The lower half of the curved wall in the powder room has faceted stone panels inset in traditional Dado style which contrast with the smooth figured marble wall above them.

This page and previous spread: For the kitchen island bench, the marble slab is deliberately cut and rotated to showcase its expressive character. The two-tone joinery fronts are also rotated to mismatch the grain, while the handcast bronze handles from Pitella add warmth and tactility.

STONE

SOMERVILLE HOUSE.

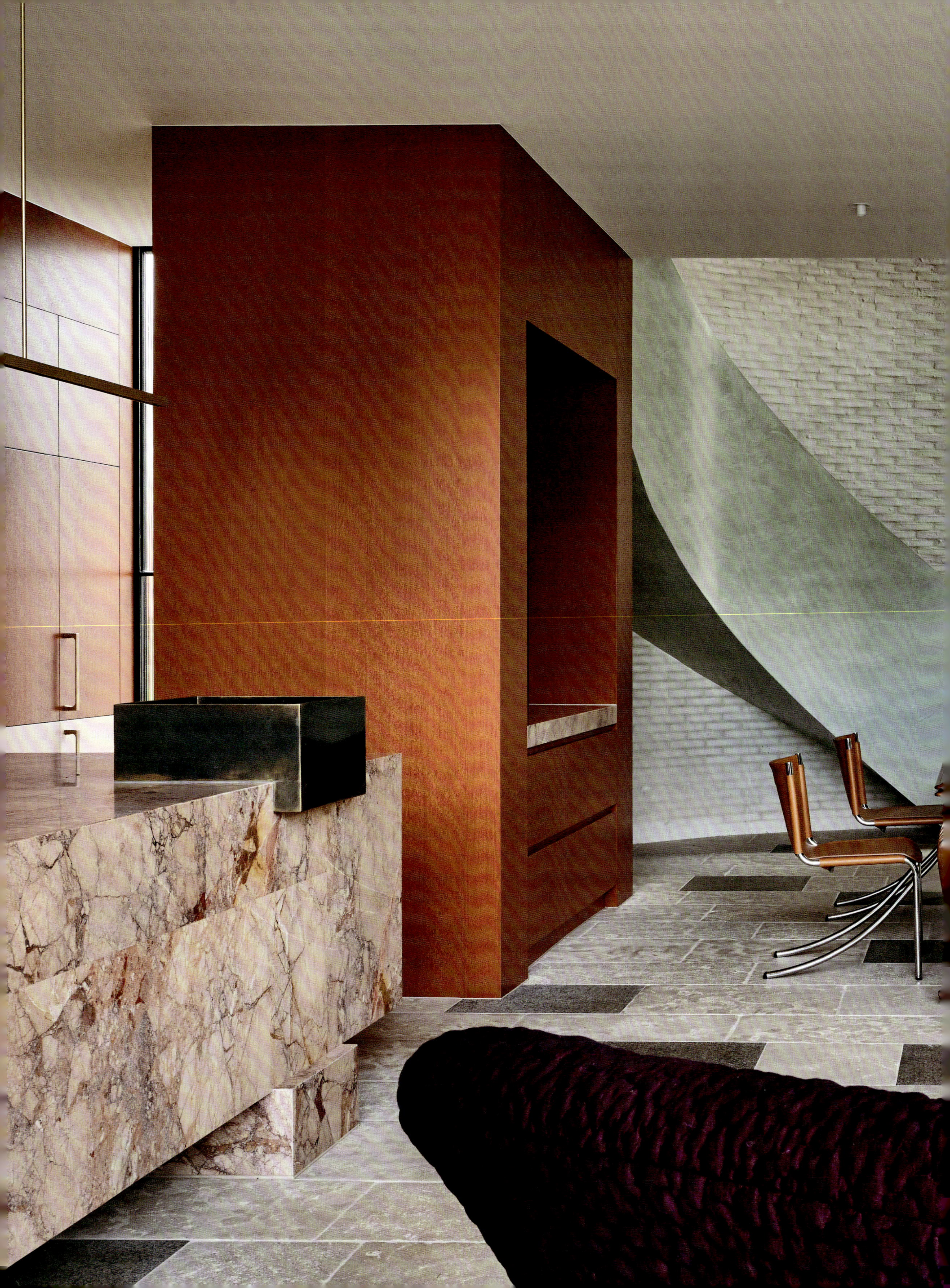

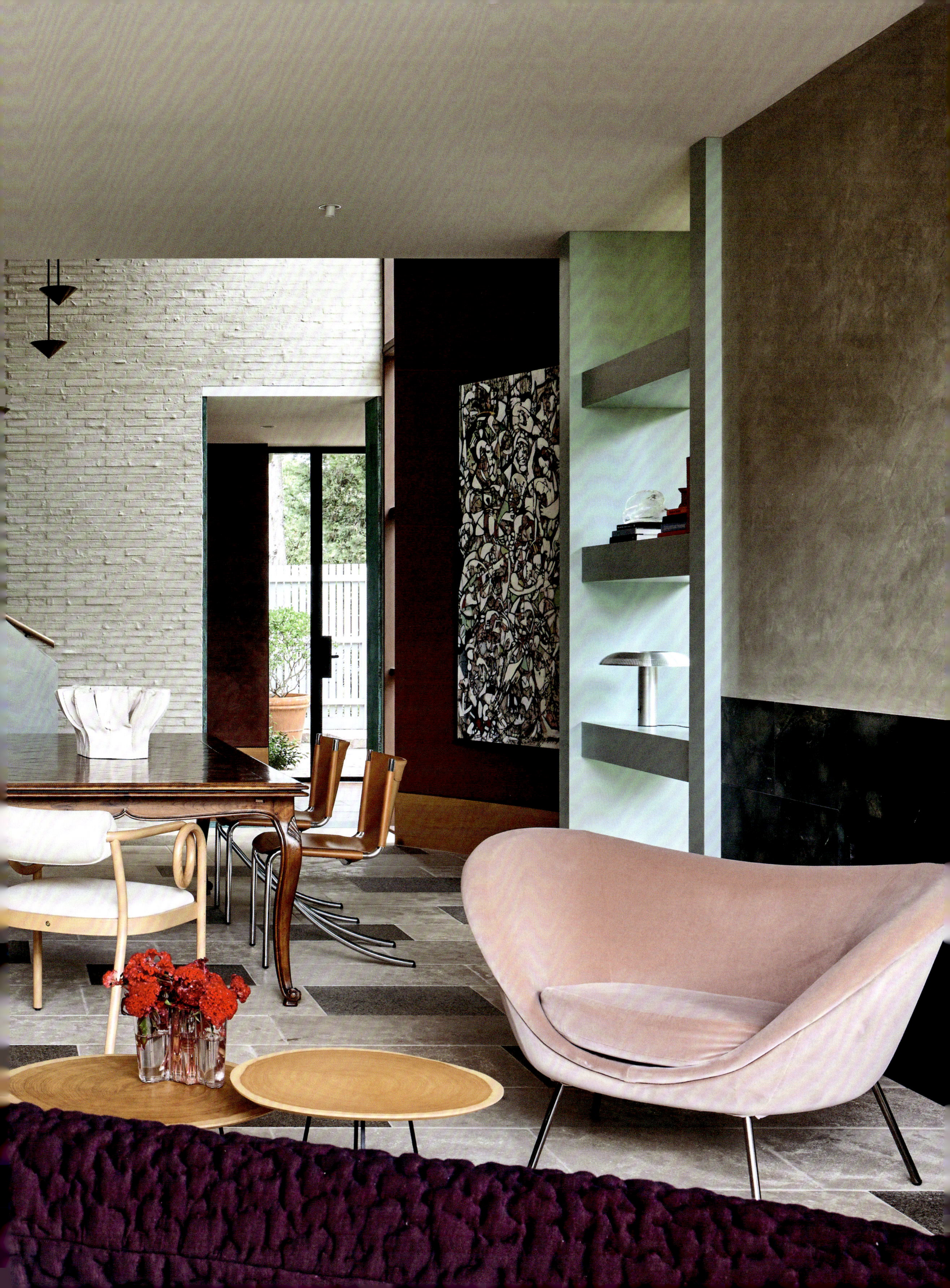

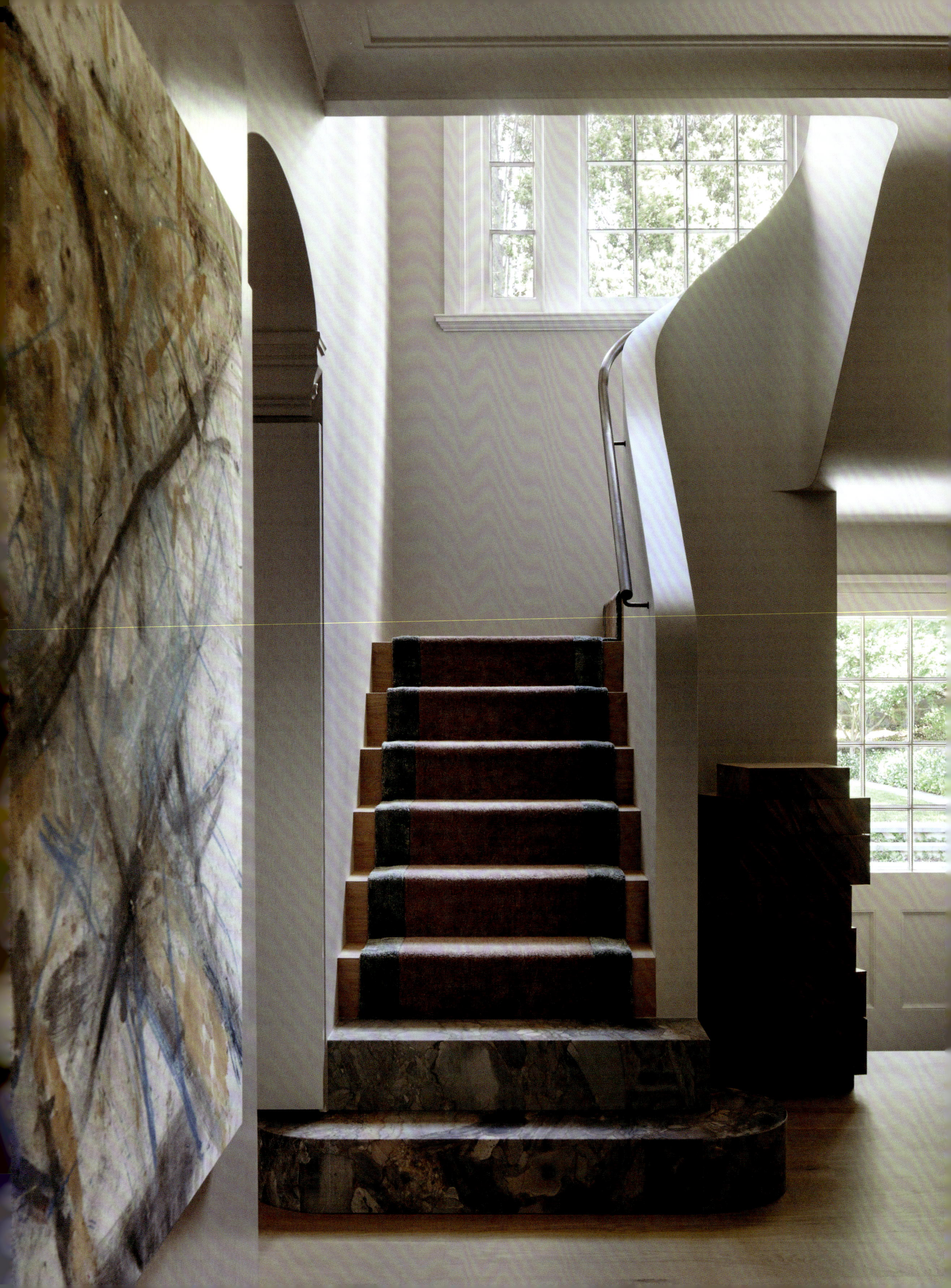

STONE

River House.

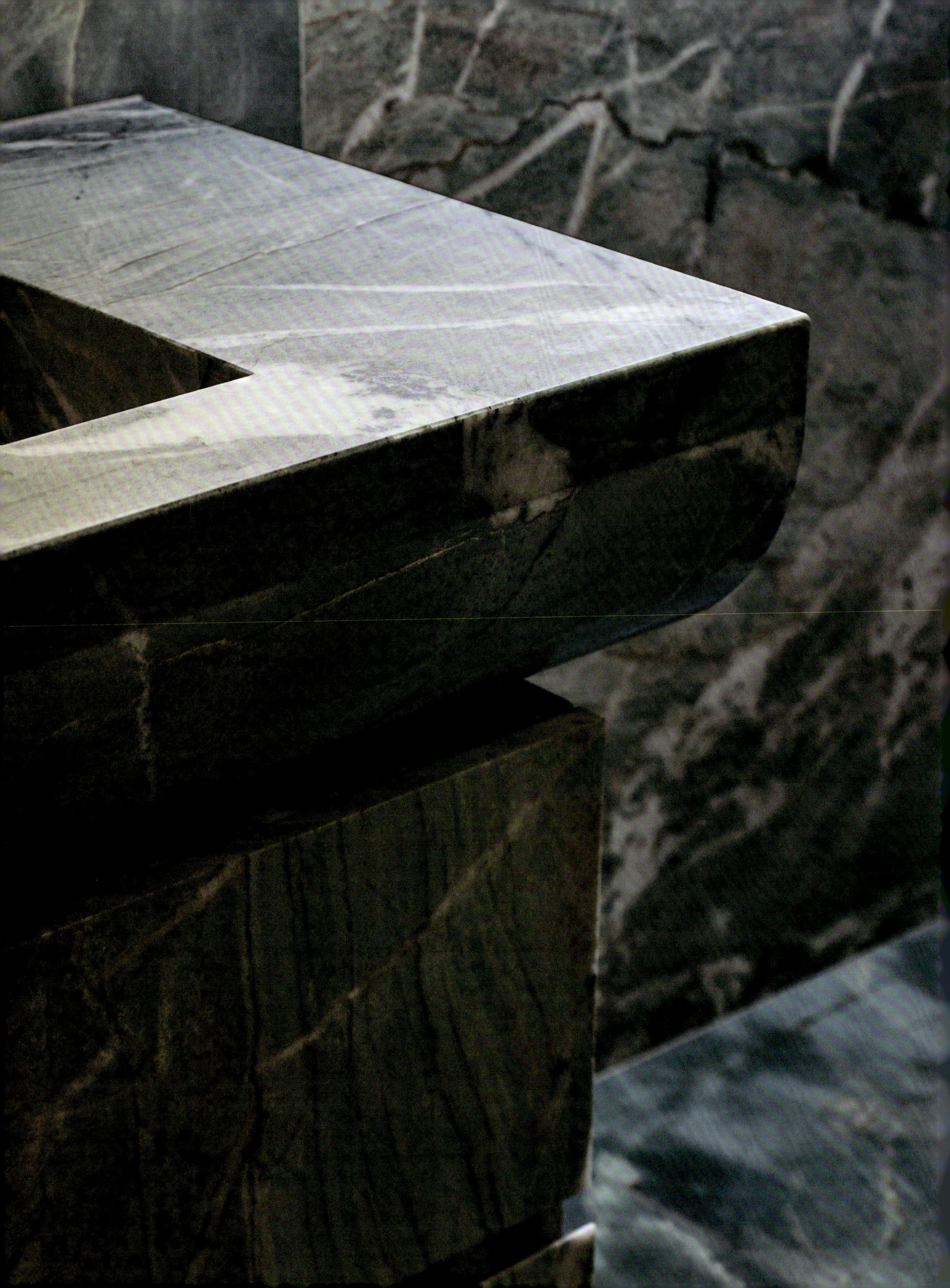

Our clients fell in love with this Georgian Revival house designed by architect Marcus Martin in the early 1930s. The house has beautiful bones and a wonderful garden originally designed by Edna Walling and more recently restored by Paul Bangay. But after numerous interventions by previous owners, the interior was tired and in need of restoration and reconfiguration.

Engaged to do a full renovation, we started by reviewing the floorplan to see how we could open up the spaces, expanding the light and connection to the outdoors. Walling was a trailblazer in landscape design, and I was inspired by the colours and textures of the garden. It's romantic and mystical, and I wanted to distil some of that whimsy to create a layered, crafted and refined home fitting of its South Yarra address.

Walls enclosing the kitchen were removed and it now feels generous and open, with views of the garden across the new dining nook. We designed a new pavilion that extends the informal living area into the landscape. This distinctly modern addition draws on the language of Mies van der Rohe's Barcelona Pavilion, with large expanses of glass and a brass canopy that will patina to dark bronze. I've visited the Barcelona Pavilion several times. It's a heroic building surrounded by verdant greenery; it has features that are quiet and understated, and others that are eye-catching and expressive. It balances them beautifully, and I've always felt our work strives to do the same.

The previous owner had renovated the kitchen, installing stainless steel joinery. I'm a strong advocate of re-using as much as possible for the benefit of the environment. Retaining the stainless steel formed a reflective metallic backdrop to the sculpted kitchen island bench. Crafted from blocks of stone and inspired by furniture, the benchtop fuses rich emerald-green quartzite and light-toned travertine and features a reverse bullnose edge – a nod to the Art Deco-era heritage of the house. The curved ends allow space for stools and evoke table legs.

The reverse bullnose edge continues in the bathroom vanities. This was another adventurous client who wanted to explore exquisite stone, and the bathrooms became an opportunity to create immersive, ornate spaces. The main ensuite has two green quartzite stones, with the bold veining in the dual vanity having a subtle distinction to that of the wall. Another bathroom is a sea of serenity, with the swirling vein direction of its green stone swapping and switching to offer a painterly quality. In yet another bathroom, pearlescent stone has violet tones running through it. This same stone anchors the base of the sculptural staircase, with a curved radius on the first step softening the approach.

As you walk down the hallways, panels of wire-brushed oak are lightly coated with pale hues of blue and lilac to offer a subtle change of colour. The formal living and dining room is light and elegant, while the wine room is rich and sophisticated with olive-green and blue-grey walls, and custom-designed aged-brass storage with accents of stone and painted oak.

Woven through River House is a story of Volker Haug lighting which illuminates spaces and surfaces with gold fittings and soft ambient light: from the Index 11 pendant at the entry and Oddment pendant over the dining table to the Anton wall lights in the bathroom. Volker also custom designed the tiered conical light over the kitchen island.

With opulent stones and a sculptural design language, we honoured the 1930s heritage of River House while reimagining it for contemporary living and its garden setting.

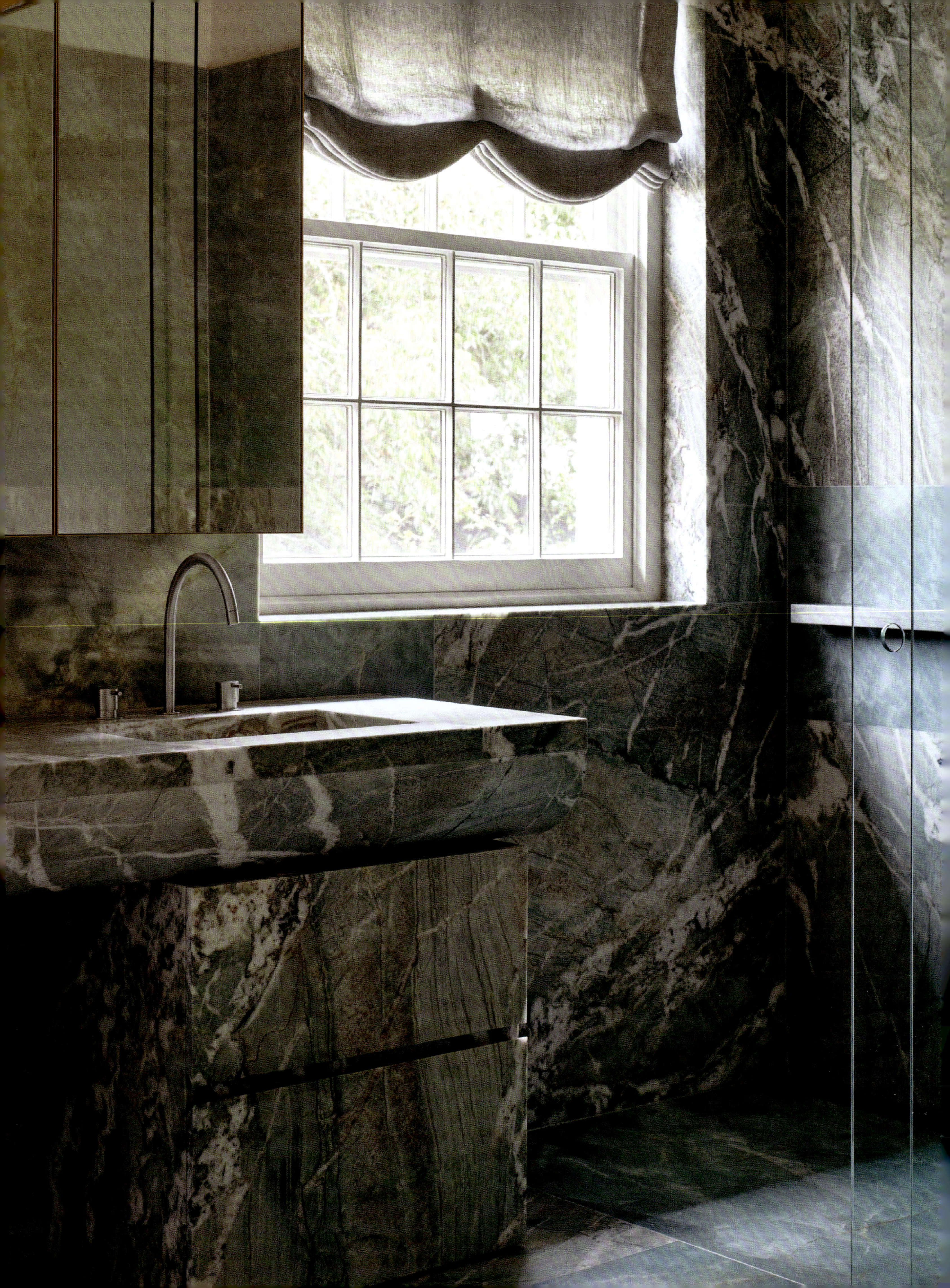

RIVER HOUSE.

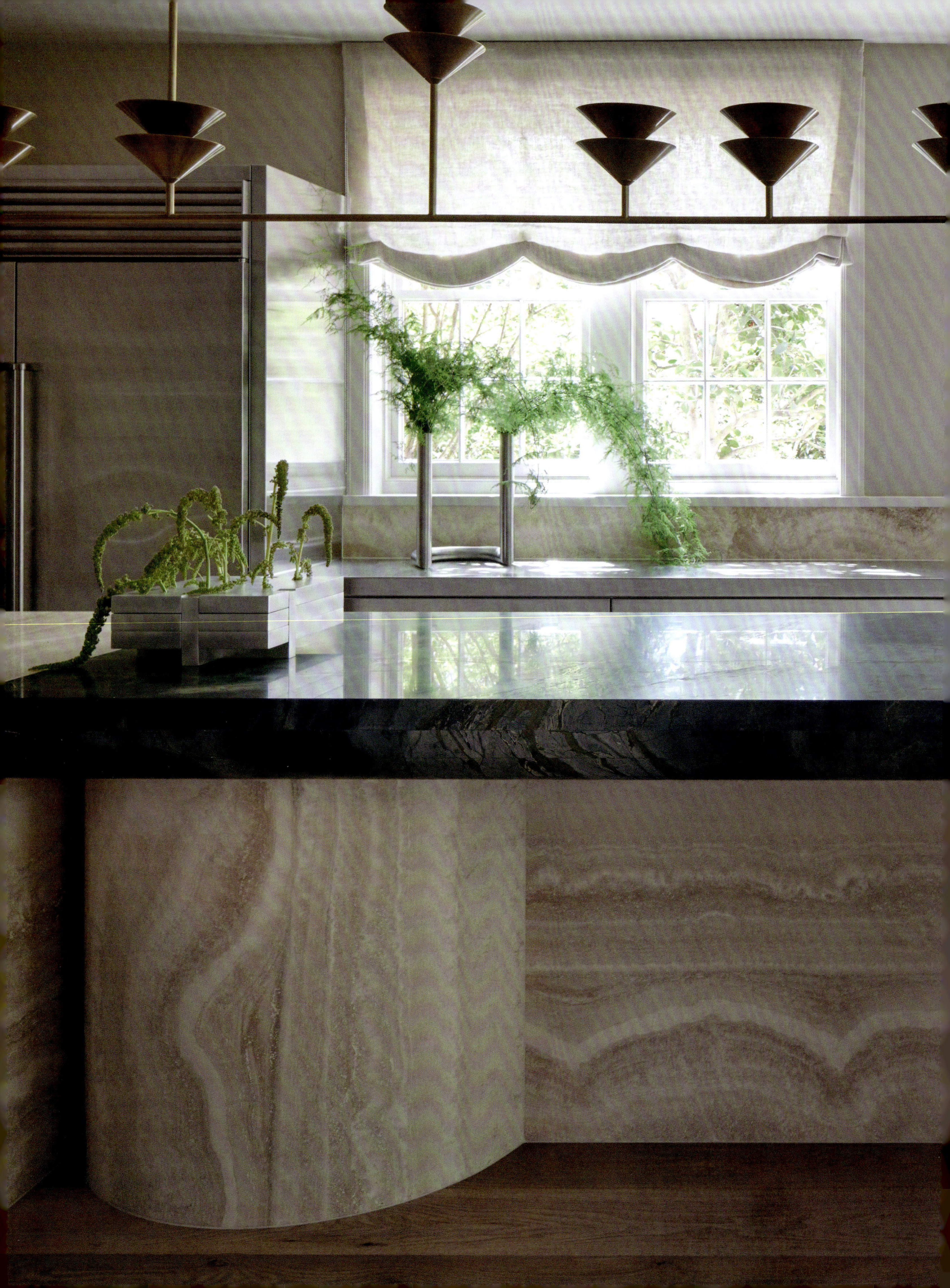

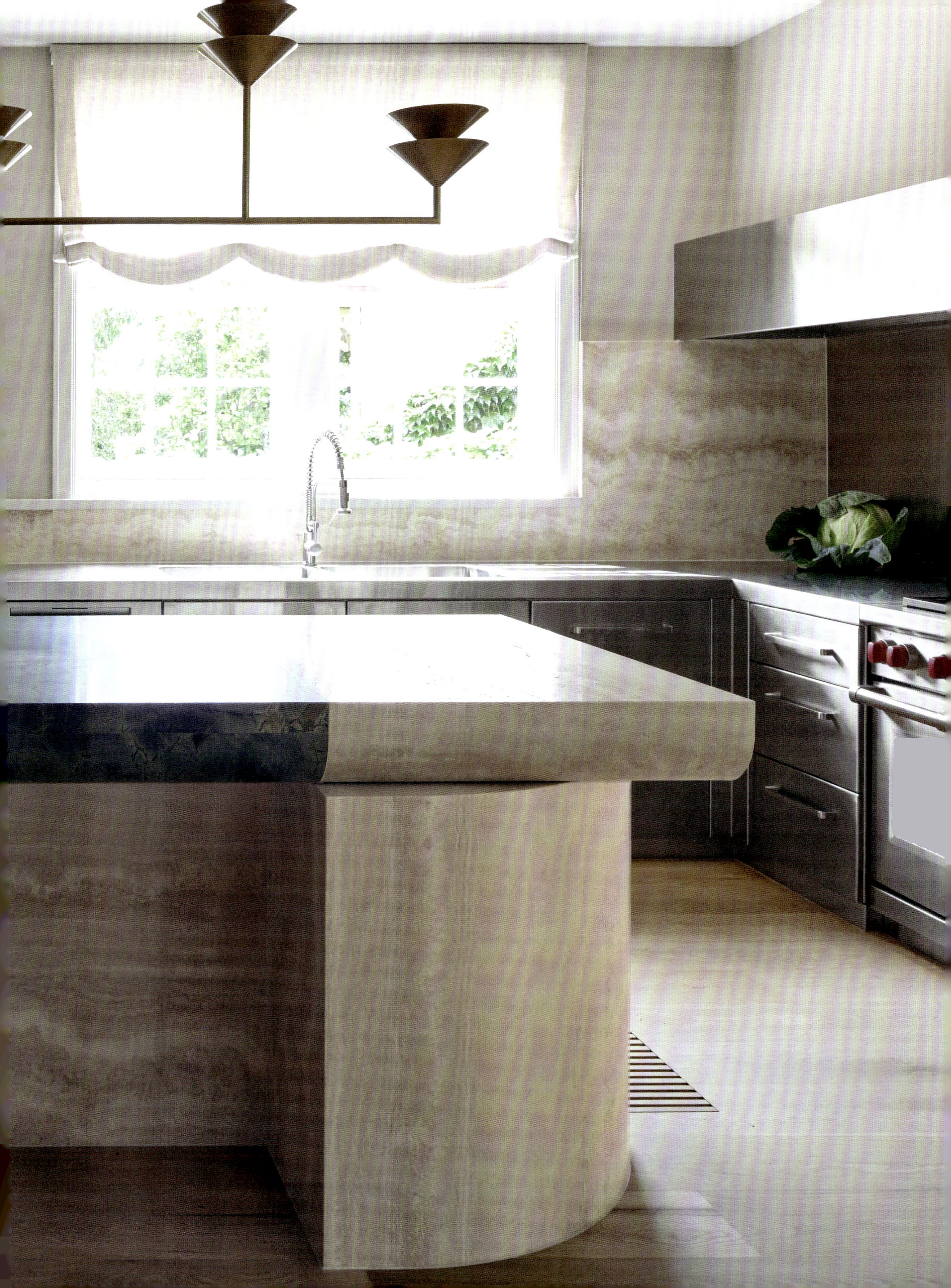

STONE

RIVER HOUSE.

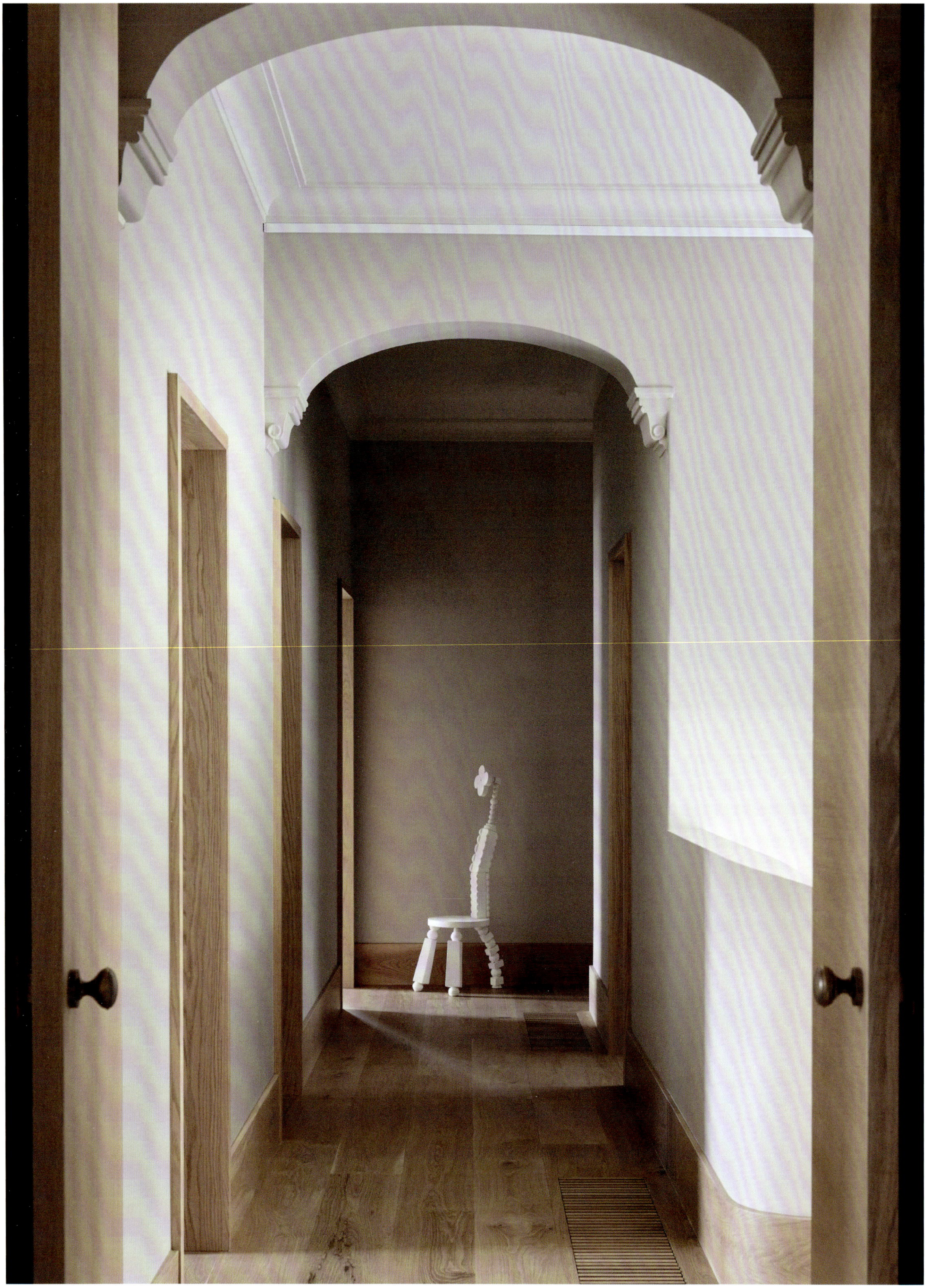

Opposite: At the end of the corridor, DenHolm's Sprout Chair is playful and sculptural, made from South Australian limestone. Doors framed with raw oak challenge the ornamental architecture of this heritage home.

This page: The powder room basin is carved from an imposing solid block of Cipollino Ondulato Rosso marble and has a reverse bullnose edge. It floats from a splashback of lavender-hued Magente quartzite within a room clad in mismatched panels of both stones.

RIVER HOUSE.

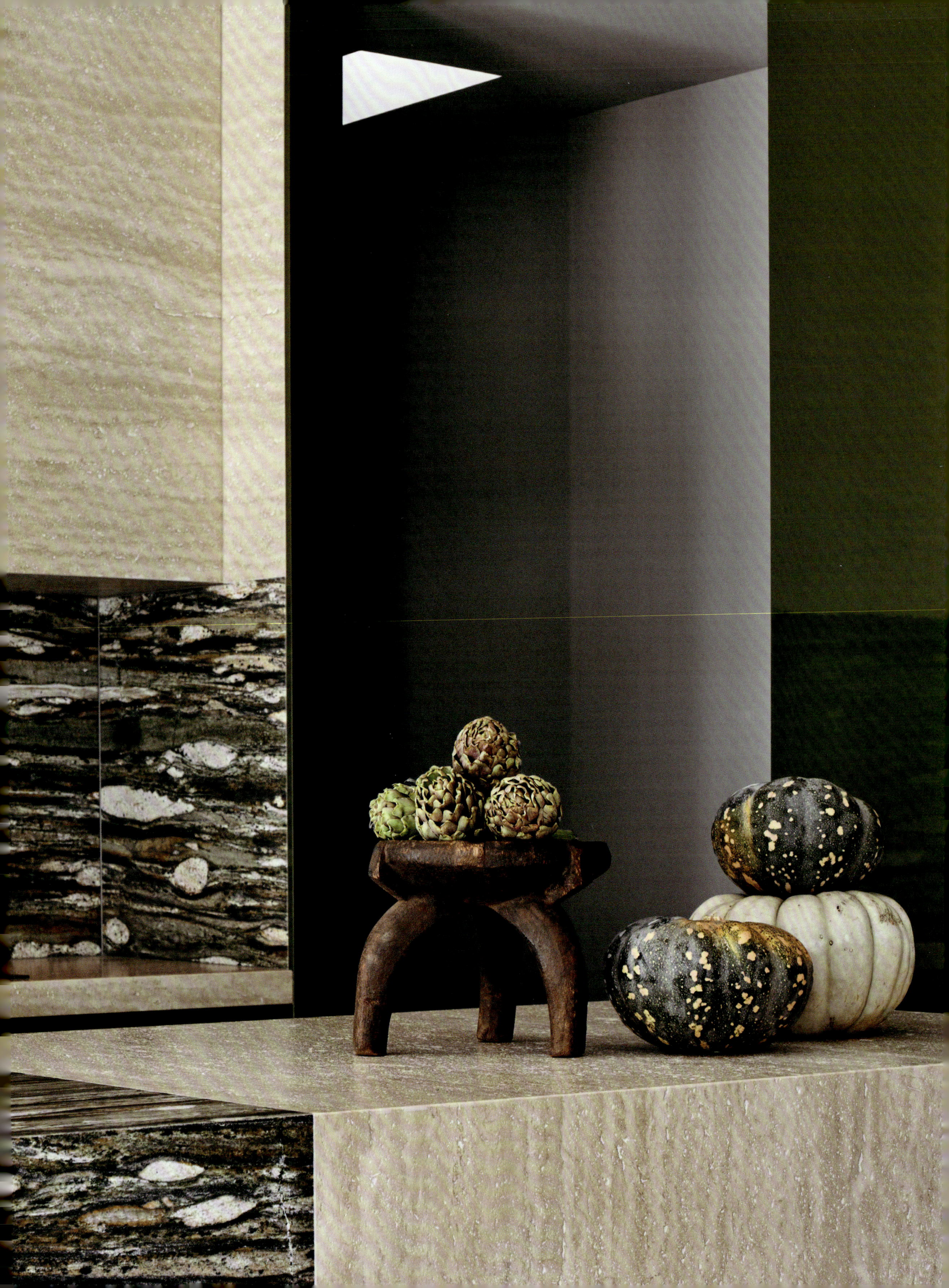

STONE

Auburn Residence.

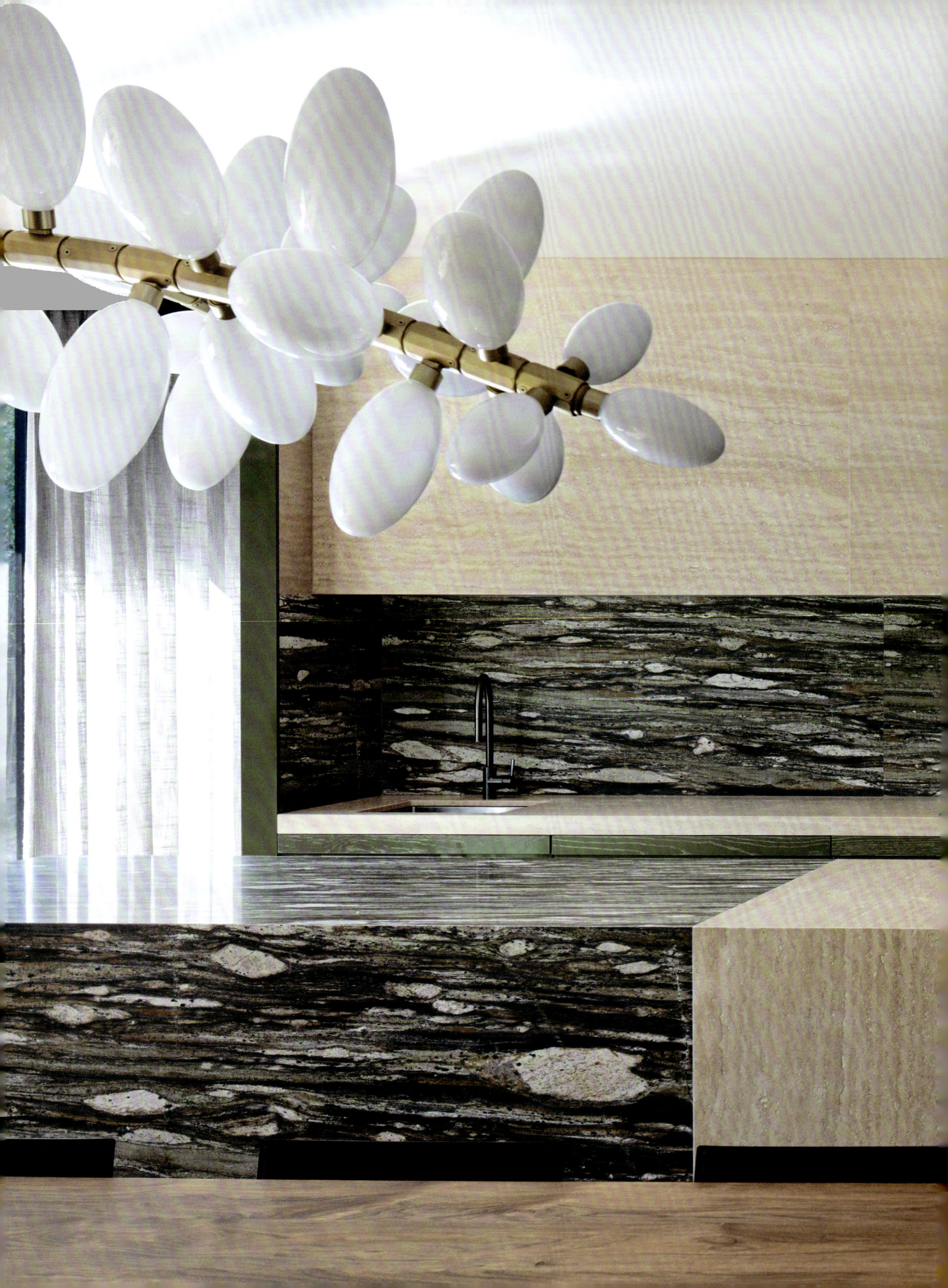

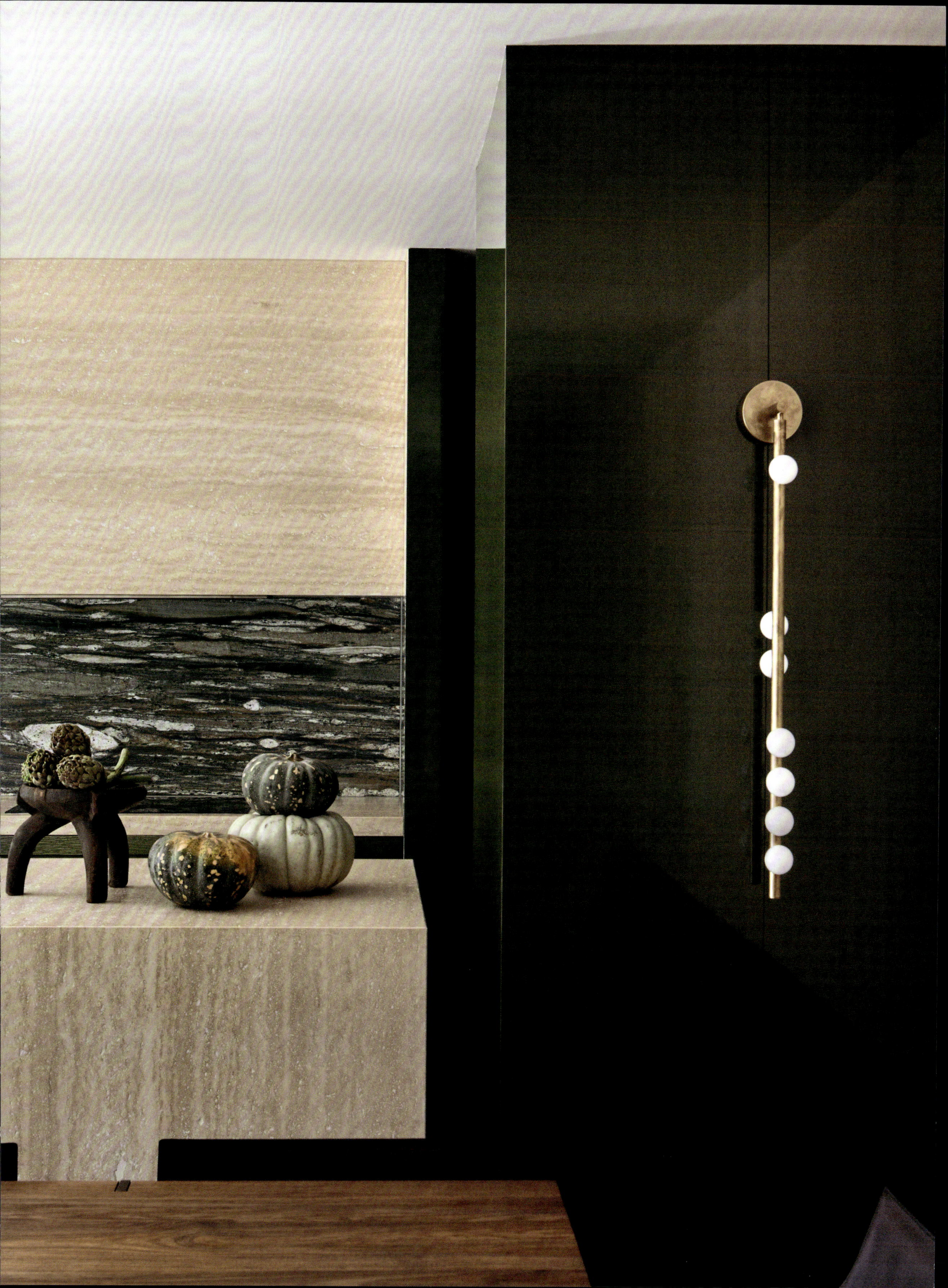

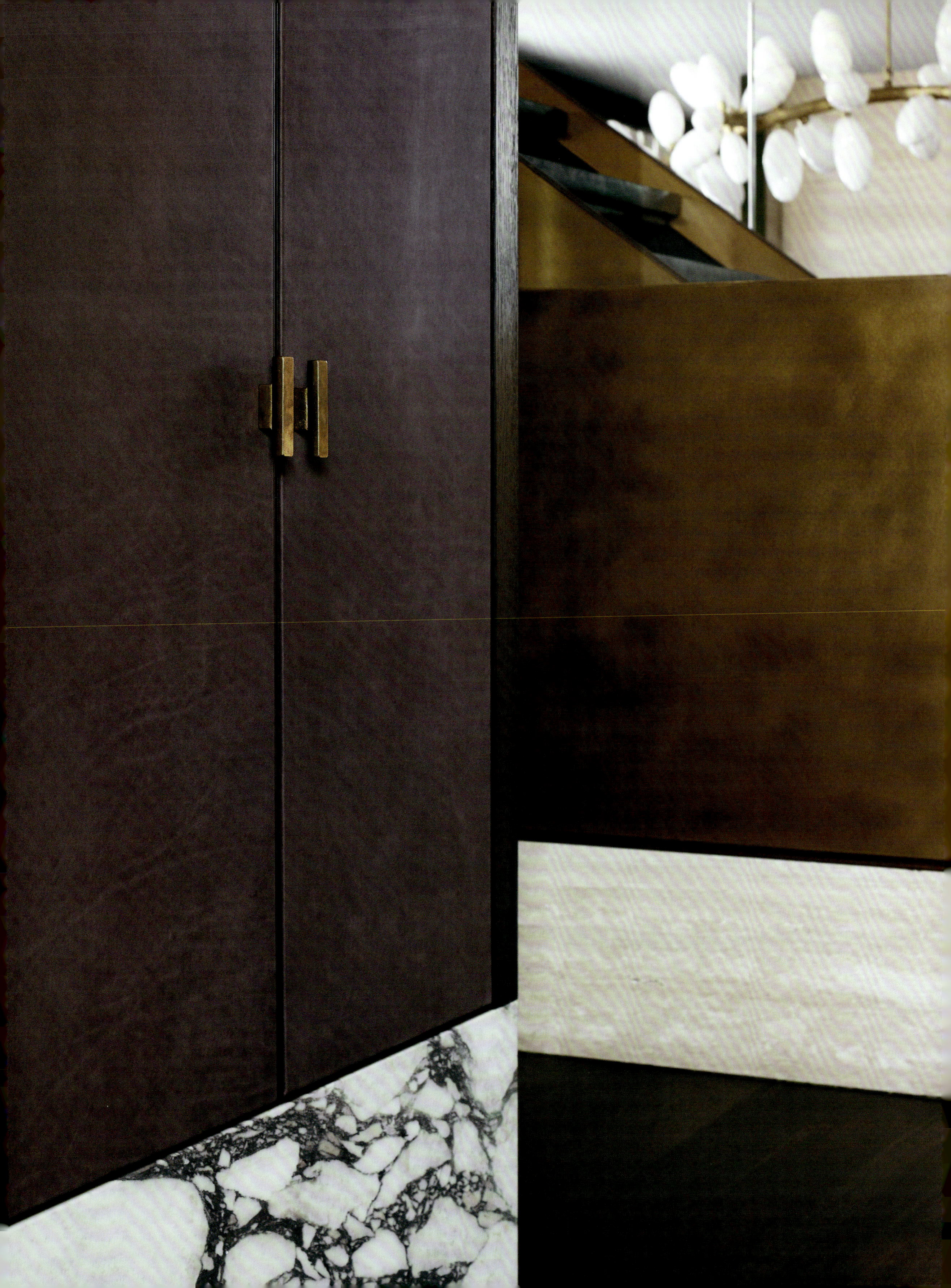

Inside the entry of Auburn Residence, an aubergine-coloured suede leather-clad closet on an opulent stone plinth is a hint of what's to come: rich colour, heroic stone and an assembly of unexpected materials.

The contemporary two-storey house is on a tree-lined street. The new owners – a retired couple – wanted their home to feel like a rich, textural sanctuary amid the verdant garden. They engaged us to do a complete renovation, and from our very first conversations they expressed their interest in colour and exploring different ideas.

Inspired by the natural surrounds of the house, we proposed an eclectic palette of green and aubergine tones. We selected a deep burgundy Calacatta Viola stone from Italy, and a Verde Bardini stone with olive, white, charcoal and gold tones from Brazil. Our clients fell in love with the colours and the stone. We expanded the palette with olive, chartreuse, forest green, aubergine and umber. Then we toned it down with travertine and grounded it with dark-stained flooring.

The house had good spatial planning with the kitchen, dining and living spaces on the ground floor opening to the outdoors, and the bedrooms and bathrooms on the second floor. We reconfigured the kitchen to enlarge the space and integrate a generous walk-in pantry, and then transformed it into the centrepiece of the home by using a striking combination of the Verde Bardini and a natural-coloured travertine. We tick-tacked the stone on the island bench, switching and turning the grain direction, and let the veining flow horizontally through both stones on the splashback and cupboards. A high-gloss viridescent lacquer on the solid oak joinery intensifies the green in the stone.

In the living room, beyond the brushed-brass staircase, the green and aubergine hues become richer, deeper and more saturated in our custom two-tone silk rug. Patricia Urquiola's Tufty-Time sofa upholstered in yellow velvet unites both colours, almost becoming one with the olive, while providing a complementary contrast to the aubergine. Travertine joinery with deep shelves displays art pieces and firewood. The softly draped, translucent curtains keep the interior intimate, while hinting at the leafy garden outside.

Upstairs, the five bedrooms have soothing dark grey and blue hues. Drawing on the design language of the entry closet, the main bedroom has a limed-oak wardrobe on a beautiful Magente stone plinth. In the ensuite, a sublime French marble with waves of aquatic-coloured veining is almost reminiscent of blue cheese. We paired it with travertine and deliberately mixed and matched the tiles – starting, stopping and rotating them – to showcase the subtle complexities of each stone across the vanity and wall surfaces.

Auburn Residence has an understated luxury and the quiet feel of an artistic retreat. As confident as it is creative, this highly personal home provides a sanctuary for its owners and leaves a lasting impression on guests.

STONE

AUBURN RESIDENCE.

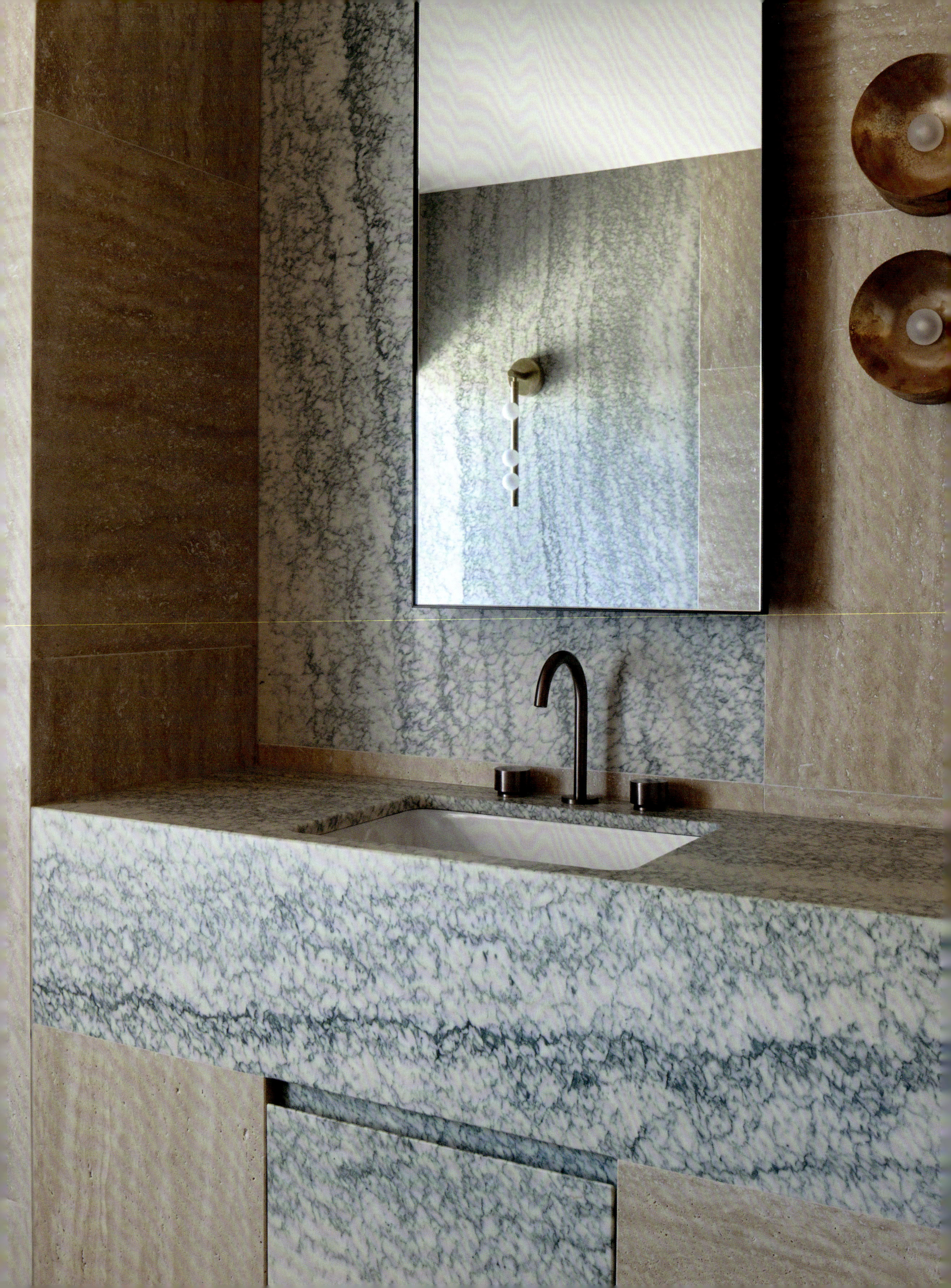

French marble and Italian travertine are mixed and matched in the ensuite, the stones rotated and pivoted in different directions to showcase subtle and delightful complexities. A 3-bulb Drop System Sconce by Lindsay Adelman casts dappled light above the freestanding Agape Spoon bathtub and Windows of Bo Bardi Side Table by Linde Freya Tangelder.

Below: In the main bedroom, the deeply pigmented pewter walls and ceilings are in a handmade paint by Bauwerk, while the Anders raffia wall light by PINCH is sculpted from layers of natural fibre.

STONE

AUBURN RESIDENCE.

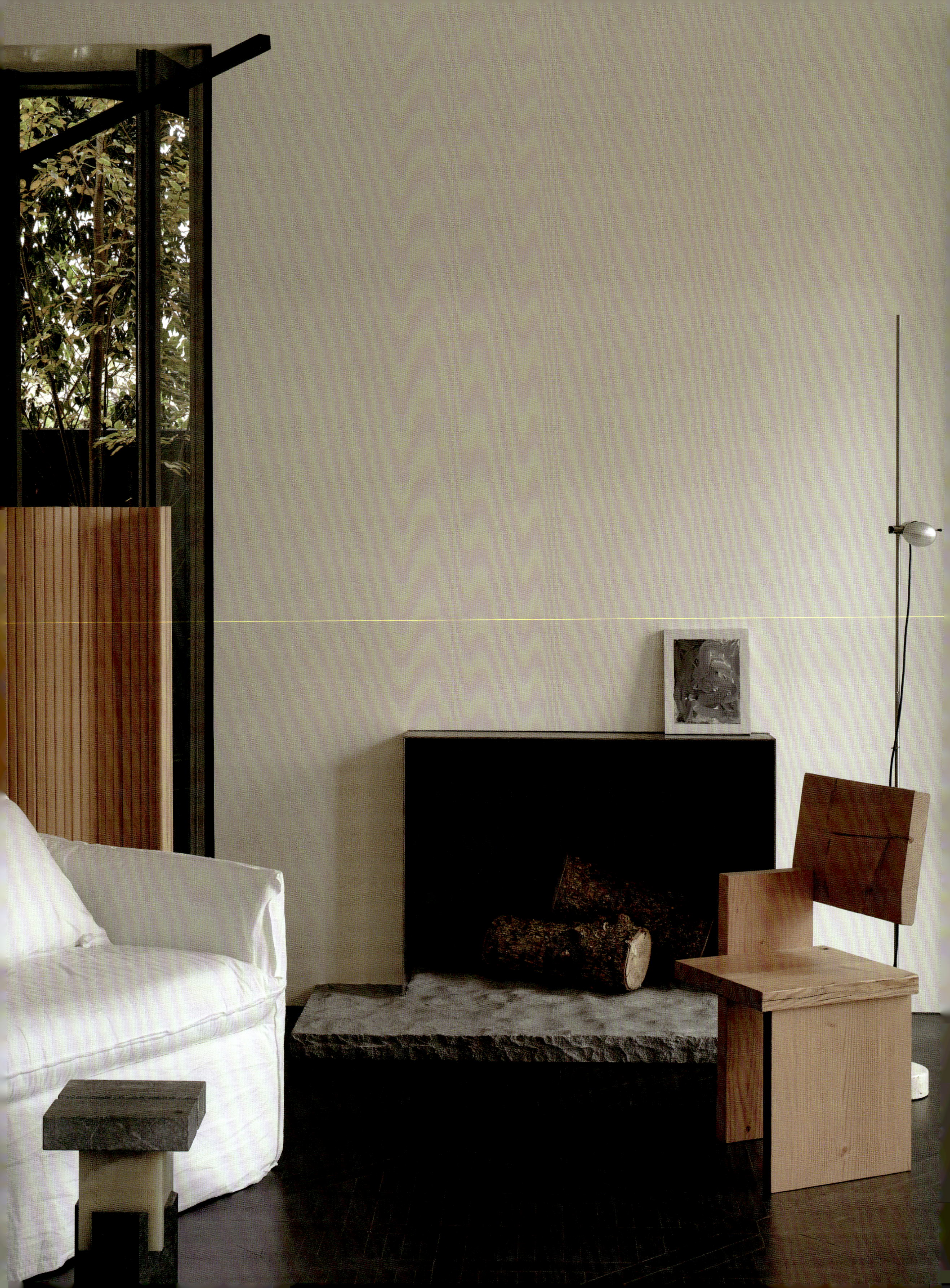

STONE

Ottawa House.

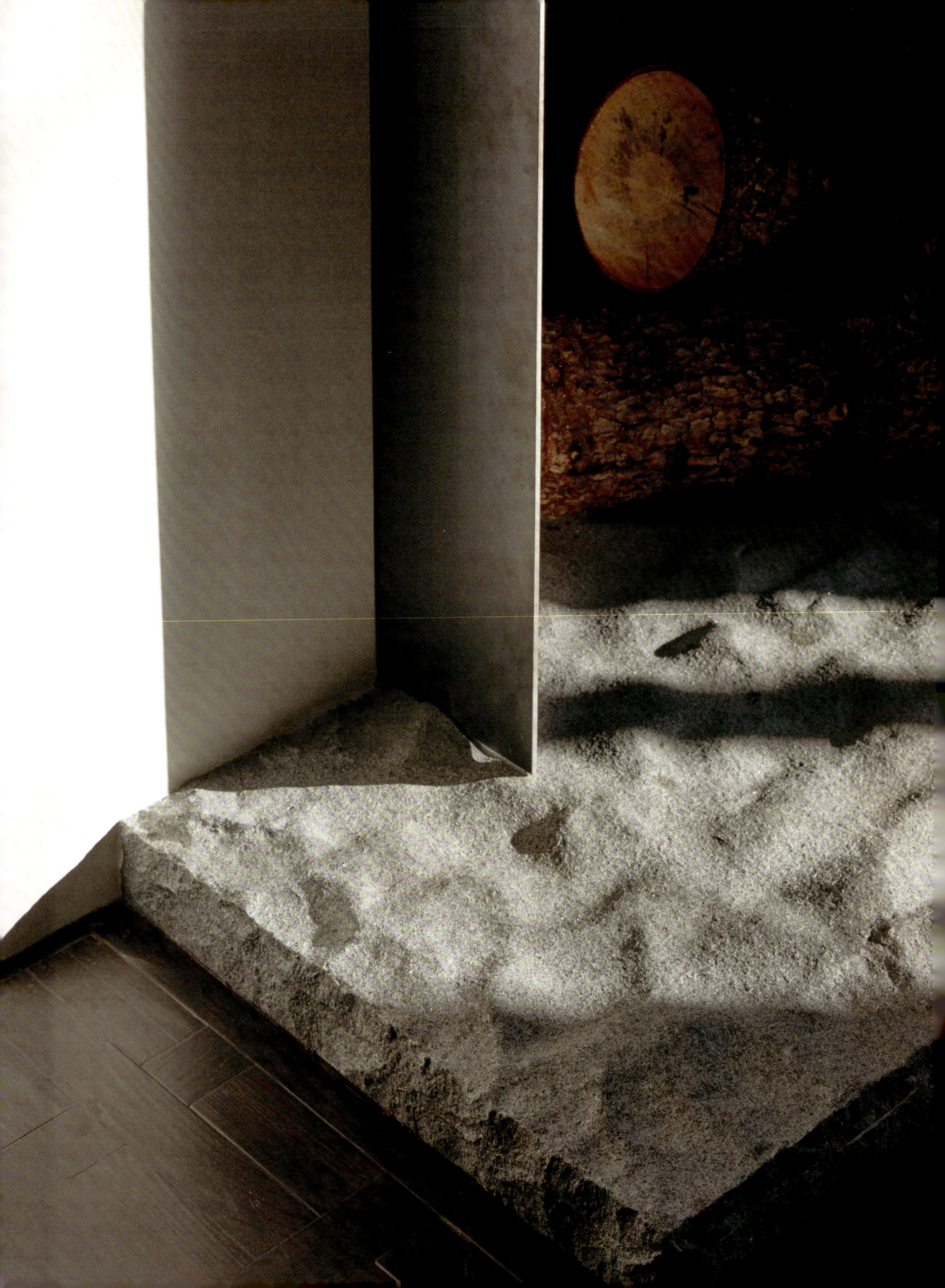

When the new owners of this house contacted our studio, I had recently met designer and artisan Henry Timi in Milan and visited the Noguchi Museum in New York. Timi's studio, Henrytimi creates incredible stone kitchens and revitalises precious craft techniques, such as chiselling stone. Isamu Noguchi also crafted amazing stone carvings with quite a chunky expression. I was inspired by both artists and wanted to bring chiselled stone into a project. This was the perfect home to do so.

The chateau-style house was designed in the early 1990s. Our clients, restaurateurs who bought the house much later, were enchanted by the evocative mini chateau – it had soaring ceilings and oak parquetry floors, which we stained jet black – and they saw the potential to modernise it.

The original stone bathtub remained in the house and set us on the journey of exploring stone. I introduced our clients to the work of Timi and Noguchi, and the idea of incorporating chiselled stone. I like to bring age-old techniques into projects to celebrate the craftsmanship and imbue the material with another layer of expression. In Ottawa House, the raw edges and rough surfaces of the handworked stone add character to the classical and contemporary elements of the architecture and interior.

The house has unusual planning, with the entry foyer opening straight into the formal dining and living room. It's a beautiful ballroom-like space with shuttered French doors and tall, elegant windows flanking two fireplaces. We wanted the fireplaces to be features that anchor each end of the room. One is framed with a block of chiselled split-face bluestone. The other is more refined, with a slim, rough-hewn hearth and fine aluminium surround. I love the connection between the two fireplaces. There's symmetry, but it's expressed differently at each end. The chiselled stone was crafted by the team at Apex Stone, who were excited by this challenge. They started with machinery and then hand finished it to achieve the rippled, textural surface and raw, coarse edge.

The chiselled stone is a recurring theme through the house. At the base of the stairs, the jagged stone edge contrasts with a polished surface on top. In the kitchen, the island bench is wrapped with a pearl grey-coloured stone. Chiselling the bottom edge softens the aesthetic and creates a ragged shadow line, as if the island is hovering just off the floor.

In the main ensuite, Arabescato Corchia marble curves around the wall surfaces. This time we matched the tiles to create continuity of the dramatic veining, and the sense that the space has been hewn from a single monolithic form. Similarly with the vanity, Gris Pearl stone lining the base of the Boffi Garden basin creates the impression of a continuous benchtop, with the Boffi Garden taps set into the vanity.

The kitchen island is often the heart of the home in today's houses, but historically it was around the fire-place that families would gather. These fireplaces, with their chiselled-stone surrounds, really give that sense in this home and help revive a traditional craft technique.

STONE

OTTAWA HOUSE.

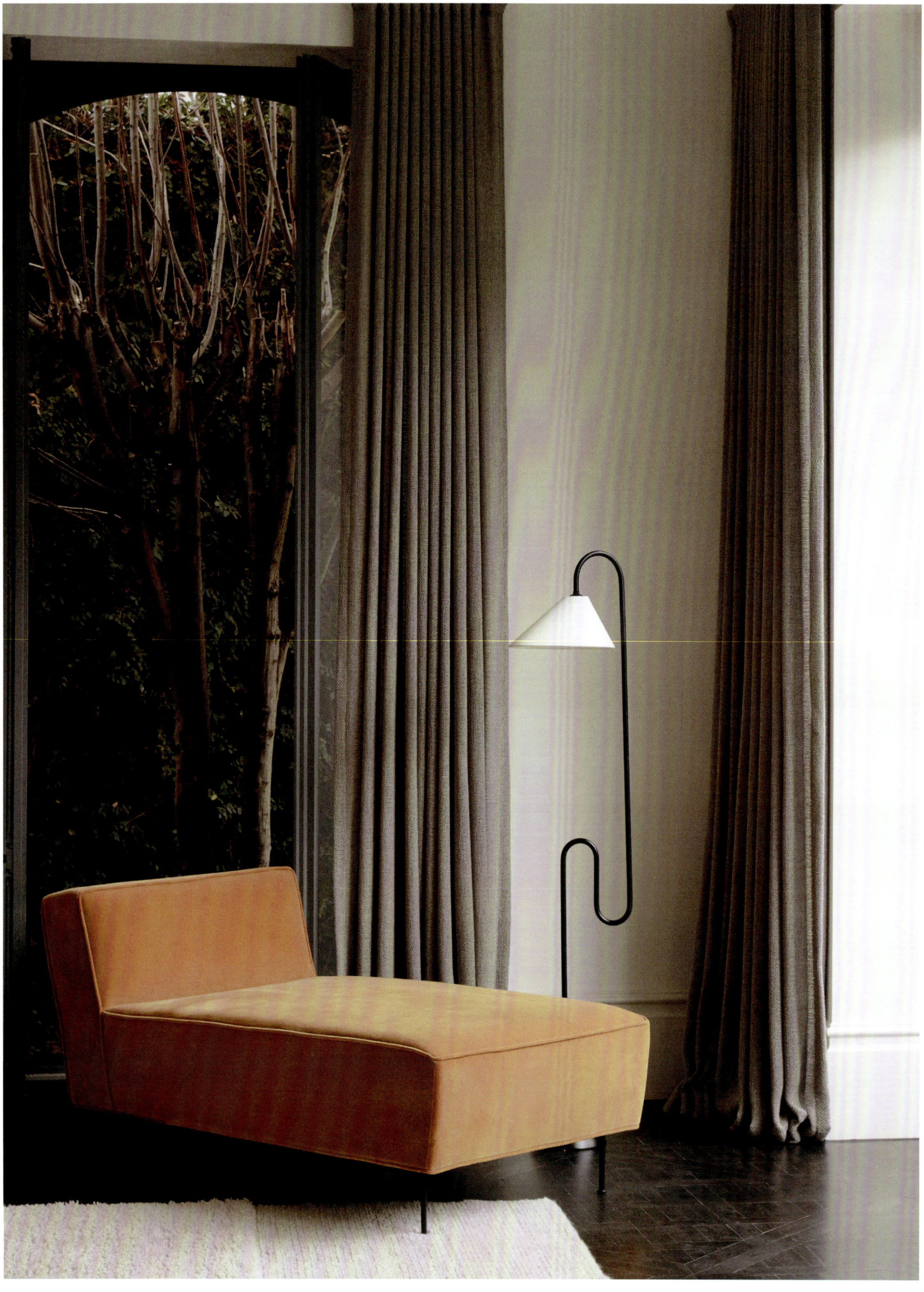

Opposite: In the corner of the living room, the sinuous Roattino floor lamp, designed by Eileen Gray in 1927, illuminates the Gubi chaise upholstered in opulent mandarin-coloured velvet.

This page: The chunky fireplace surround is chiselled from split-face bluestone, granting it the appearance of crudely moulded clay. At the base of the stairs, the hewn stone plinth contrasts raw, jagged edges and a smooth polished surface.

STONE

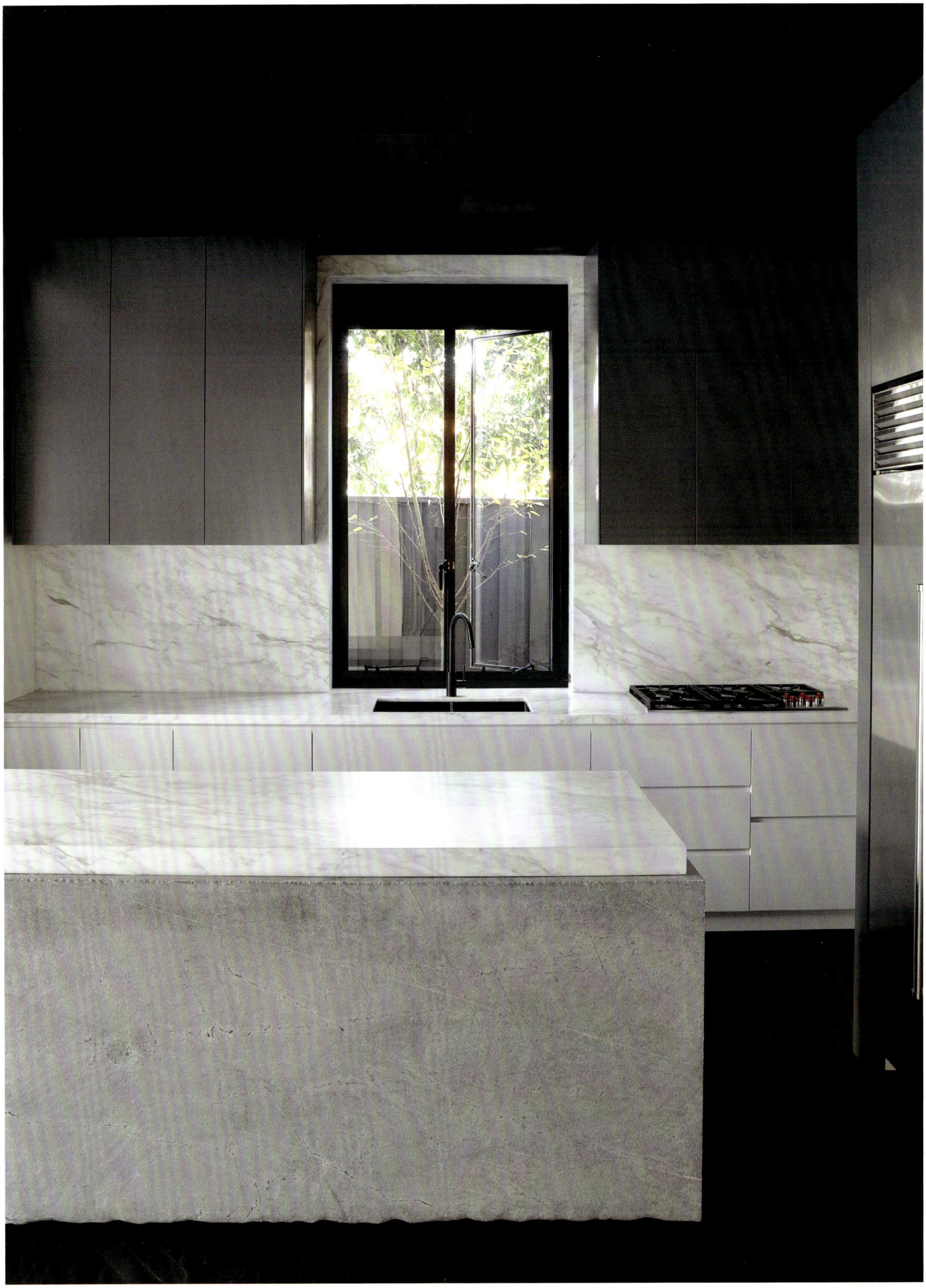

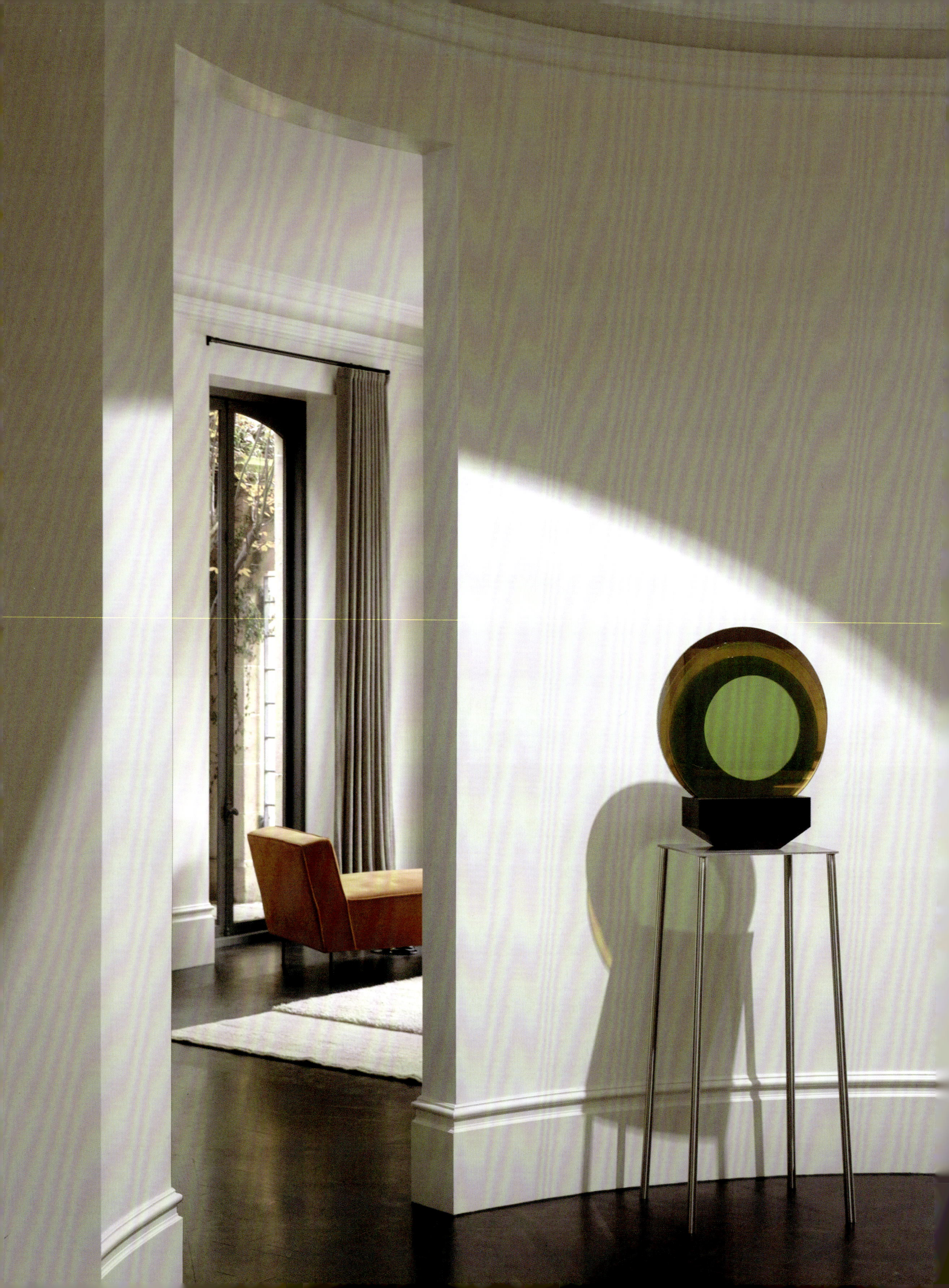

OTTAWA HOUSE.

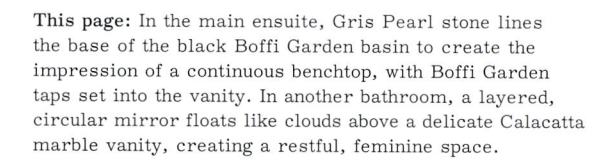

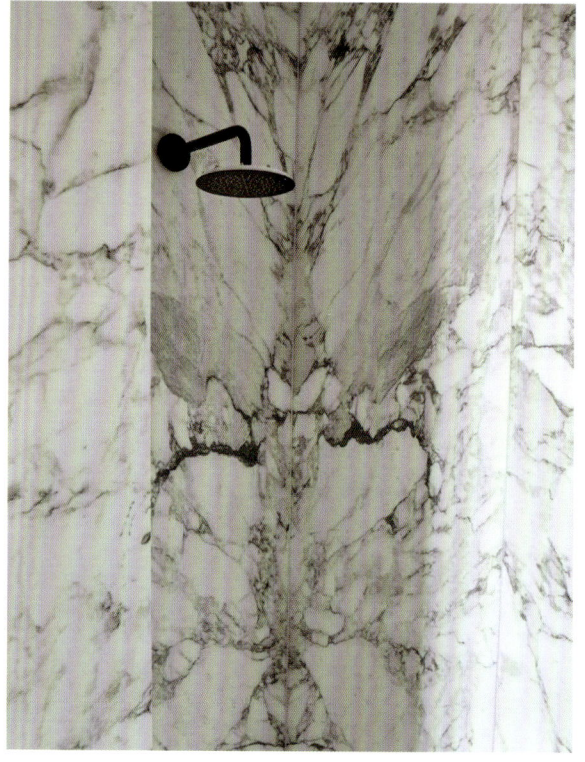

This page: In the main ensuite, Gris Pearl stone lines the base of the black Boffi Garden basin to create the impression of a continuous benchtop, with Boffi Garden taps set into the vanity. In another bathroom, a layered, circular mirror floats like clouds above a delicate Calacatta marble vanity, creating a restful, feminine space.

Opposite: The imposing stone bathtub takes centre stage in the second-level bathroom (adjacent to the main bedroom as it was to be our client's special ensuite). It pays homage to the chateau-style architecture and was the starting point for exploring stone.

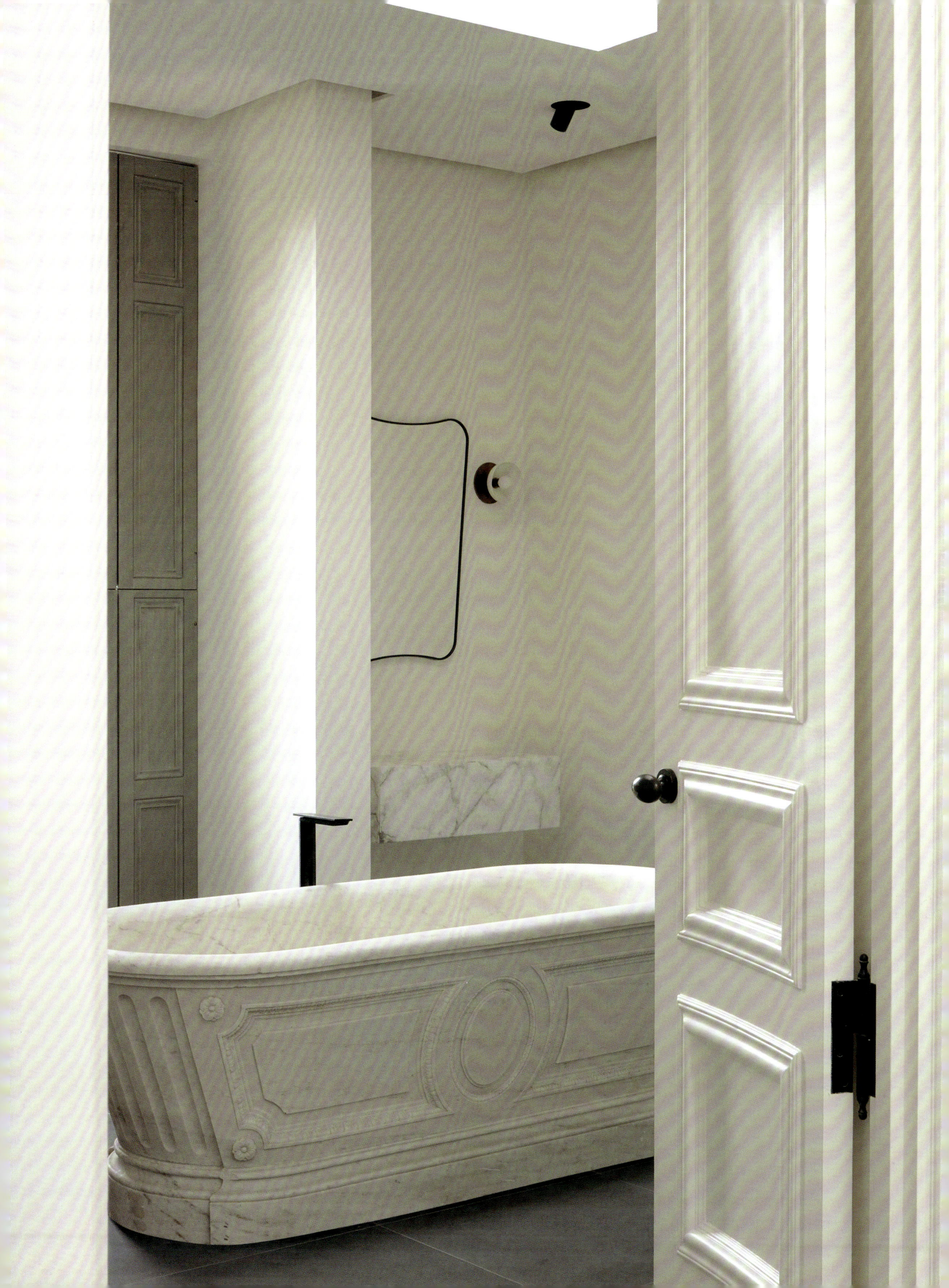

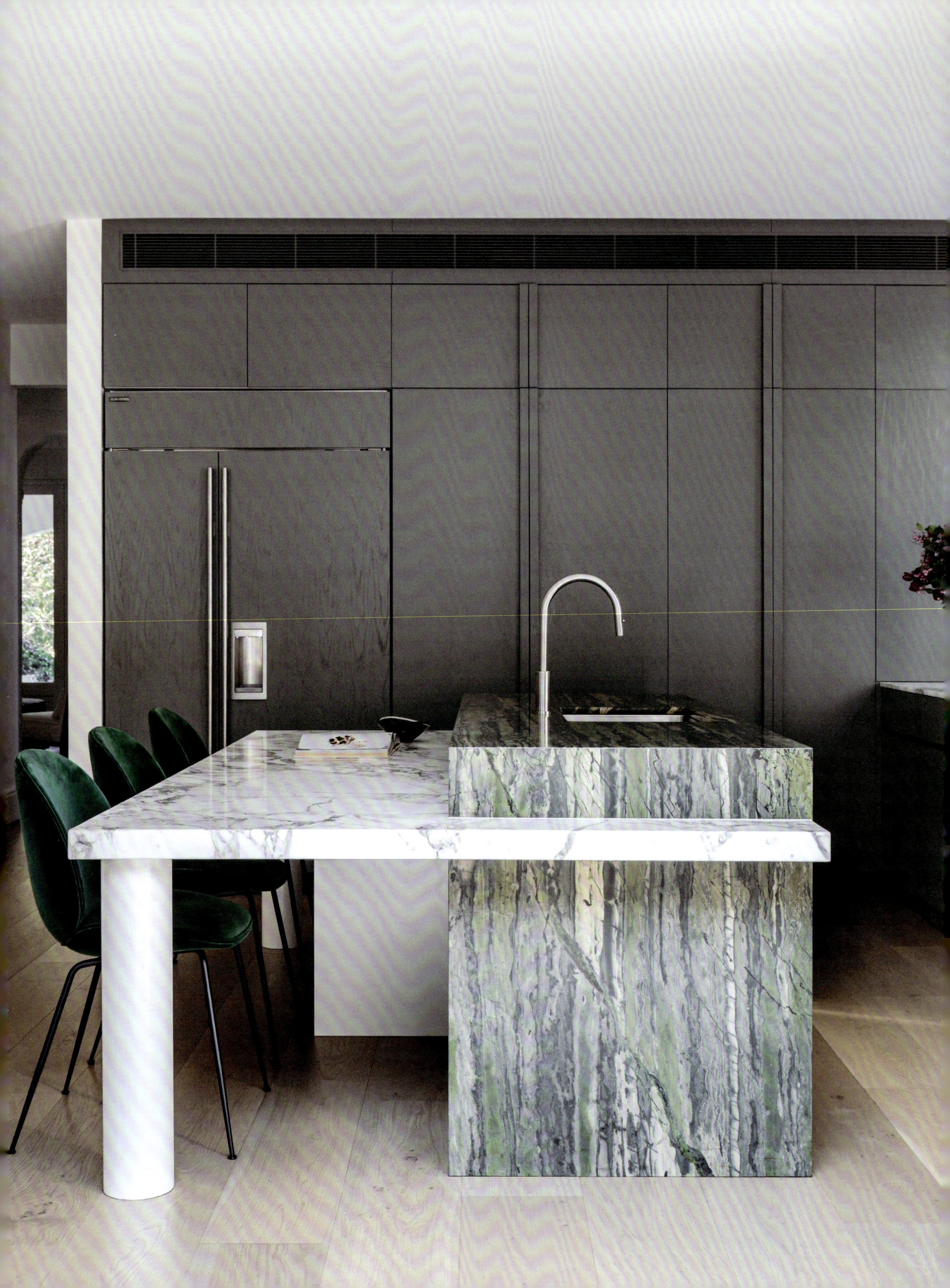

STONE

Rose Bay House.

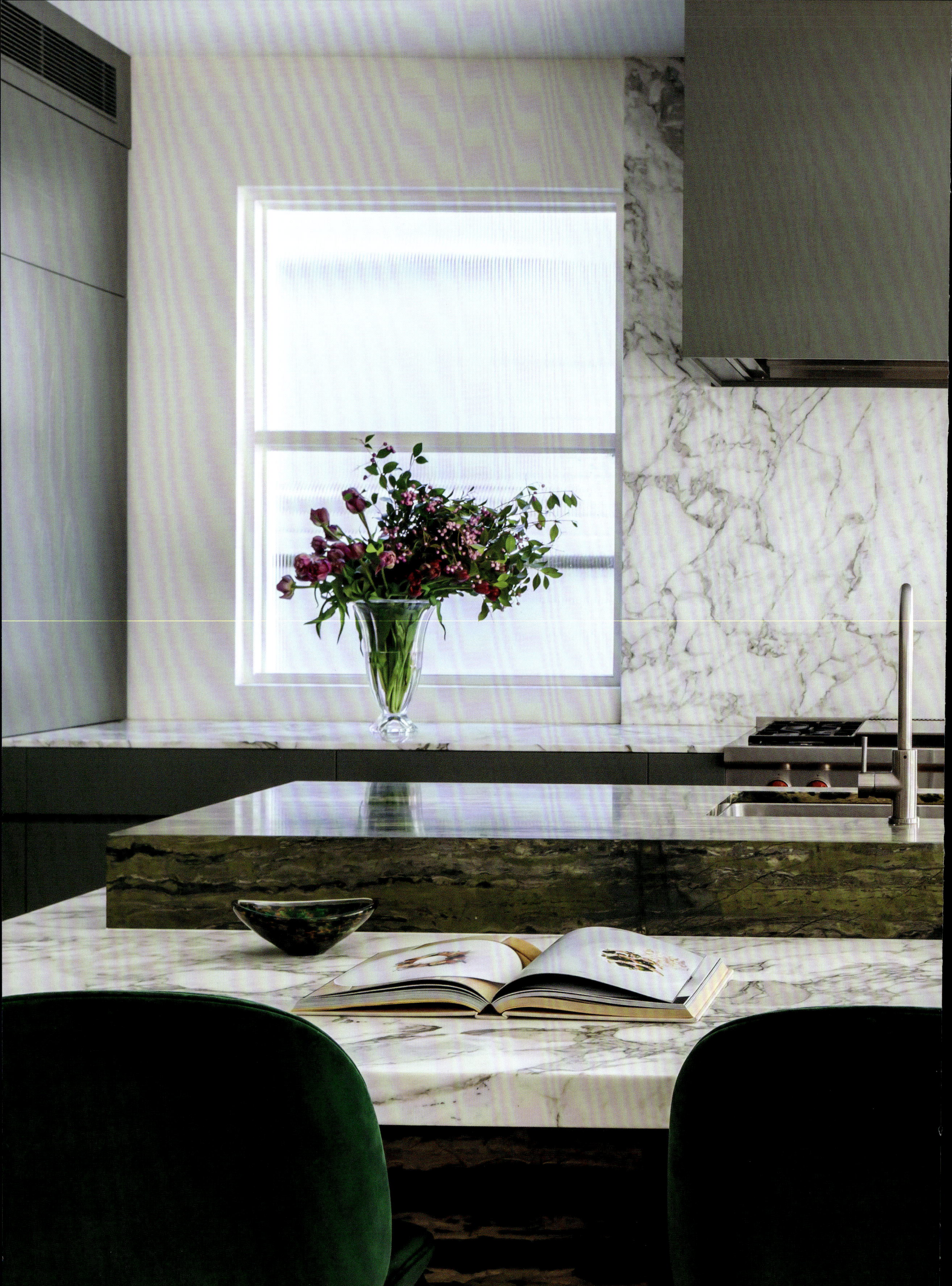

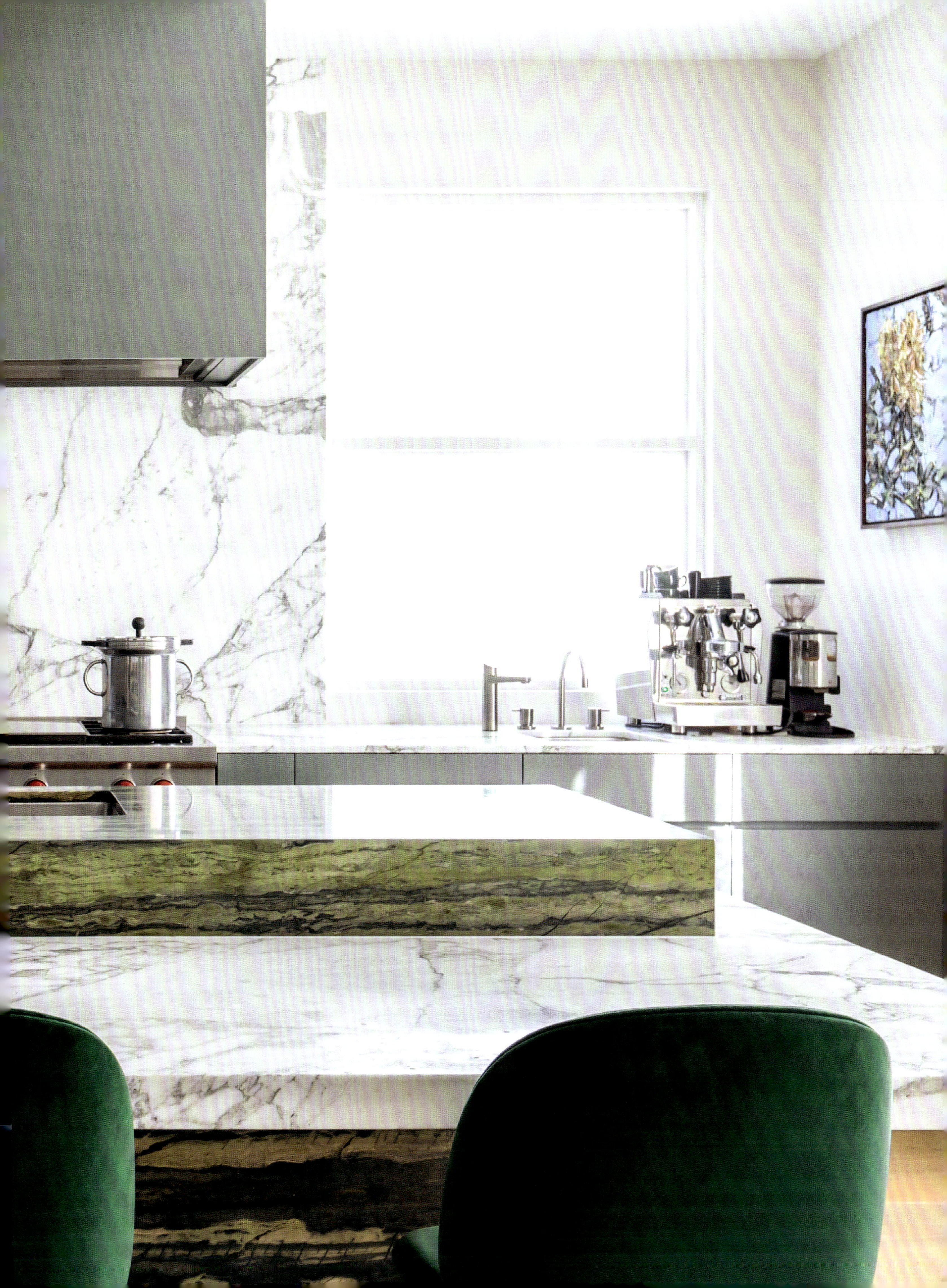

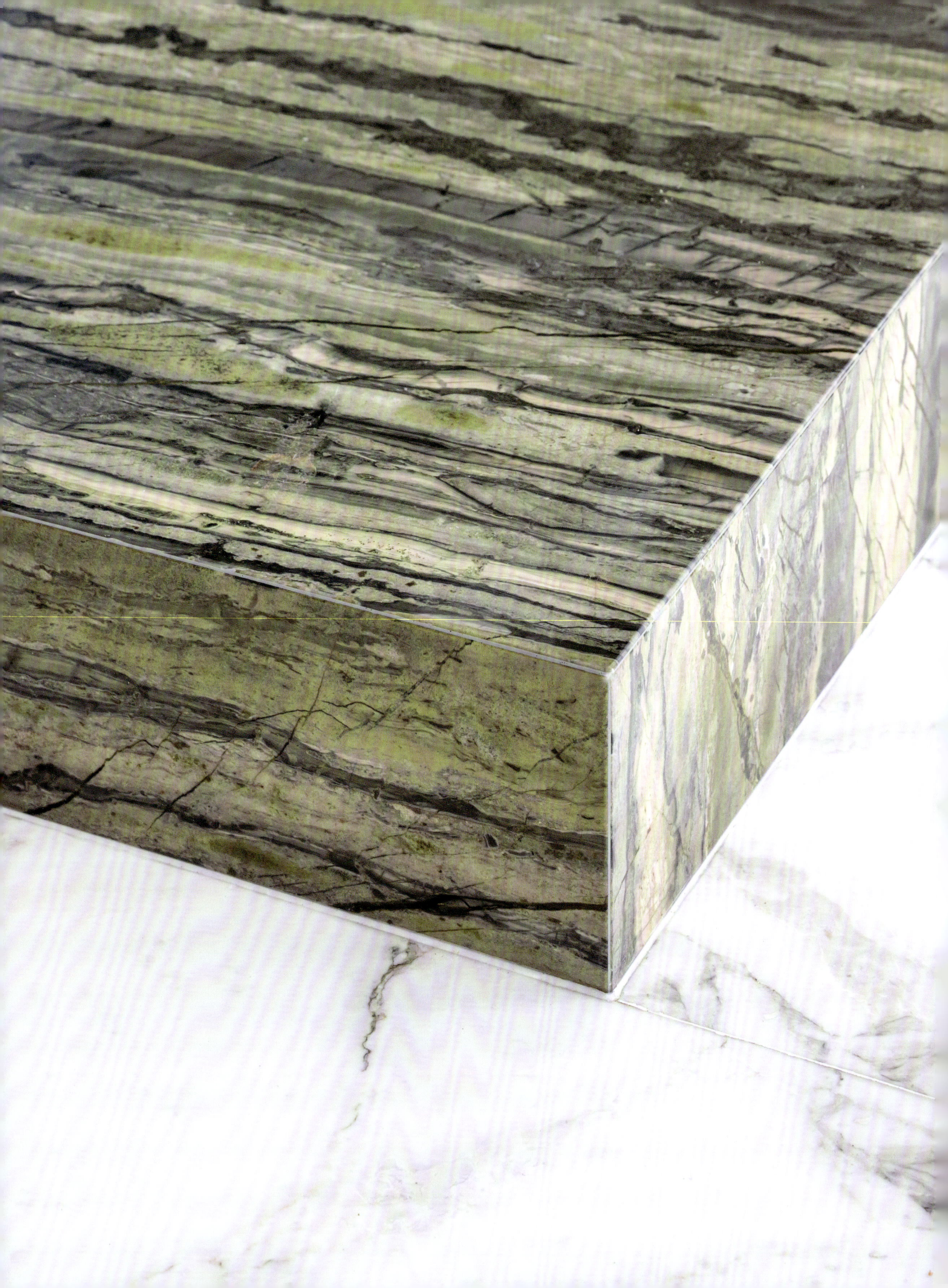

Bold design decisions can drive striking outcomes. Rose Bay House in Sydney is the first project where I used an unusual stone. White and neutral stone was the popular choice then, but we wanted to take a brave approach and explore different stones and uncommon pairings. We've continued to do this ever since and it never fails to excite and inspire us and our clients.

We were engaged to do a partial renovation of this 1920s home. Our clients, who are a high-profile Sydney chef and restaurateur, wanted a social and welcoming kitchen that would serve as an extension of their professional life. The brief also entailed a light, airy ensuite offering an indulgent retreat.

The kitchen is on the ground floor of the two-storey Art Deco house and opens to a beautiful courtyard garden. We wanted to create a practical, elegant, versatile kitchen that encouraged interaction and conviviality. It's the clients' everyday spot for having breakfast and lunch, and hosting family or friends for casual get-togethers.

We designed a two-tiered island bench combining a dining table and an elevated work surface. A sculptural centrepiece, it provides a friendly area for guests to sit with a glass of wine and engage with the hosts and the spectacle of cooking. The robust work surface is the banded South American marble Gardano, a variegated landscape of bottle and olive greens. Extending from the island, Vagli Argento stone forms the dining table, surrounded by Gubi Beetle chairs upholstered in rich, emerald-coloured velvet.

Beyond the island, the deep-red knobs of the Wolf oven and cooktop provide pops of contrasting colour. Full-height lacquered oak cabinetry conceals the fridge and pantry, its soft eucalypt hue drawing out the green-grey tones of the marble work bench.

Upstairs, the main bedroom and generous walk-in robe open to a light-filled ensuite. Honouring the timeless elegance of the house, we created an atmosphere of sanctuary and seclusion. While the floor-to-ceiling windows bathe the room in magical sunlight, they posed a challenge for the vanity as it needed to sit in a space with a window behind it. We anchored the floating Calacatta Vagli marble vanity – echoing the kitchen palette – with a brass-clad wall crowned with a brass-trimmed mirror by Gio Ponti. Designed in 1933, its gentle curves hark back to the decorative era of the home.

The heritage-inspired Agape Ottocento bathtub is a modern interpretation of a classic cast-iron bathtub. Beautiful sheer curtains soften the light and open for a restful view of the garden beyond.

This page and opposite: Soft eucalypt-coloured joinery panels line the walls of the kitchen, providing a subdued and relaxed backdrop to the two-tiered island bench clad in Gardano and Vagli Argento. Gubi Beetle chairs upholstered in sumptuous emerald-green velvet provide a comfortable observation post for kitchen companions.

ROSE BAY HOUSE.

STONE

ROSE BAY HOUSE.

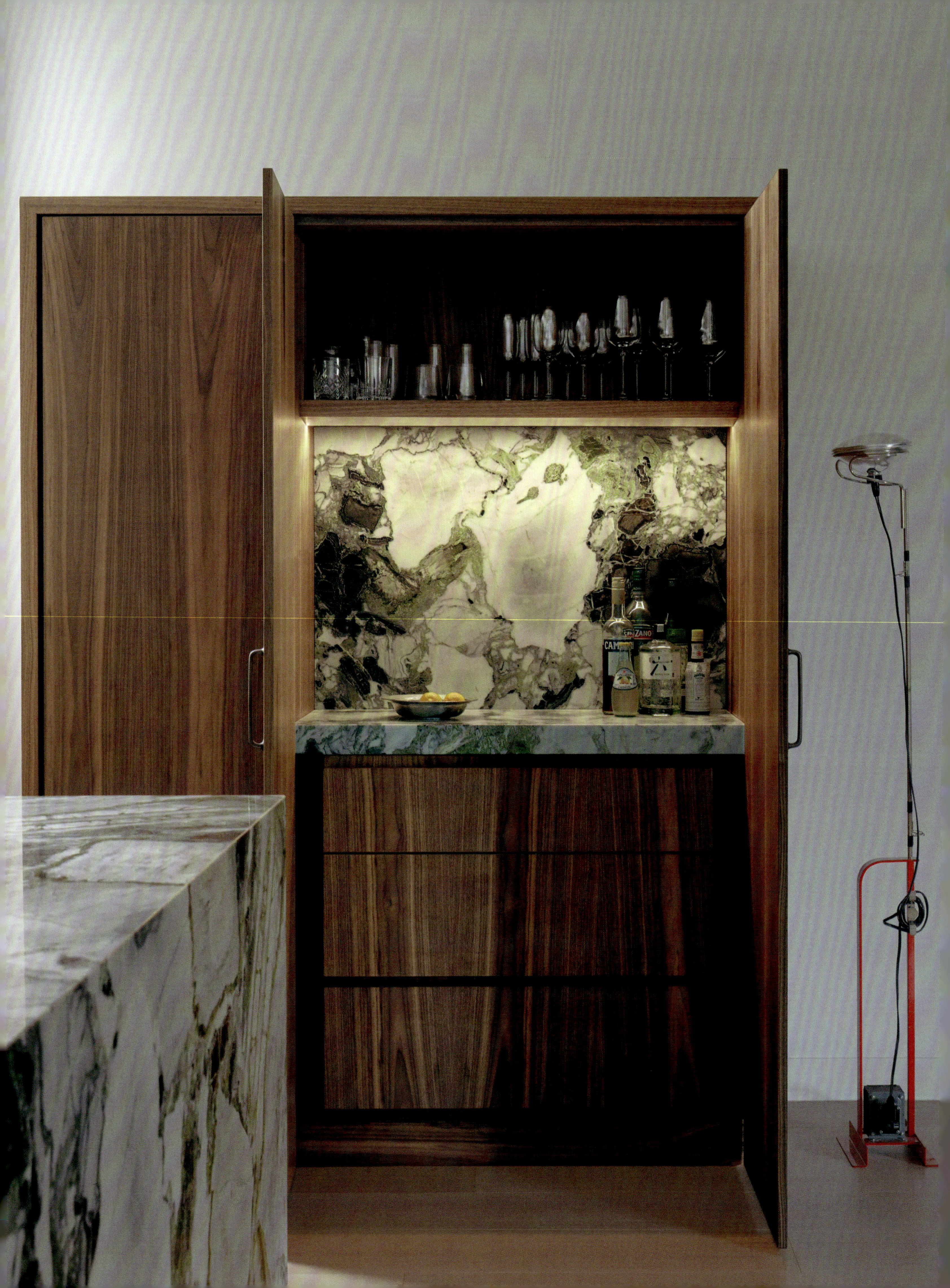

STONE

St Kilda Apartment.

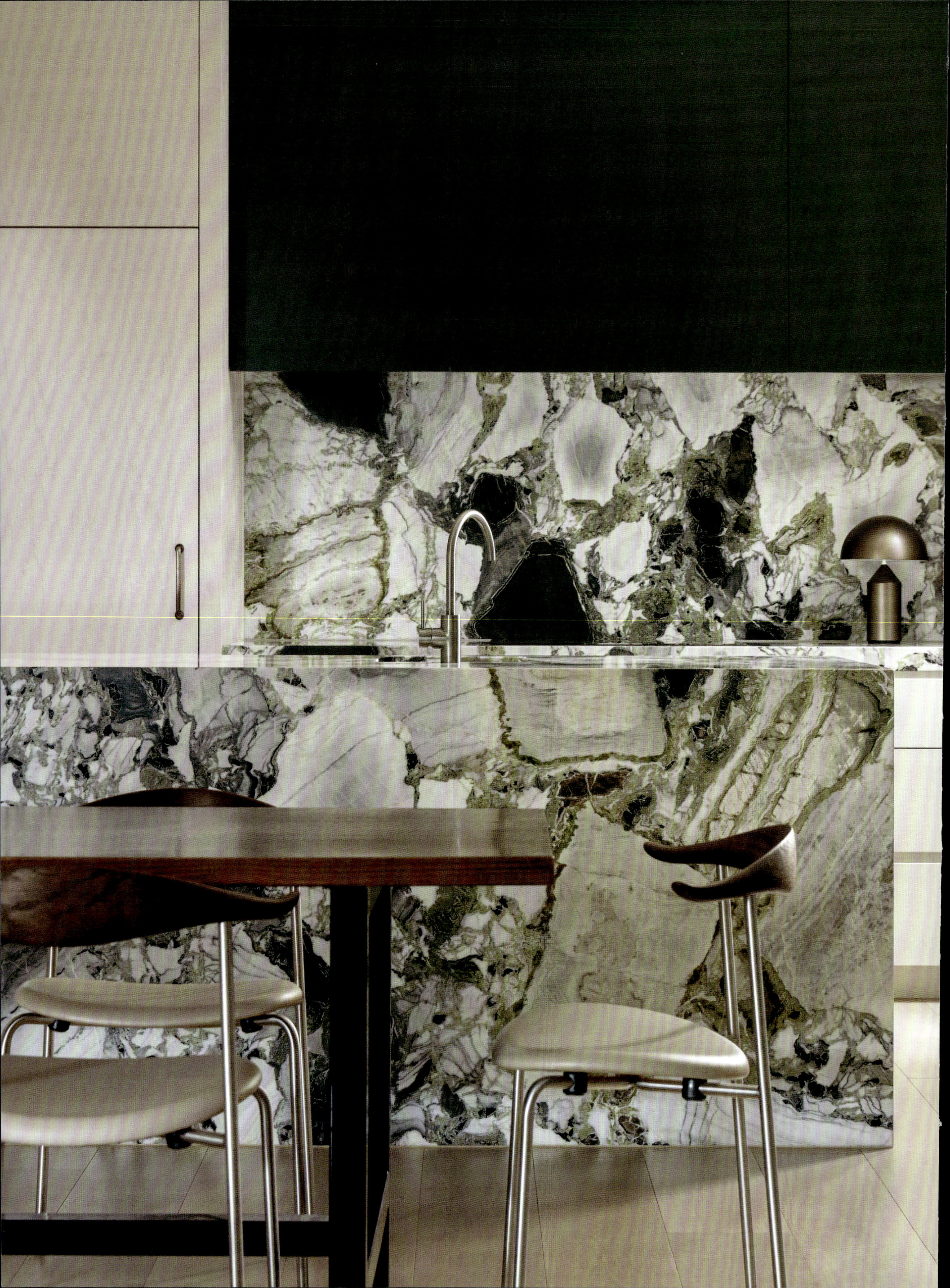

A peaceful spirit infuses St Kilda Apartment. Olive-green gums outside the apartment, viewed through picture windows, create the impression of a treehouse, imparting this home with a feeling of restfulness and elegance.

The brief for the redesign of the sizeable apartment was to transform the tired, dark and stifling interior into a light and graceful home that nourishes and refreshes its adventurous owners. Their personal objects are dotted throughout to reflect the story of their lives and the much-loved family apartment.

We took inspiration from the apartment's elevated position amid the tree canopy, bathing the interior with calming tones of ink, straw and the greens of nature. Wide, pale floorboards and a wheaten-hued custom bamboo silk rug in the living room provide the foundation for curated materials throughout. Rich White Beauty stone is splendidly baroque within the kitchen, embellishing the island bench and splashback, as well as the tailor-made cocktail cabinet. Joinery of striated walnut wood is offset with muted block colours of olive, blush and ink.

The apartment is soothing, yet alive with colour. A landscaped wall of greenery, designed and nurtured by the owner, draws nature inside via the generous all-weather tiled balcony. Selected objects provide pops of blue, while crisp white linen, buff-coloured leather and textural window furnishings in subdued greys and drab greens take their cue from the heroic stone that wraps the monolithic kitchen island and sculpturally adds a focal natural element.

Purposefully reclusive, the apartment turns away from the frenetic bustle outside, offering its occupants a whisper-quiet reprieve from the urban locale. Textural wall treatments and fabrics soften robust edges and reinforce the air of understated luxury. Heavy drapery brings a sense of theatre, the sumptuous swish of fabric blurring the boundary between inside and out.

In St Kilda Apartment, richly textured layers combine with an expressed architecture of rawness to create a hotel-esque style of home, a haven and retreat for its owners.

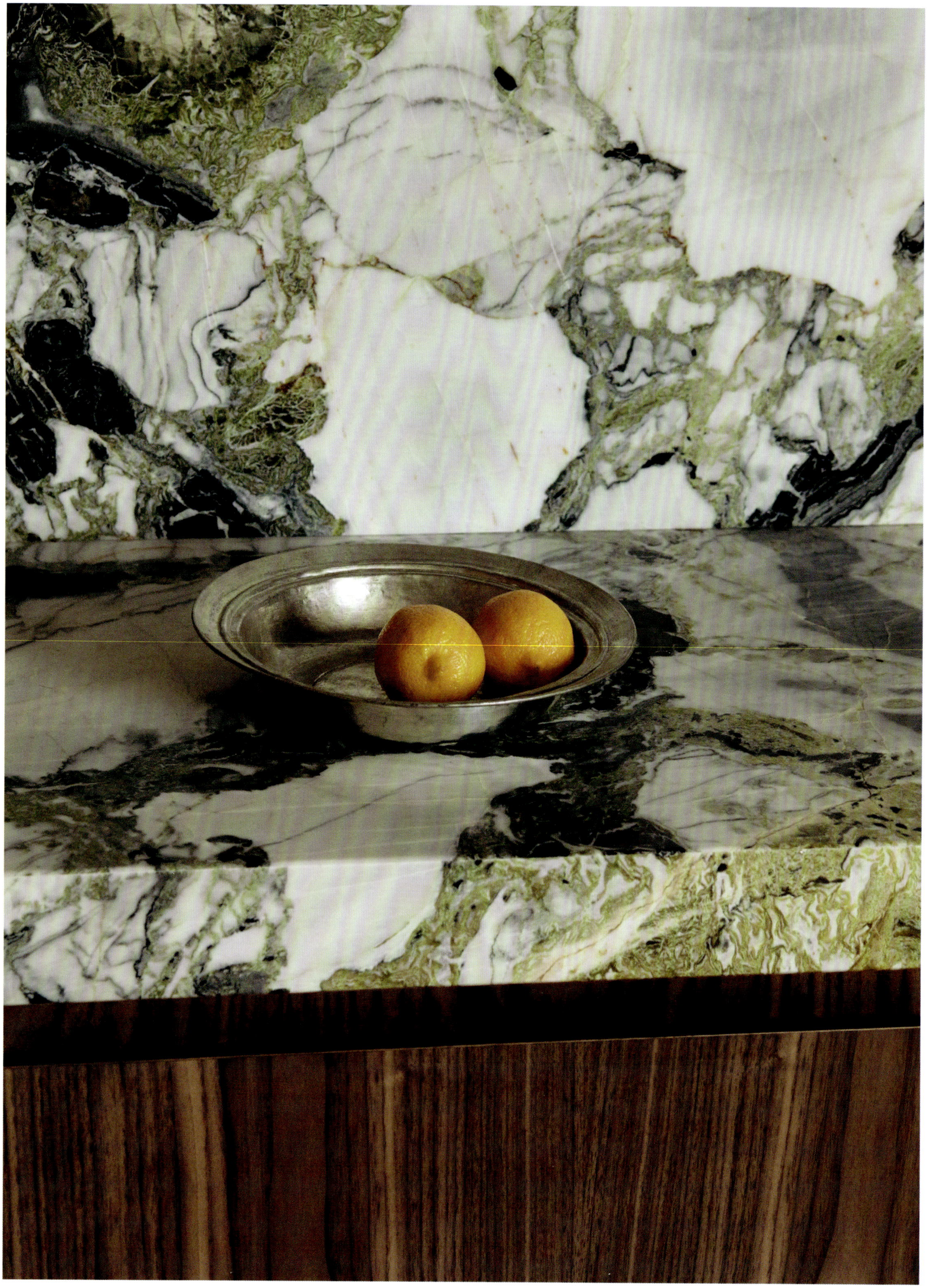

ST KILDA APARTMENT.

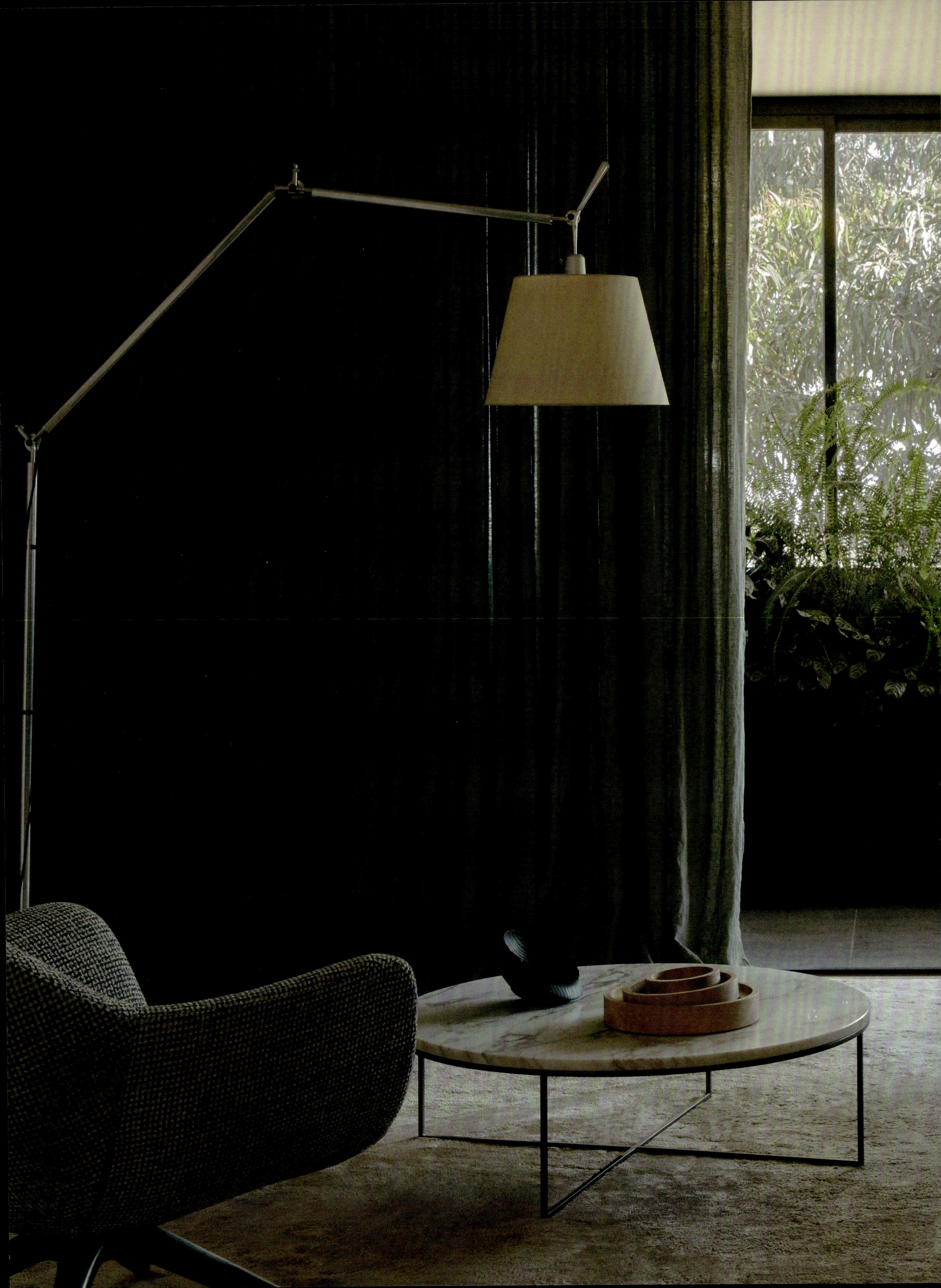

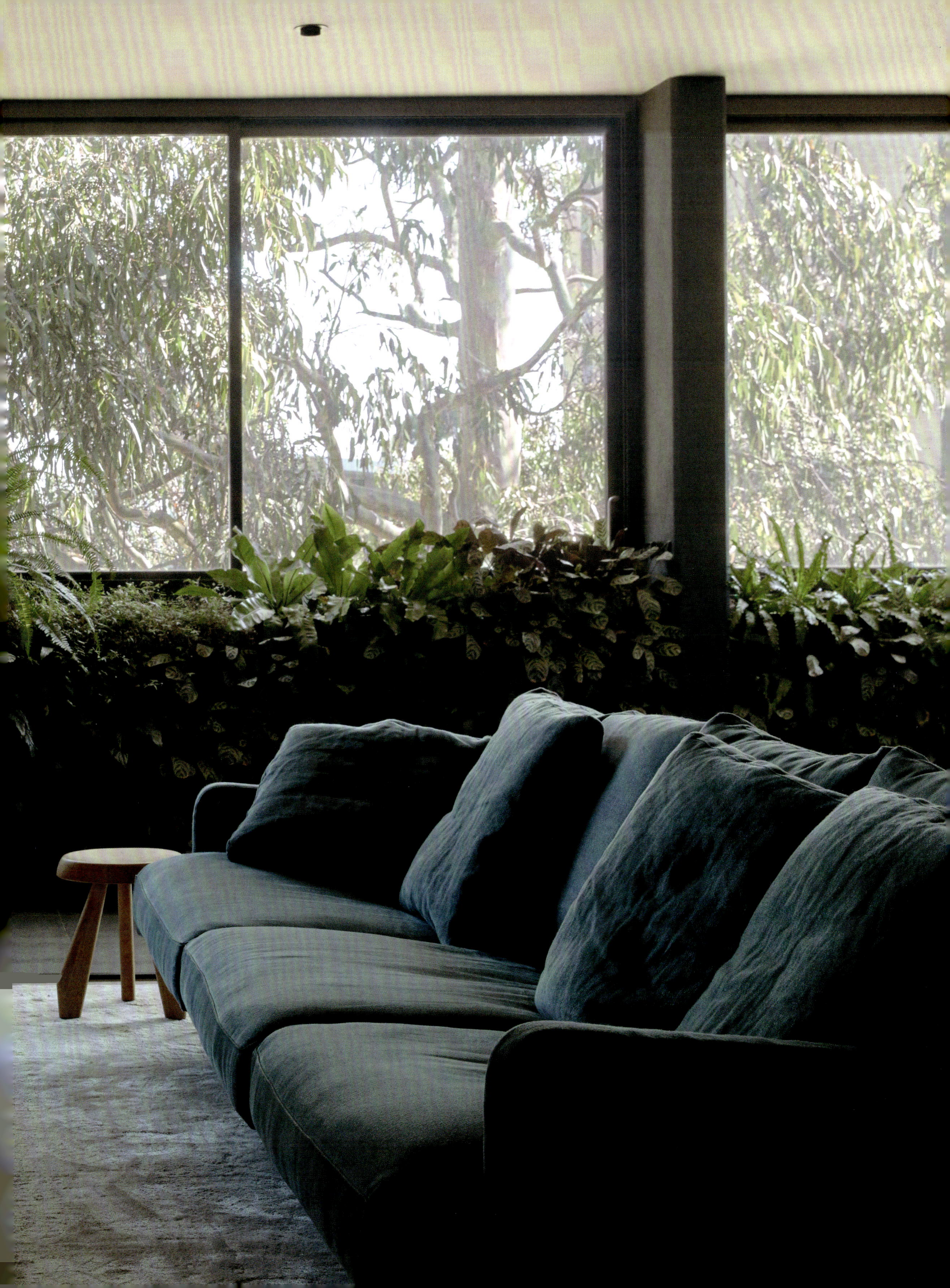

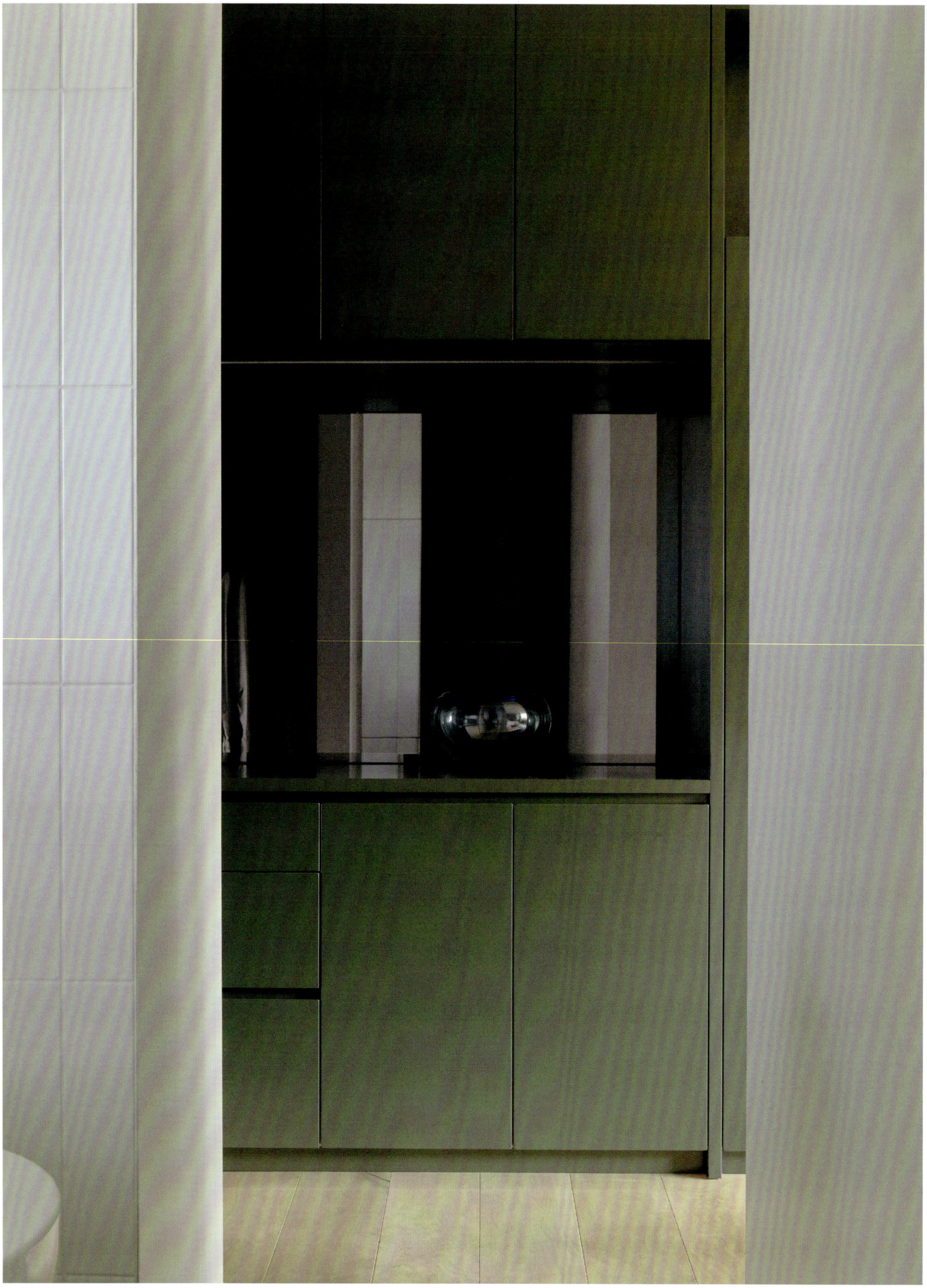

Swathes of green in the bedroom elicit a mood of quiet harmony, from the sage linen curtains to the mellow bedding and muted olive-green joinery. Tan leather wraps the bedhead frame with timber oak detail.

ST KILDA APARTMENT.

STONE

GIANT STEPS

Our brief for the Giant Steps tasting room was to pay homage to the landscapes of its single-vineyard sites in the Yarra Valley. At the time, the tasting room only occupied the second floor of the two-storey building. We convinced our client that incorporating both levels would better reflect their expansive offering. The downstairs would be a relaxed and light space to enjoy their new releases in a fresh and casual setting, and upstairs would be moodier and robust to complement their premier vintage wines with a fuller-bodied ambience.

Our vision was to create a space that harmoniously blended the verdant hues of the landscape and the taste sensations of Giant Steps' chardonnay and pinot noir. We developed a palette of stone, wood, metal and textiles to connect the levels through materiality and colour but at the same time provoke a transformative experience.

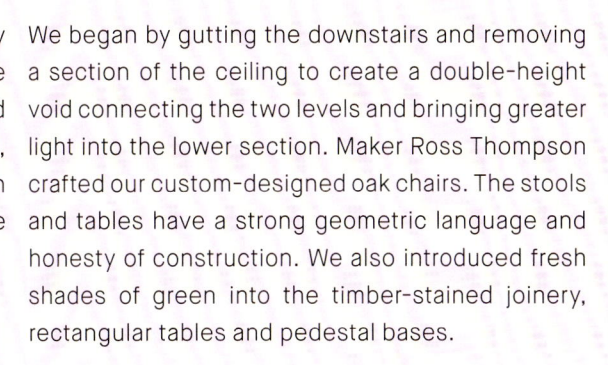

We began by gutting the downstairs and removing a section of the ceiling to create a double-height void connecting the two levels and bringing greater light into the lower section. Maker Ross Thompson crafted our custom-designed oak chairs. The stools and tables have a strong geometric language and honesty of construction. We also introduced fresh shades of green into the timber-stained joinery, rectangular tables and pedestal bases.

We designed the central bar to be appealing and welcoming. We selected the exquisite Silver Cloud granite and sandblasted and brushed it to create a textured surface. Its mottled silvery shade symbolises the cool-climate origins of the brand's wines, and its elaborate wavy motif is almost like a fine textile weave. At the end of the bar, a hand-finished box is a versatile vessel for displaying flowers or wine. The opulent stone bar provides a heroic backdrop for an exceptional experience.

The Cuff seating and chairs are upholstered in deep-olive leather with raw open seams. The chairs sit atop rich lilac-coloured rugs, bringing to life the gorgeous combination of green and aubergine. Glossy, round side tables introduce bursts of vinous red.

Giant Steps is a harmonious, integrated expression of natural materials and artisanship. The stone, metal, wood and textiles celebrate the Australian landscape and animate the tasting room with inviting appeal.

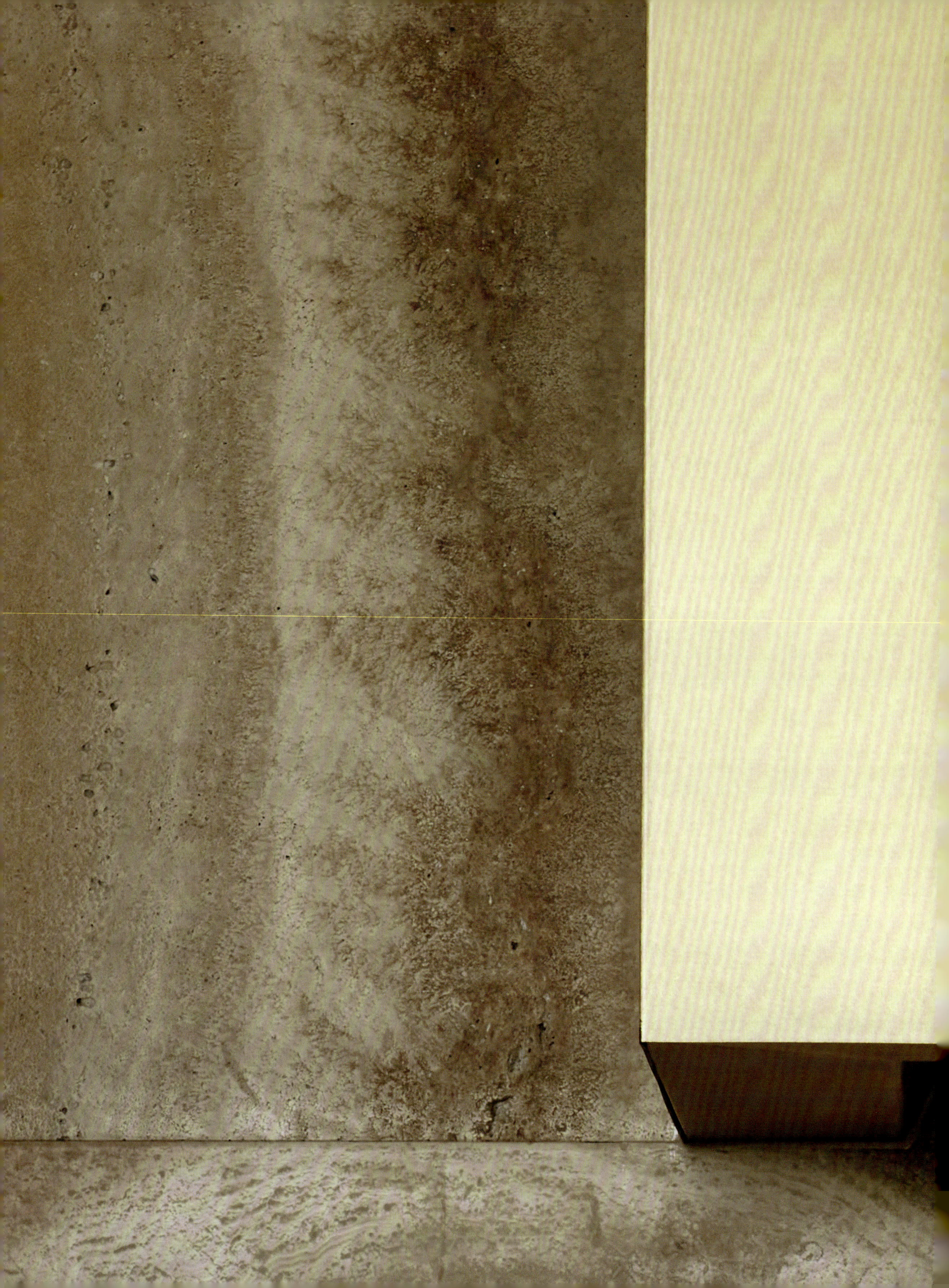

METAL

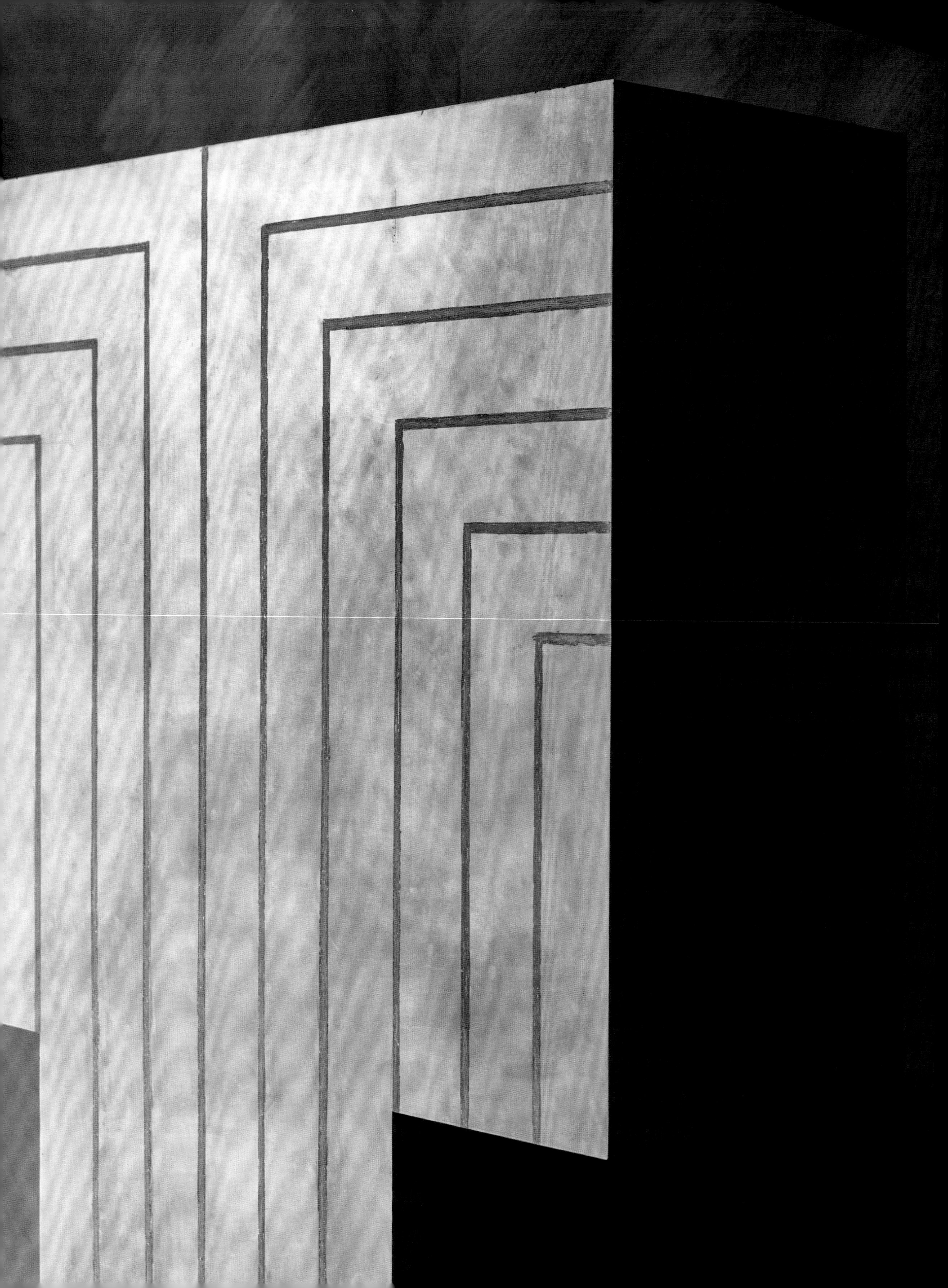

The metal shed on our farm was an adventurous place to play when I was a kid. I relished the rawness of the space and the way the wind would whistle through the building. Brass, aluminium and blackened steel mixed to create a jangled mishmash of metal. It's a memory that has influenced my design work with metals.

Two renowned makers have also inspired the use of metals in our projects: the American sculptor David Smith and the Australian sculptor Inge King. David Smith would manipulate metal by hand, making it far more tactile. I first discovered his work in a book that contained wonderful photographs of his sculptures. The images were shot in the snow and this backdrop made his work feel monumental yet approachable at the same time. Inge King's creations, too, are powerful – immense in scale and impact. Both artists used hand-worked metals and minimal forms to make metal the hero material.

Aluminium is one of my preferred metals. It is an oily material that keeps changing – it takes on your fingerprints when you touch it. By sanding it, then hand waxing it, it becomes a soft, evolved metal. The Melbourne Penthouse features aluminium panels dipped in acid to create an ombre effect; to achieve a different effect for the same project we took recycled brass filings, heated them up and sprayed them onto aluminium panels. These two metal panels, each with a distinct look, sit alongside each other. Adjacent to these is an exquisite Vincenzo de Cotiis freestanding wall unit in sandcast aluminium. A medley of different metal explorations make the Melbourne Penthouse feel modern and eccentric at the same time. It's a seductive combination.

In developing projects, we collaborate with craftspeople and artists to create an interplay between art and design. The projects that showcase metal are often the result of experimentation and teamwork, an approach that creates robust spaces.

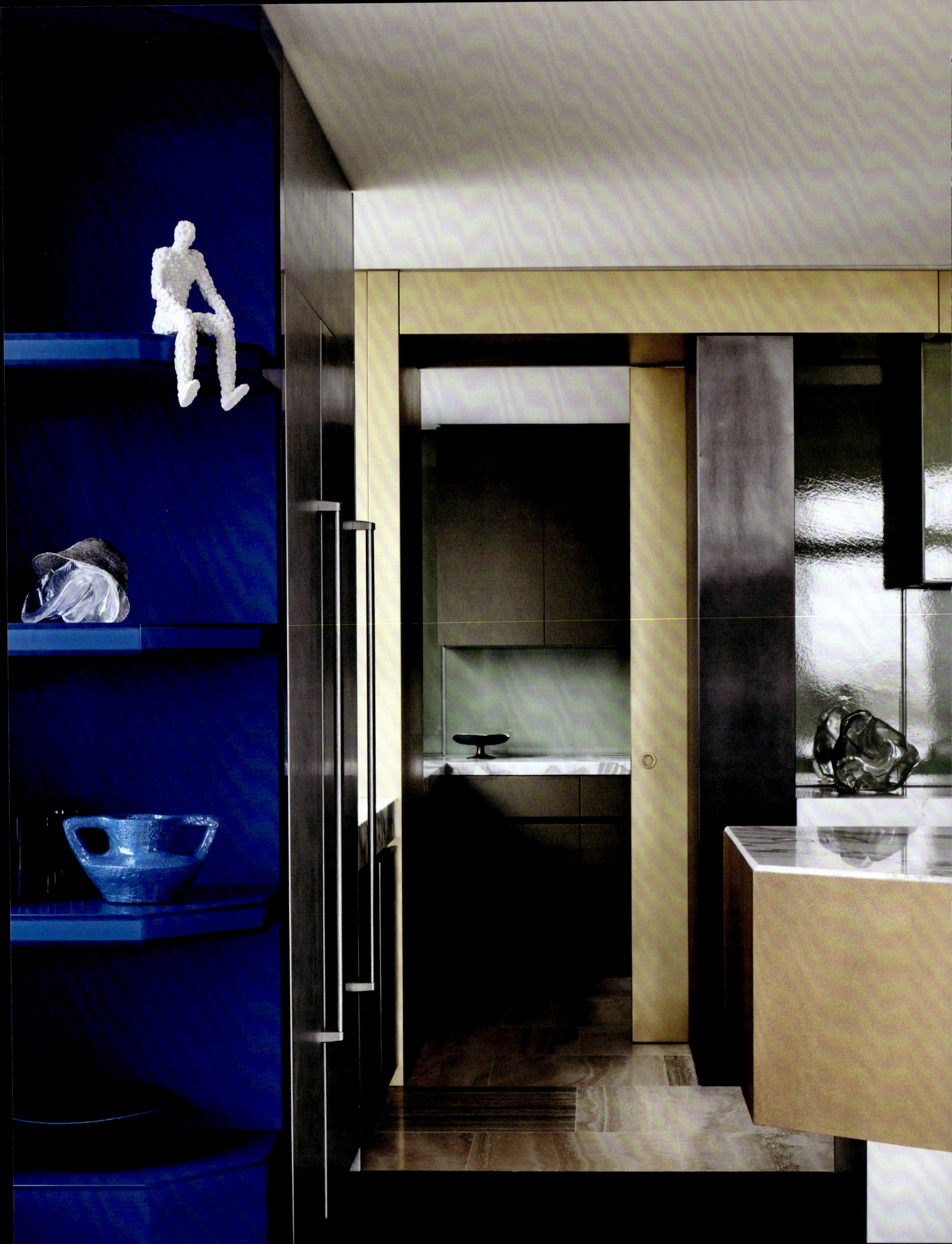

METAL

Melbourne Penthouse.

METAL

MELBOURNE PENTHOUSE.

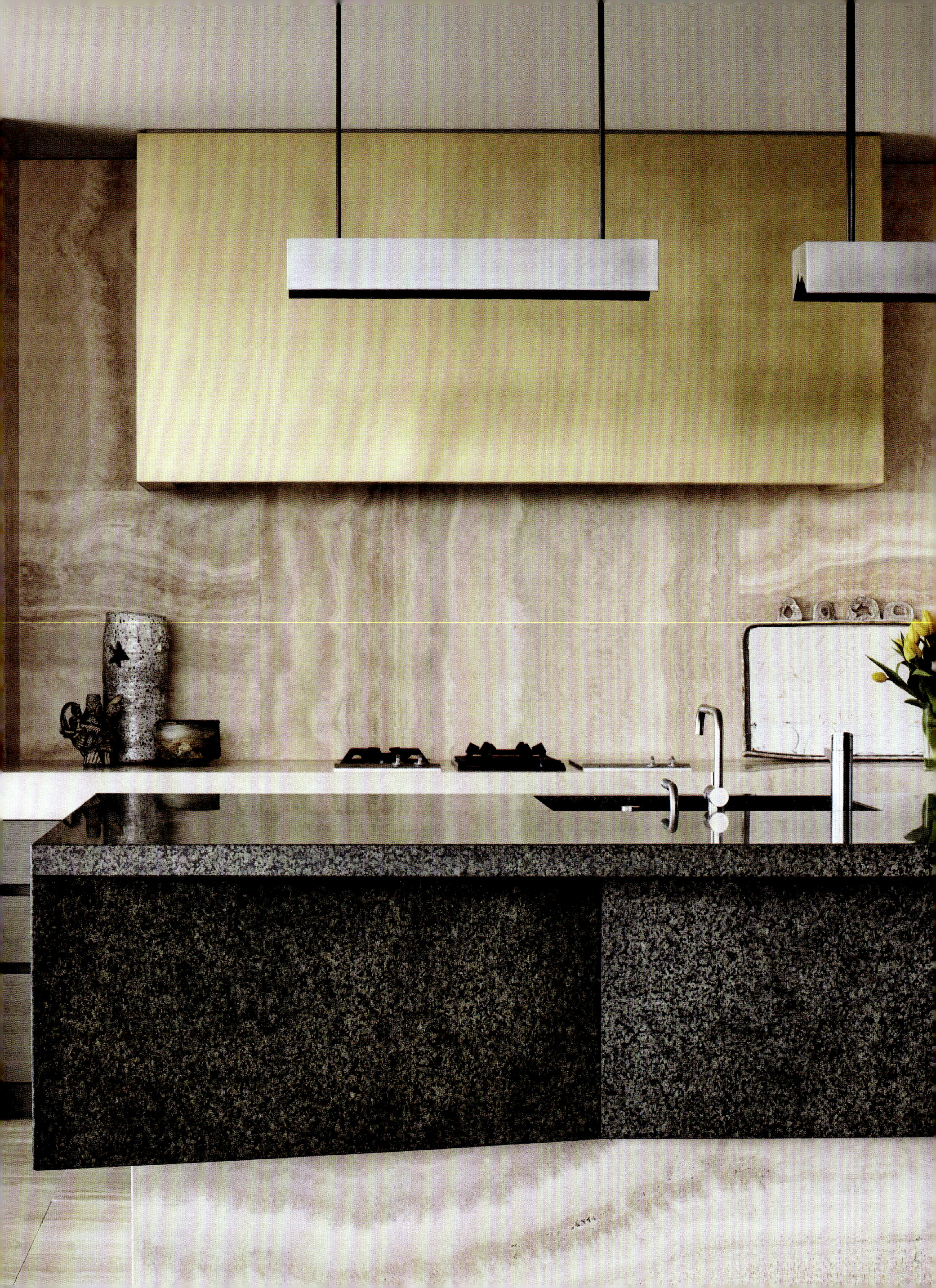

Travertine and bluestone flooring set the foundation for our layering of materials and exploration of artisanal techniques in this impressive penthouse. It's home to a retired, sociable couple who enjoy entertaining and have a strong interest in art and culture. I lent them a collection of art, architecture and design books from which to draw ideas and inspiration, and through that they discovered the work of one my favourite designers – French architect Charles Zana. His use of metal and stone helped set the direction for our approach.

The penthouse has two kitchen, dining and living spaces – one at each end of the apartment, capturing the expansive views of Fawkner Park and the city to the east, and Port Phillip Bay to the west. The initial scope for the project was to uplift the west-facing kitchen where the couple entertain, to create something special that engages with its context. However, the scope quickly expanded to the whole apartment, thus ensuring a cohesive flow within the space. I wanted to give it texture, depth and personality, and the sense that it could be in any great city in the world. We developed a bold architectural language referencing the built and natural environment of Melbourne, and accentuated the sculptural forms with tactile surfaces, dramatic patterning, surprising colour and bespoke statement pieces.

We began with the floor and paired blue-veined travertine with creamy-toned travertine, deliberately mixing the tiles and orienting the veining in different directions. This is a common practice in Italy when they patch damaged stone, and I find it endearing and beautiful. Tick-tacking the patterning amplifies the unique beauty of each tile and stone, and it feels more approachable and organic, as it breaks down the monumentality. We also rotated the travertine tiles on the built-in shelving in the living room and study, and left the natural holes in the stone, as the clients appreciated how beautiful it is untouched and unfilled.

The kitchen island bench is the jewel of the space. Floating on an aluminium plinth, it has a front clad with folded aluminium that has been sprayed with brass filings. It's an old technique that plumbers used to seal taps, and it gives a subtle, textured finish. Behind the island, blackened steel frames the ceramic-glazed lava stone splashback and rangehood. Quarried and finished in France, the stone has a gorgeous soft-green glaze that reflects the light, ever-changing as the sun moves throughout the day. Bright resin shelving in International Klein Blue, by French artist Yves Klein, is an unexpected shot of colour at one end of the kitchen.

The strong geometry of the kitchen island and built-in shelving is offset by the curved de Sede modular sofa and the jagged edges of the superb aluminium Vincenzo De Cotiis limited-edition bookcase. The cast-bronze beauty is a statement piece upon entry, maintaining views and openness through the living room.

A South Australian Balmoral Green granite and Italian travertine in the second kitchen, and an extraordinary Calacatta Vagli marble encasing the main bathroom, add to the dramatic effect. We designed the vanities as bold, monolithic structures, carved from a single block of Italian stone and wrapping around a cylindrical base.

It's a joy to work with clients who are so brave and adventurous with their choices. The result is an arresting, immersive home where they can enjoy life and entertain. They love to spend mornings on the east side of their home soaking up green views of the park and the city beyond, and evenings on the west side, overlooking the expansive bay.

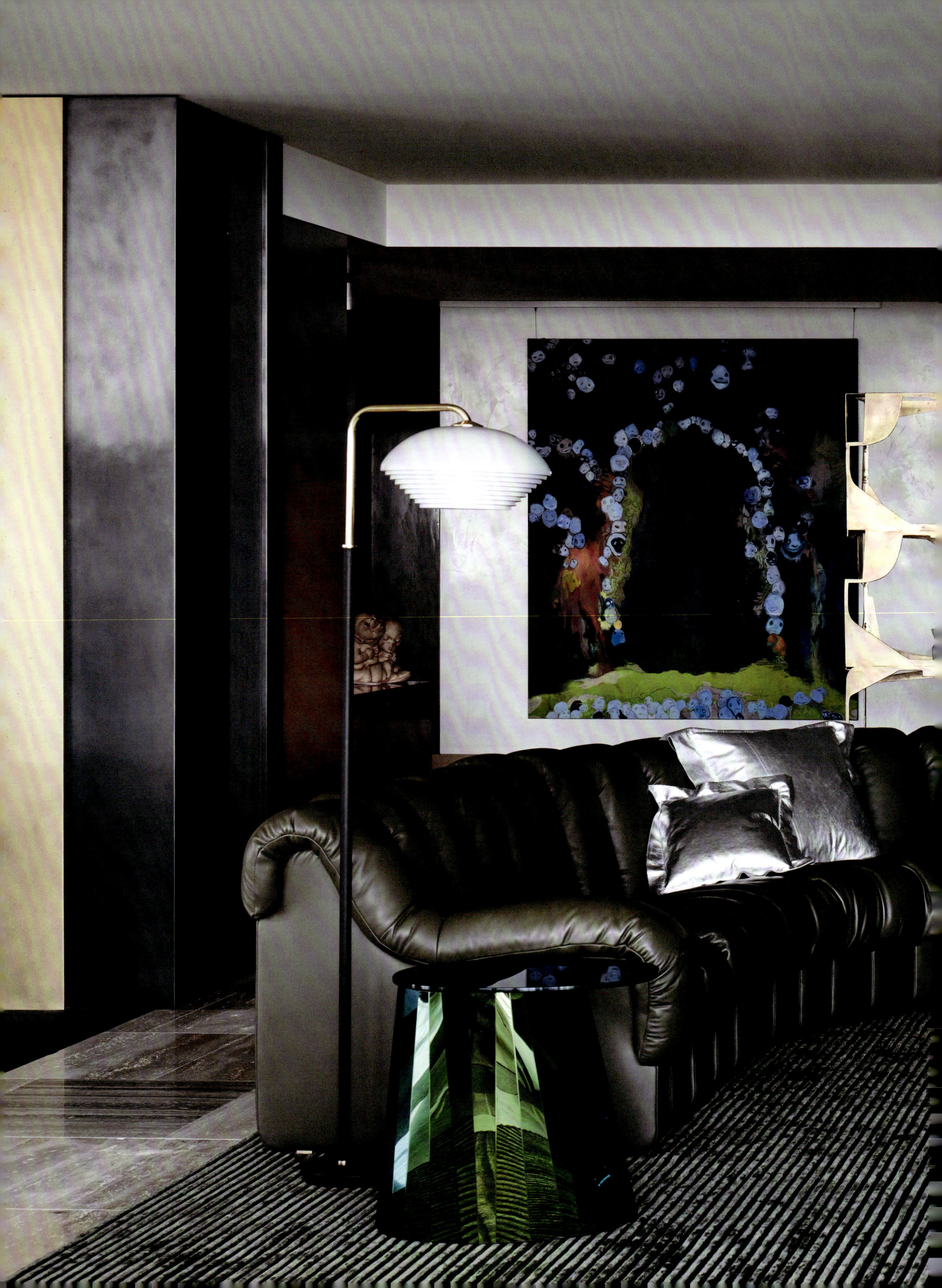

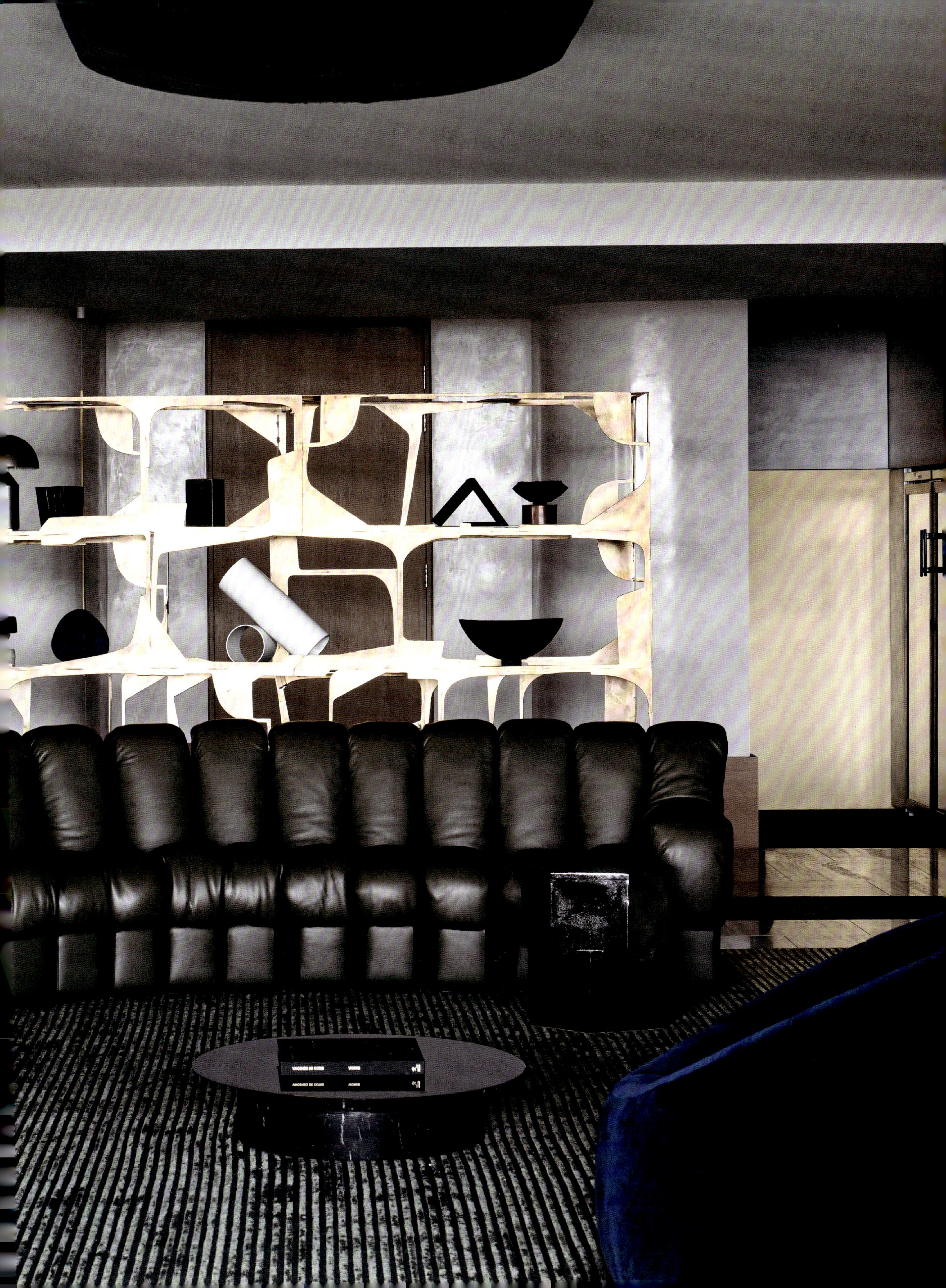

METAL

MELBOURNE PENTHOUSE.

METAL

MELBOURNE PENTHOUSE.

METAL

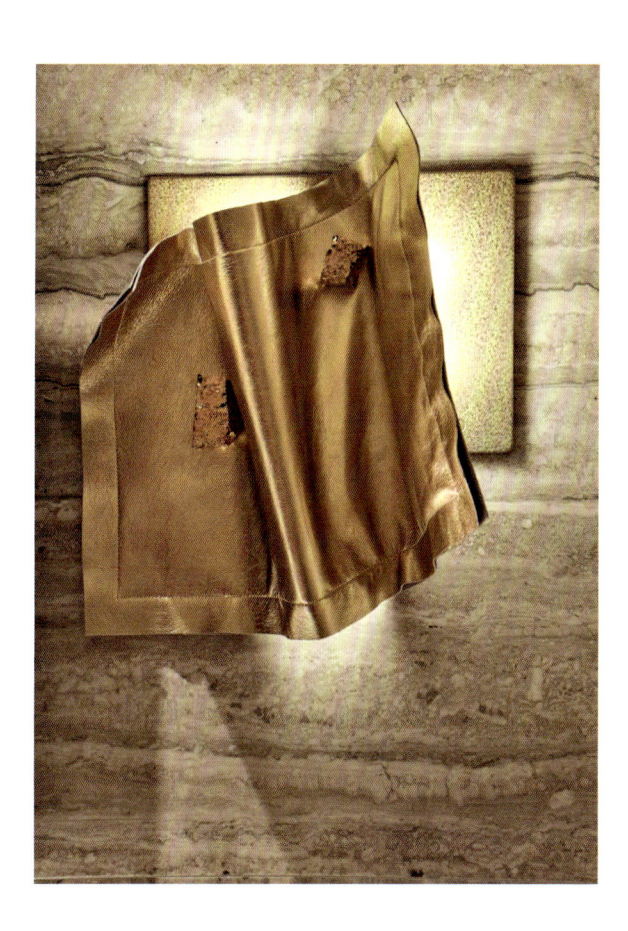

Opposite: Imposing twin pedestal vanities are carved from blocks of Calacatta Vagli marble in the main ensuite. Custom streamlined brass joinery and Formanova divides them, enhancing the gilded veins of the stone.

This page: Adorning the powder room, a custom leather wall light with recycled brick fragments is finished in a gold ceramic glaze by our studio. Concealed magnets allow the leather to be moved on the cast brass wall plate.

MELBOURNE PENTHOUSE.

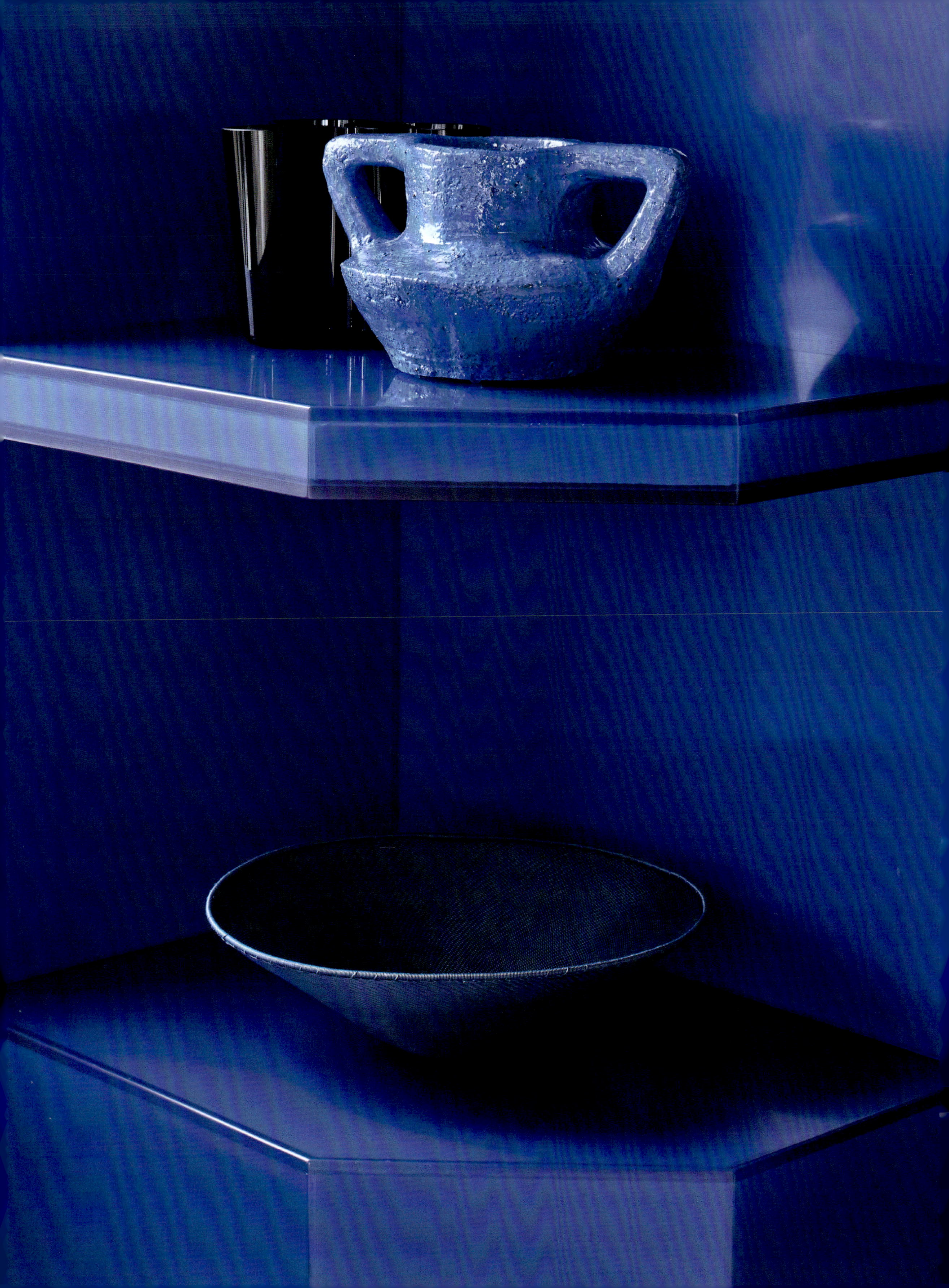

MELBOURNE PENTHOUSE.

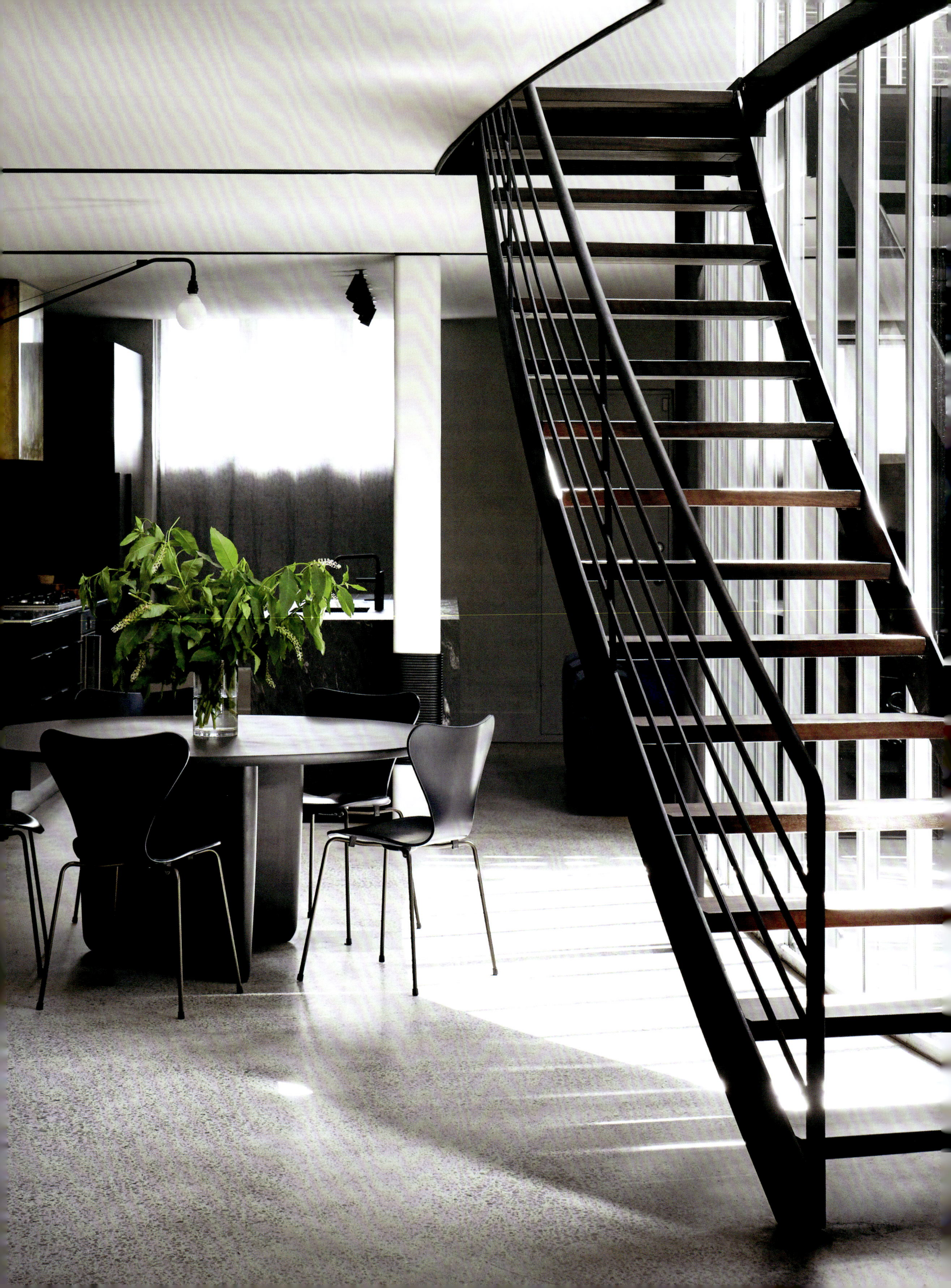

METAL

Fitzroy House.

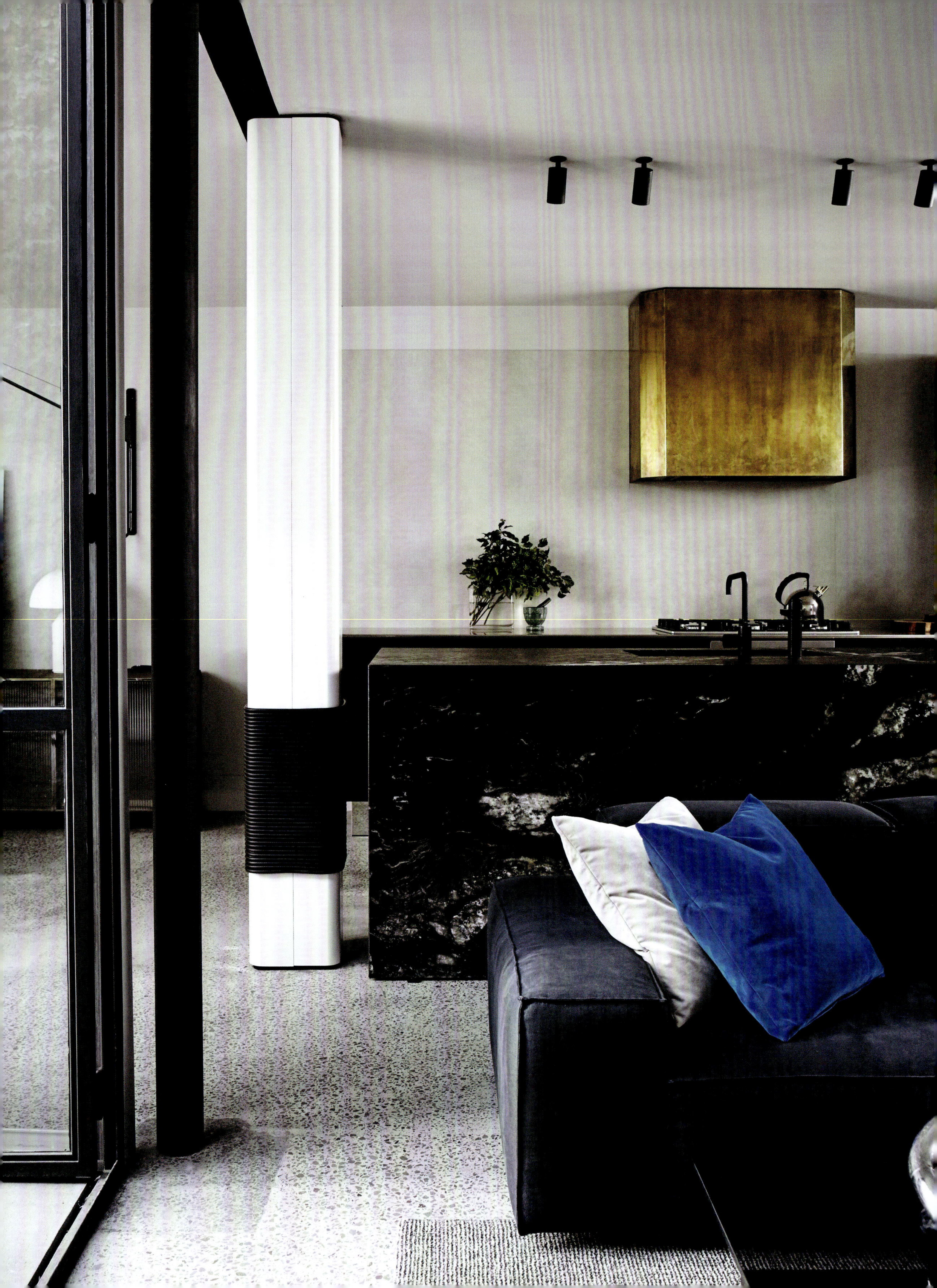

In the late 1980s, experimental architect Ivan Rijavec converted a former shoe factory in Fitzroy into a two-storey home and office. The then-pioneering warehouse conversion featured a double-height glass atrium, graphic steel, and gently curved and skewed walls. Many of these architectural elements remained when our client – a former dairy farmer and keen mountaineer and adventurer – bought the house about twenty years later. He approached us to create a private, introspective and understated inner-city sanctuary that provided extensive joinery for his collection of art and books, and ample storage for hiking equipment.

Inspired by our client's interests in farming, mountaineering, art and literature, we developed a dark and robust palette that balanced ruggedness and refinement: a moody, masculine backdrop of black granite and dark-stained timber detailed with lustrous, metallic elements and enlivened with richly coloured soft furnishings and artwork.

We modernised the awkward layout to create open spaces connected to the courtyard, while respecting the architecture. The stepped ceiling was levelled out to achieve one continuous ceiling plane, and some of the walls were removed or square set, while others were curved even more. Bush-hammering the existing concrete floor enhanced its texture, and painting the walls a soft putty-grey created a light contrast to the dark materials without being stark and clinical.

Upon entry, a new curved wall and black-stained oak cupboards with leather handles elevate the sense of arrival. The curve is a nod to Rijavec's original design and encloses a powder room, where the walls are enveloped with ribbed timber wall panelling and grey mosaic tiles to evoke the feeling of a dark, luxurious cave. A delicate aged-brass towel rail wraps around the black granite vanity, and concealed strip lighting in the timber panelling illuminates a long corner mirror, giving the mirror the appearance of floating.

We redesigned the kitchen in an island layout and accented the space with an oxidised brass rangehood. Its patinaed metallic finish glistens in the morning sun. We selected a leathered Nero Marquina granite for the island bench. With snowy white tones set deep within black rock, this monumental block evokes memories of the European mountains our client has climbed.

Next to the island, a structural column is partially wrapped with matte black rubber cord, paying homage to the building's shoe factory origins, and inspired by architect Alvar Aalto's Villa Mairea, where he wrapped the columns with rattan.

A wall of shelving ascends the two levels, from the ground-floor library to the first-floor study, and is scaled with a custom ladder. Upstairs, the desk overlooks the crevice where the floor stops short, allowing the joinery to flow up the wall. In the main bedroom, we designed a sumptuous inky-blue silk carpet to create a luxurious feel to the space, and counterbalance the grey rendered brick walls and the graphic steel beams of the existing structure.

Given our client's keen interest in furniture, we sourced classic and contemporary pieces in shades of black and grey, including the B&B Italia Toby-Ishi dining table and Arne Jacobsen's iconic Series 7 dining chairs. The Molteni & C Strand sideboard has shimmering metallic and glass doors, and Jean Prouvé's Potence pivoting wall lamp for Vitra has an industrial aesthetic, yet with a fineness to it.

At the entry, Tracey Deep's She Chair is a reinterpretation of the Series 7 chair for Cult Design. Wrapped with metres of raw, knotted rope, the chair encapsulates the ruggedness and refinement that continues throughout the design and furnishing of the home.

METAL

FITZROY HOUSE.

METAL

Classic and contemporary furniture pieces include
a B&B Italia Toby-Ishi dining table, Arne Jacobsen's
Series 7 dining chairs and Jean Prouvé's Potence pivoting
wall lamp in the dining room. The living room features
a Marechiaro sofa by Mario Marenco, the Kalos armchair
by Antonio Citterio, and Tracey Deep's She Chair nestles
in the entry.

FITZROY HOUSE.

METAL

FITZROY HOUSE.

ARMAND HAMMER
THE FIRM
SOROS
TITAN
BLACK ANGUS
KATE MOSS
RALPH LAUREN

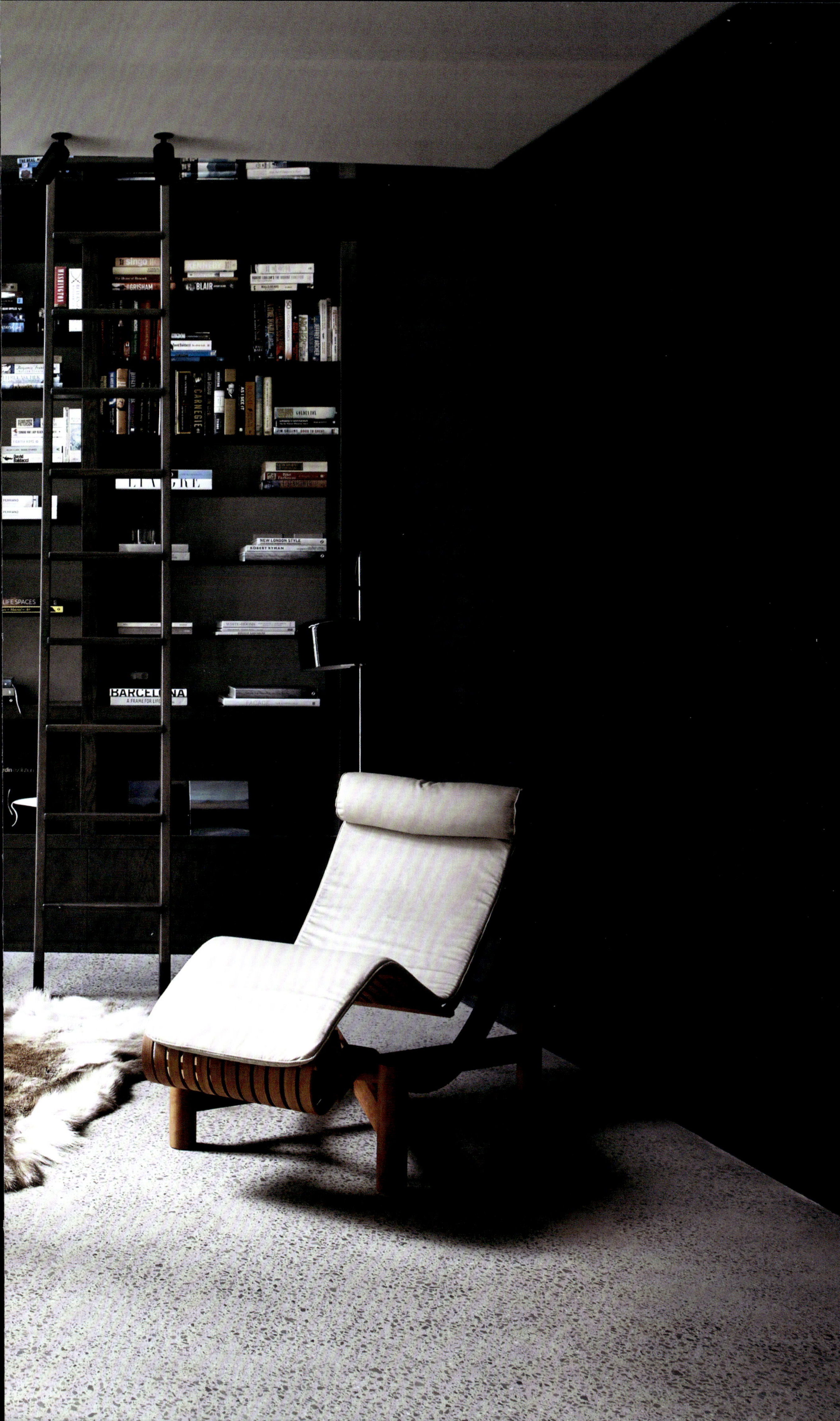

METAL

Opposite: The library, in stained oak joinery, ascends through a void to the second floor and is accessed via a custom rail ladder.

This page: The atmospheric powder room features a honed Grigio Carnico stone vanity with a delicate brass rail detail. Timber panelling behind the vanity has a custom shelf.

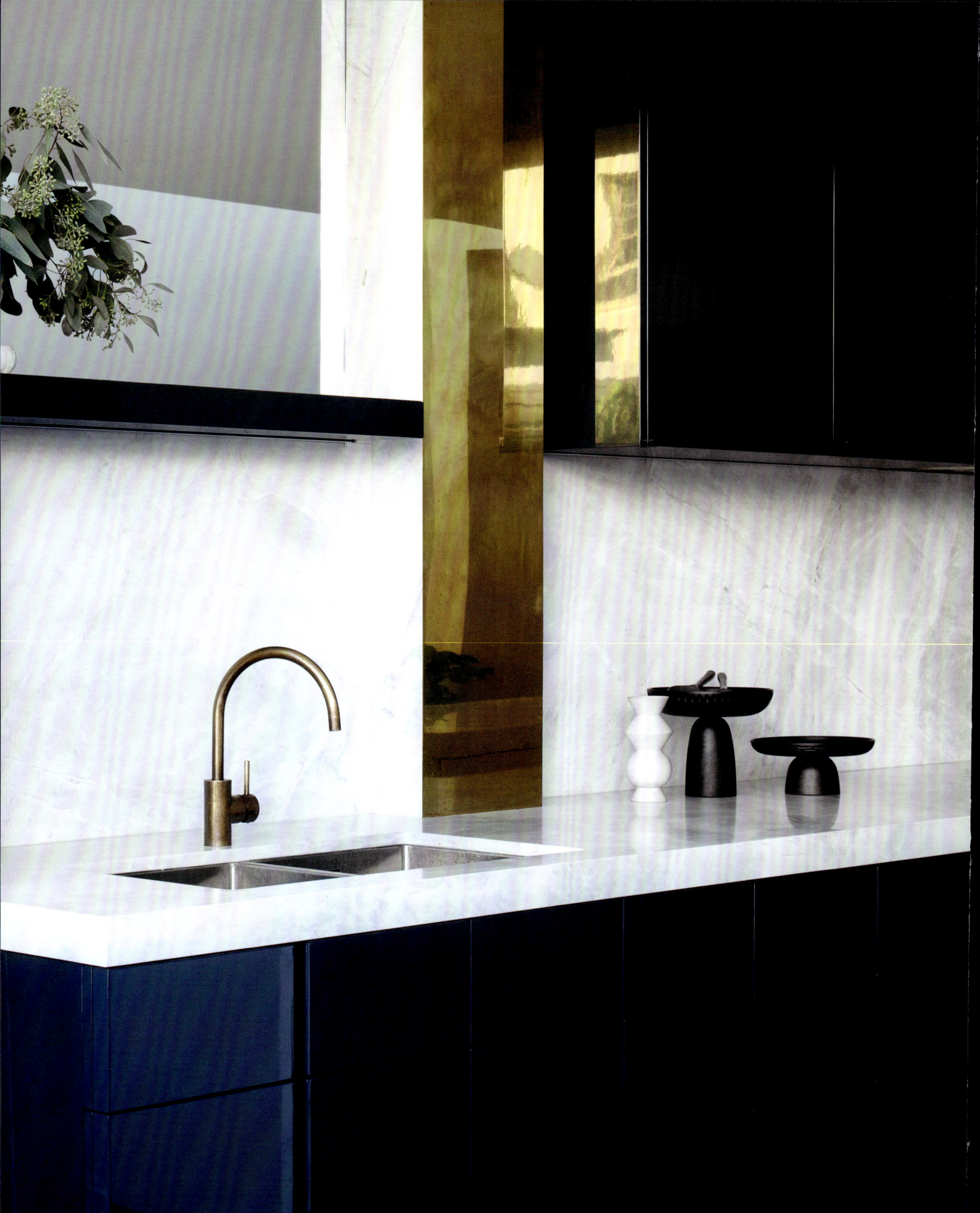

METAL

Surry Hills House.

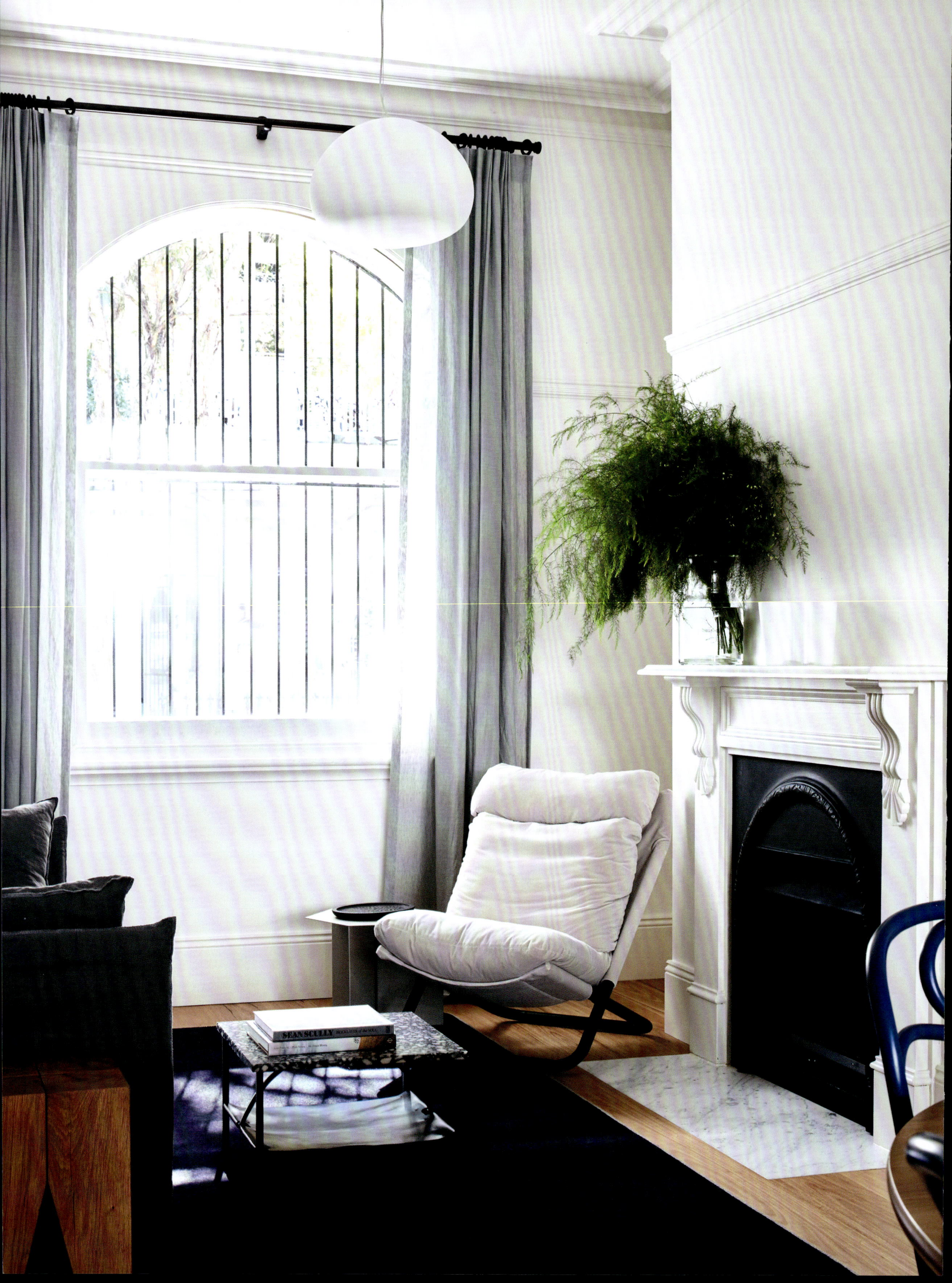

Our clients commissioned us to complete a total renovation of their 150-year-old Victorian terrace in Surry Hills. The passionate cooks sought a design resolution that would include entertaining areas and a functional, elegant kitchen befitting their lifestyle.

Like many Sydney terraces, this one was narrow. We remapped the floorplan within to maximise available space. Our aim was to achieve a light-filled home that capitalised on the attractive period features of the terrace, but created a clean, timeless feel in the home's working areas, especially the kitchen and bathroom.

The colour palette was kept simple and bright, with shades of white applied to the walls, woodwork, balustrades, skirtings and cornices. This predominance of white elevates the original ornate mouldings that appear through the home, in archways and mantels. The exception to the light colour scheme was the dramatic use of high-gloss navy blue cabinetry in the cooks' kitchen, coupled with glowing brass panels and tapware. A mirror, cleverly installed on a section of wall in the kitchen, reflects light and adds to the sense of depth and space in the room. With entertaining and cooking being a significant and pleasurable part of our clients' lives, we designed the kitchen to be the central focus of the house, opening to a courtyard that offers further entertaining space.

A handsome selection of materials, including natural stone, terrazzo and brass, combines to create a feeling of stylish luxury. Contemporary furniture was chosen with a focus on scale, ensuring that it did not overwhelm the narrow width of the terrace. Crisp cobalt blue bentwood dining chairs catch the eye, hinting at the blue to come in the rear kitchen. Soft fabrics dress the windows, adding privacy and textural comfort.

This terrace, while limited in space, showcases what can be achieved with inventiveness, a well-resolved footprint, meticulous planning and carefully selected materials.

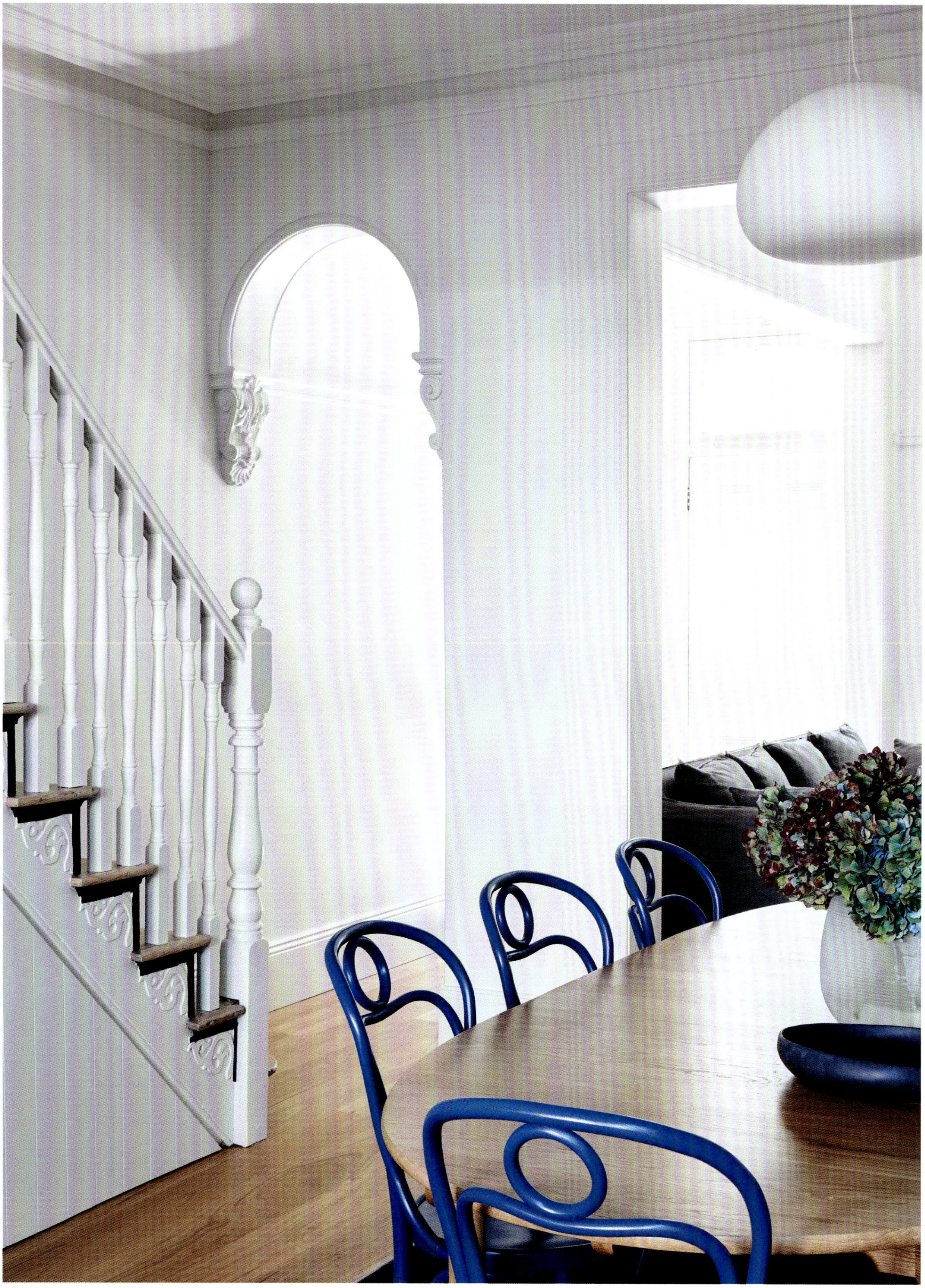

Bright blue Cobalt blue Fureau chairs by Thonet infuse
the dining area with fun, vibrant colour, the sinuous
bentwood frames echoing the elaborate heritage mouldings
and arches. The Pandul VIP Wall Sconce casts a soft glow
that reflects off the hand-finished unsealed brass panel
in the elegant kitchen.

SURRY HILLS HOUSE.

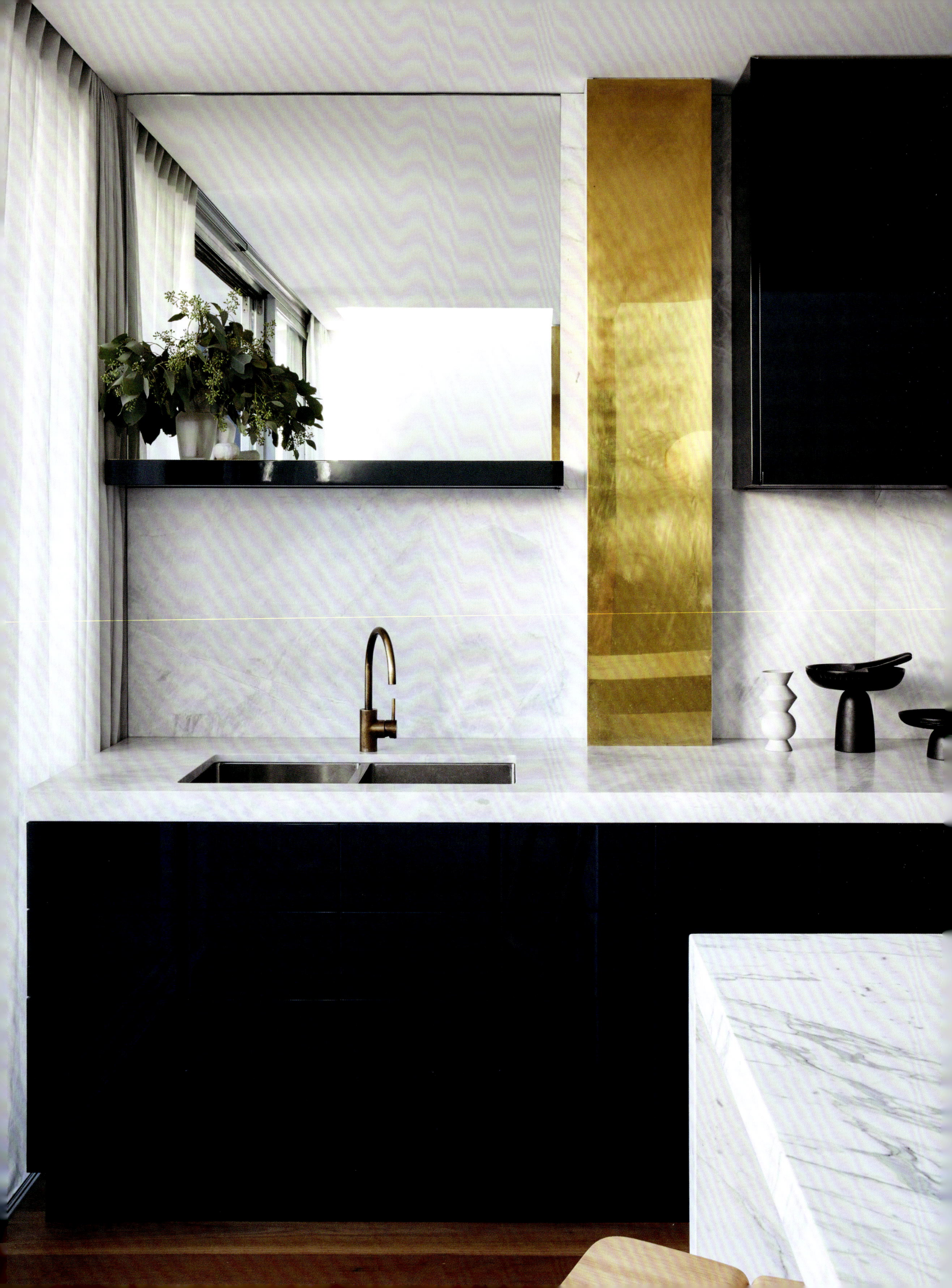

SURRY HILLS HOUSE.

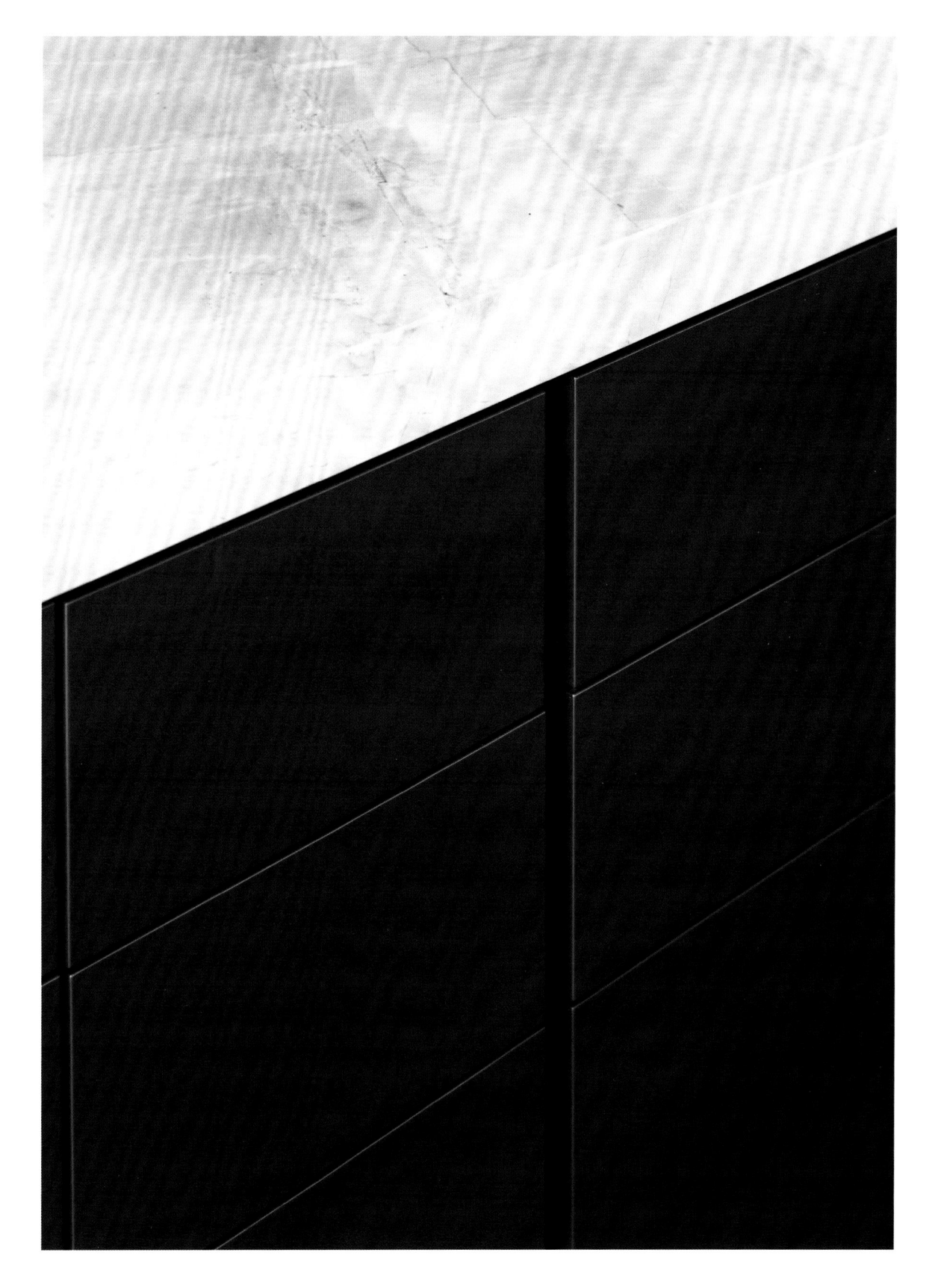

METAL

SURRY HILLS HOUSE.

140 METAL

LEE MATHEWS

Lee Mathews is an artist and clothing designer, whose globally renowned fashion aesthetic is both classic and experimental. The Lee Mathews store in James Street, Brisbane, is one of the first projects for which we commissioned artists to create large pieces as part of the interior fabric. As Lee has a strong personal interest in design and art, the fit-out not only reflected the Lee Mathews brand, but also her artistic pursuits.

Lee had recently been to Marfa, Texas, when we started the project, and had returned home inspired by Donald Judd's minimalist work and his repeated geometric forms. She also had several pieces on her desk by local ceramicist Alana Wilson, a long-time collaborator of Lee's. This counterplay between Judd's and Alana's work – between the polished and the raw – guided the design direction and the pieces we commissioned. The approach also complemented Lee's clothing, as some pieces are quite architectural in their detailing, while others are softer, feminine or more expressive. We wanted to emulate that duality, bringing in the sharpness and minimalism alongside looseness and tactility.

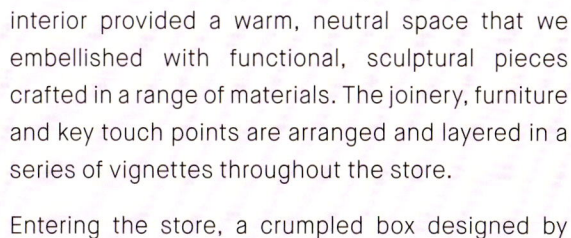

The cream- and sandy-coloured palette of the base interior provided a warm, neutral space that we embellished with functional, sculptural pieces crafted in a range of materials. The joinery, furniture and key touch points are arranged and layered in a series of vignettes throughout the store.

Entering the store, a crumpled box designed by metalworker Michael Gittings serves as a display plinth. Michael creates striking works exploring light and form and incorporating contemporary and age-old techniques. He also created the patinaed blackened-steel counter with gold laminate overlaid on the inside surfaces. Behind the counter, timber joinery inspired by Japanese Tansu chests has an honesty of materials and construction that expresses the beauty of the solid oak.

The series of stacked, floating wall shelves are a nod to Judd. The highly polished stainless steel chrome is filled with coloured resin that refracts honey-hued light onto accessories.

During the early stages of the project, Lee and I had the idea of commissioning a monumental artwork from Alana to wrap around the corner of the mirrored box, accentuating the dynamic interplay between raw and polished surfaces. Alana also created the clay vessels that are suspended on metal chains in a mobile-like display in the front window.

Around the store, sinewy and elegant rails contrast with thick, textural finishes. Paint applied directly to the walls has a dense impasto finish, and rails are anchored with hand-moulded clay footings.

Collaborations with artists and artisans bring something unique and distinctive to interior design. I believe the future of design lies in giving opportunities to makers and artists to create pieces on a larger scale. As Lee Mathews' store demonstrates, our interiors are so much richer for it.

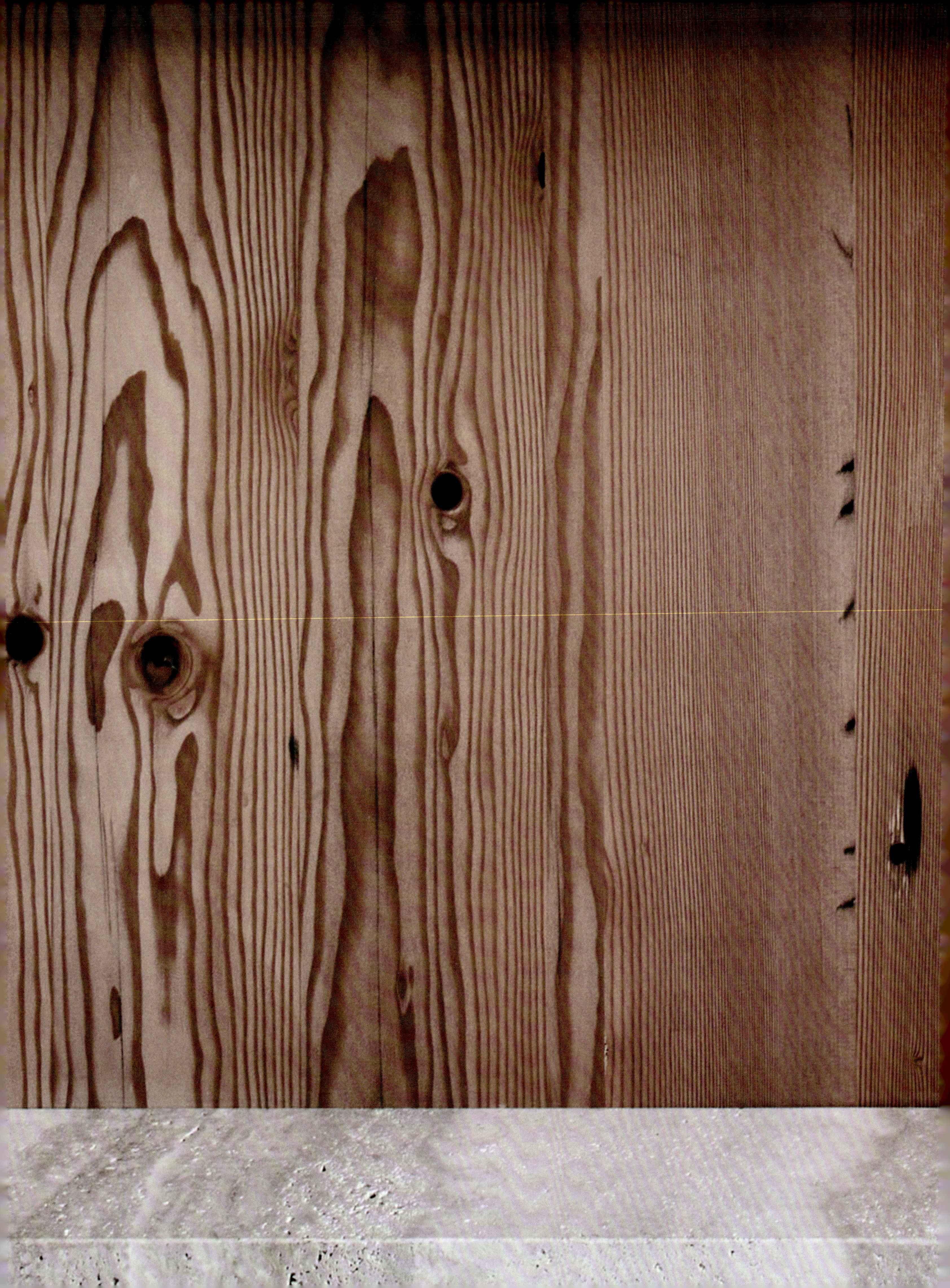

WOOD

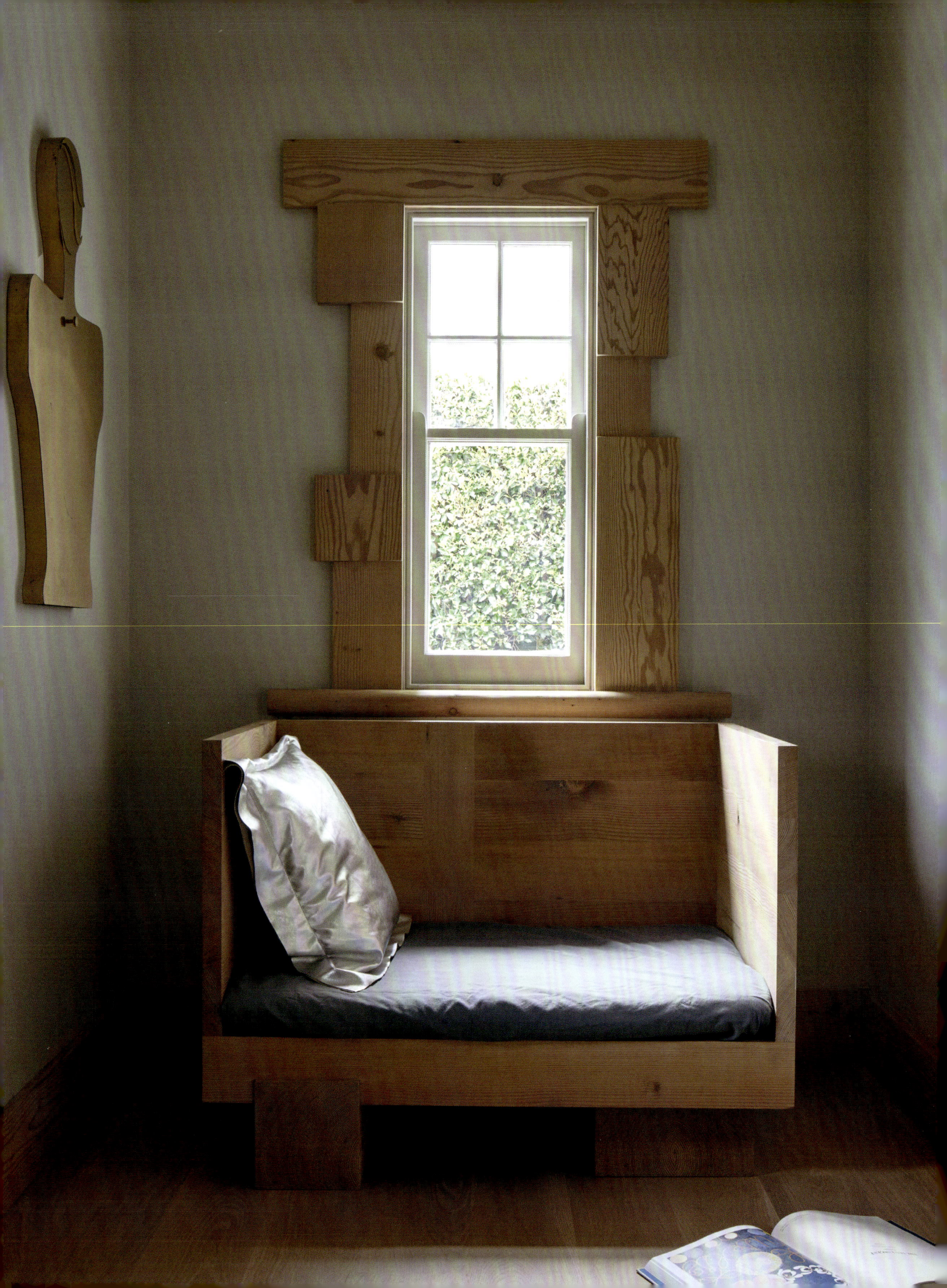

Wherever we see an opportunity to incorporate existing materials, we will seek to reinvent them in a way that recognises their history and complements our design vision. The natural durability of wood lends itself to repurposing and recycling, meaning that many older timbers can enjoy an extended life in contemporary design projects.

Donald Judd, one of my design heroes, used a broad sweep of materials in his work; however, he was a strong proponent of wood, which he integrated into both his furniture design and his art. Visiting the Judd Foundation at his former home and gallery on Spring Street, New York, I could fully appreciate his use of Oregon or oak timber in most of his furniture.

My own home, Hill House, had original Oregon beams that needed replacing. When the house was built in 1910, most timbers came either from Oregon in the United States or the Baltic region of northern Europe. When remodelling the house, rather than removing and discarding the beams, I had an idea to have them re-milled, then wrapped around a window and doorway opening into our living room – a functional design outcome that built on the 'story' and history of the house while minimising waste.

Our commitment to repurposing is visible in our fabrication of furniture and in the creation of art installations for projects. In each of our projects there will be a wood moment. Wood always makes me feel grounded and connected to the world.

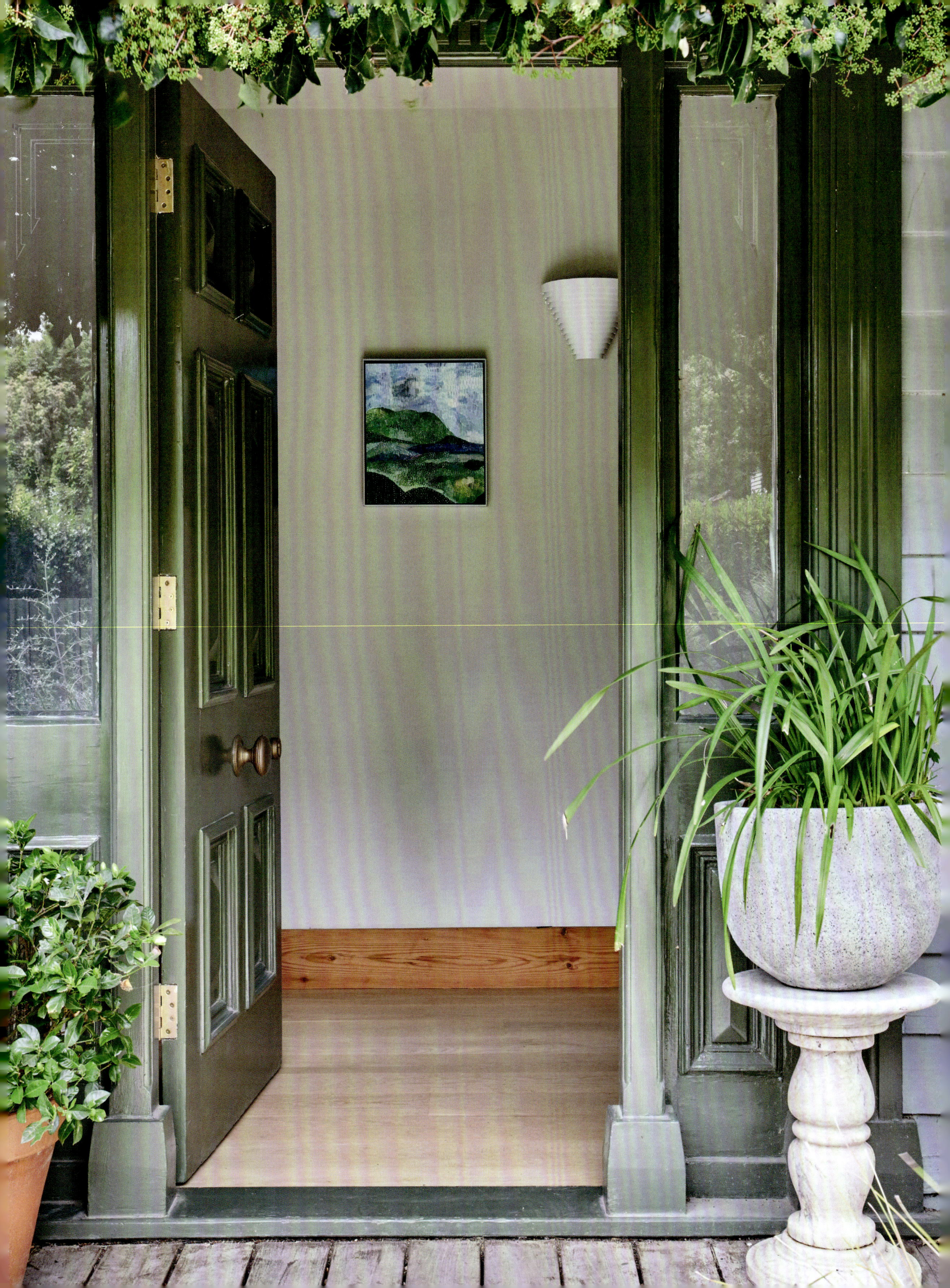

WOOD

Hill House.

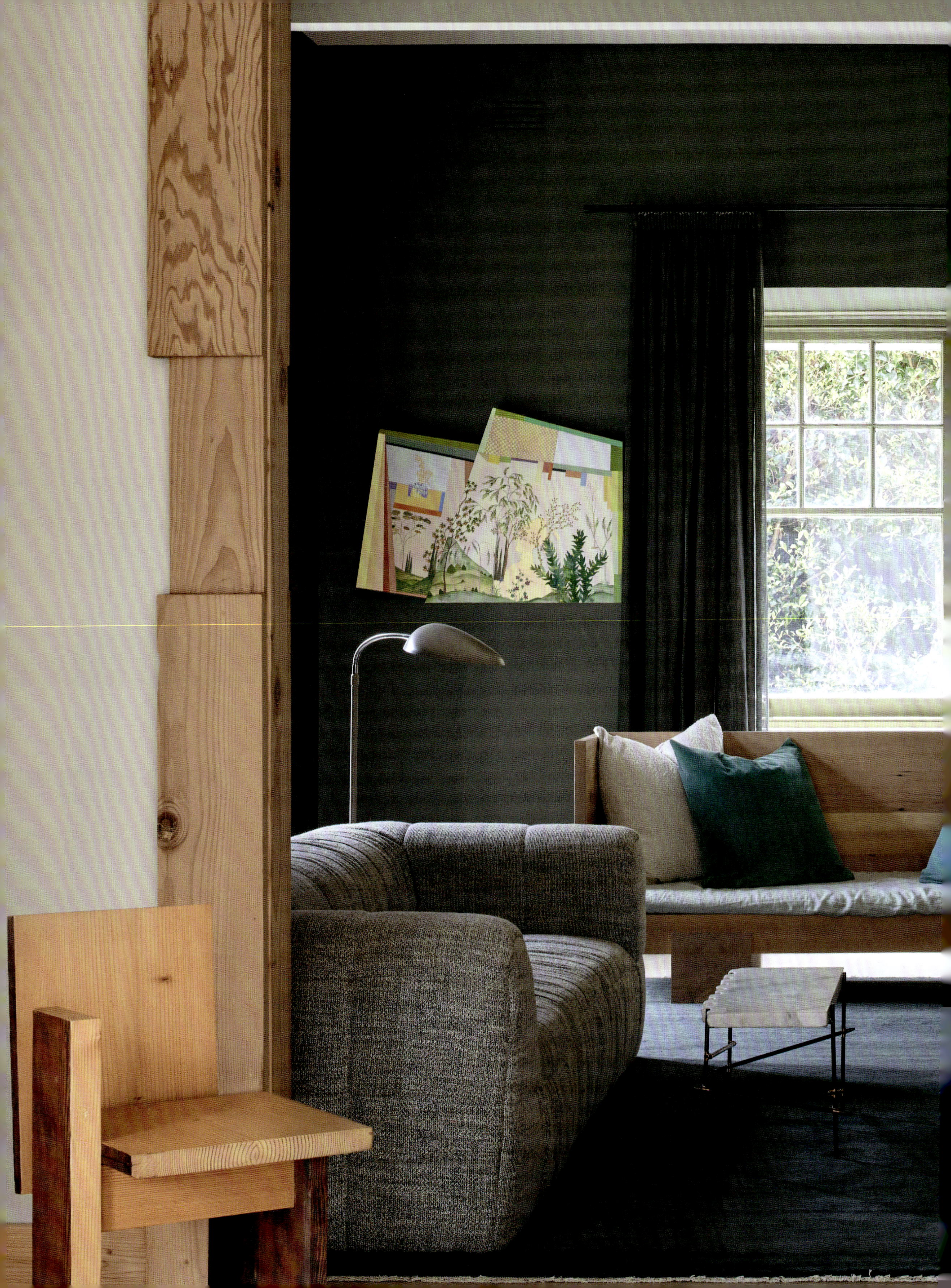

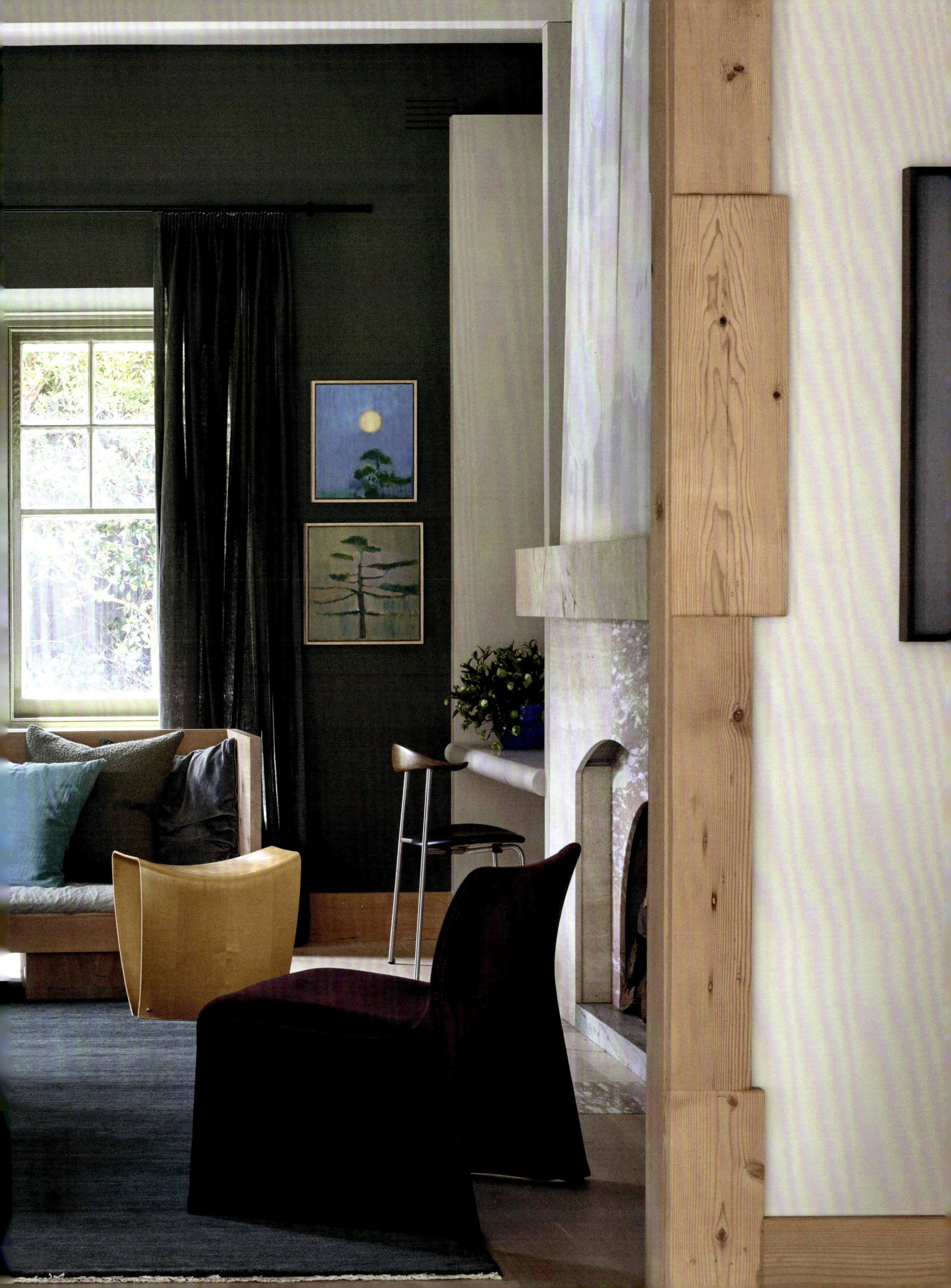

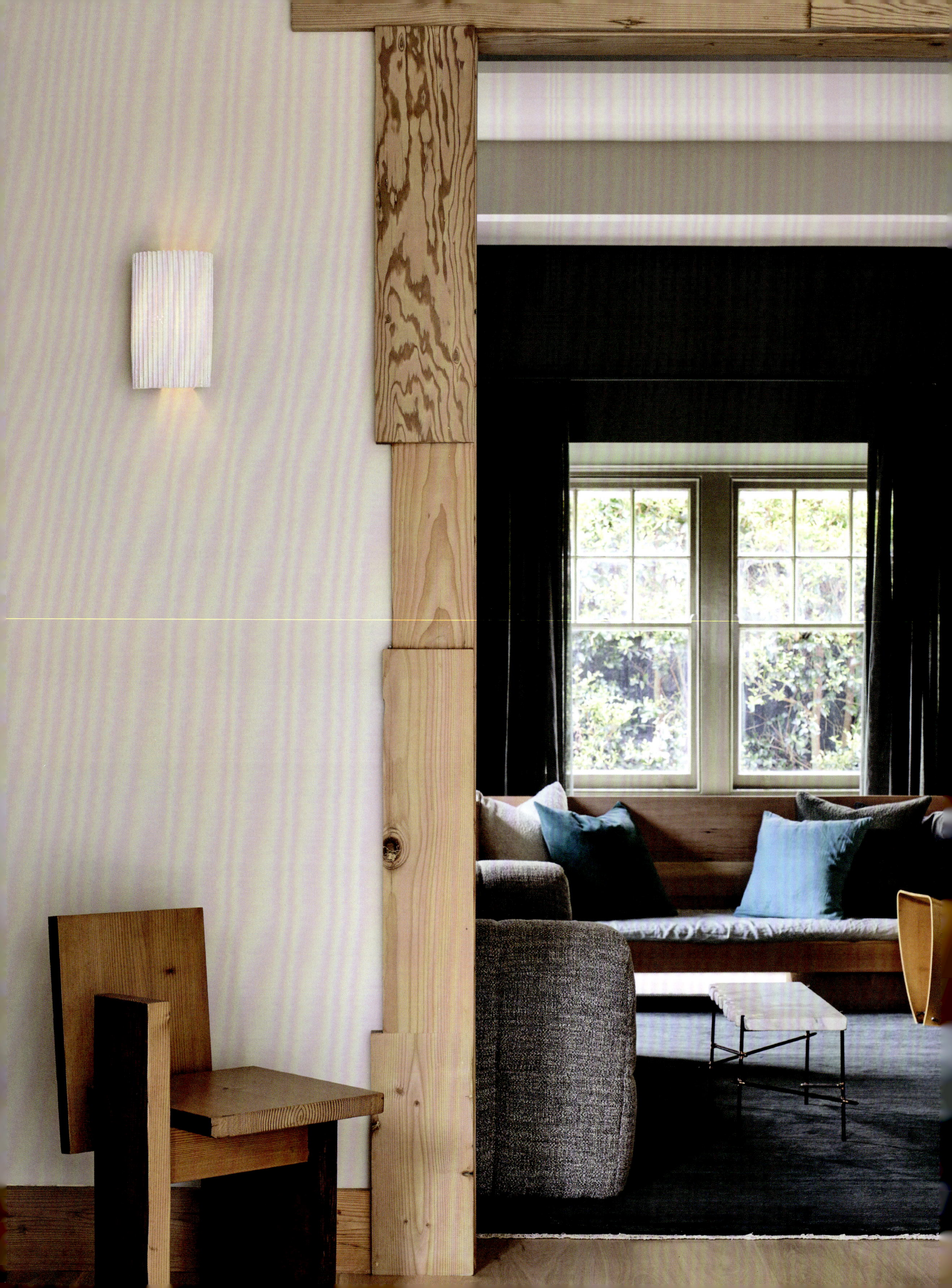

Hill House is my home. It was a wonderfully eclectic house when we bought it, as it's not at all conventional in its layout. Originally a scout hall, it was constructed in 1910. As various owners renovated the building, adding walls and ceilings to create a home, the layout became quite unusual. There's no hallway, unlike a traditional house, and there were lots of little spaces in the attic, which our children used to love to explore.

After living here for thirteen years, we decided it was time to renovate and make it our own. I drew up plans to improve the flow and connections in the house. When our builder started removing the low plasterboard ceilings, we discovered extra volume and space. It revealed such a ramshackle structure, with about eight different timbers, that we had to rebuild much of the interior.

We replaced the Oregon pine beams with large steel beams to support the house, and re-used the timber as a feature, paying homage to the heritage of the scout hall. Oregon pine was one of the most popular building materials for Australian houses in the 20th century. It was imported from the United States and Canada until the 1980s, when the popularity of Oregon surpassed its natural sustainability and the use of Australian timbers became more prevalent. While it has since become a valuable timber because of its scarcity, the demolition and renovation of older houses means there is still recycled Oregon available.

I had the timber machined and segmented into different widths and lengths to create layered, asymmetrical frames around the entry to the living room and the window in the reading nook, where there's a gently curved bullnose on the windowsill. There's something naive about the articulation of the timber; it's welcoming and comforting.

The design of the timber sofas evolved during work on the Kiln project, for which I drew inspiration from the straight lines and rectilinear forms of pieces by Wright, Schindler and Judd. I also looked at the tradition of Shaker furniture and the integrity of materials and construction. Our sofas express design in its purest form. Furniture-maker Ross Thompson crafted several pieces for our studio's first capsule collection, launched at Melbourne Design Week in 2022. The sofas are made with recycled Oregon pine and have large solid, asymmetrical blocks of timber for the feet.

The dining table – another American timber, maple – bookends the rear wall of the kitchen, where I've paired Cristanza stone and brass. I love brass because you don't have to be precious with it, and it accrues a beautiful, warm feel with age and use. Tick-tacking the stone on the island bench gives it an expressive, painterly quality, as if the veining is abstract brushstrokes.

We deliberately played with different stones for the fireplace in the living room. I worked with a stonemason to select various offcuts from his factory, then we wrapped the existing brick fireplace and constructed a mantelpiece using pieces of stone. Offcuts are a sustainable and cost-effective approach, as you only buy and use what you need. It also produces a more interesting, imperfect design.

We raised our children in this house and look forward to spending many more years here. It's even more magical and wonderful now that we've truly made it our own.

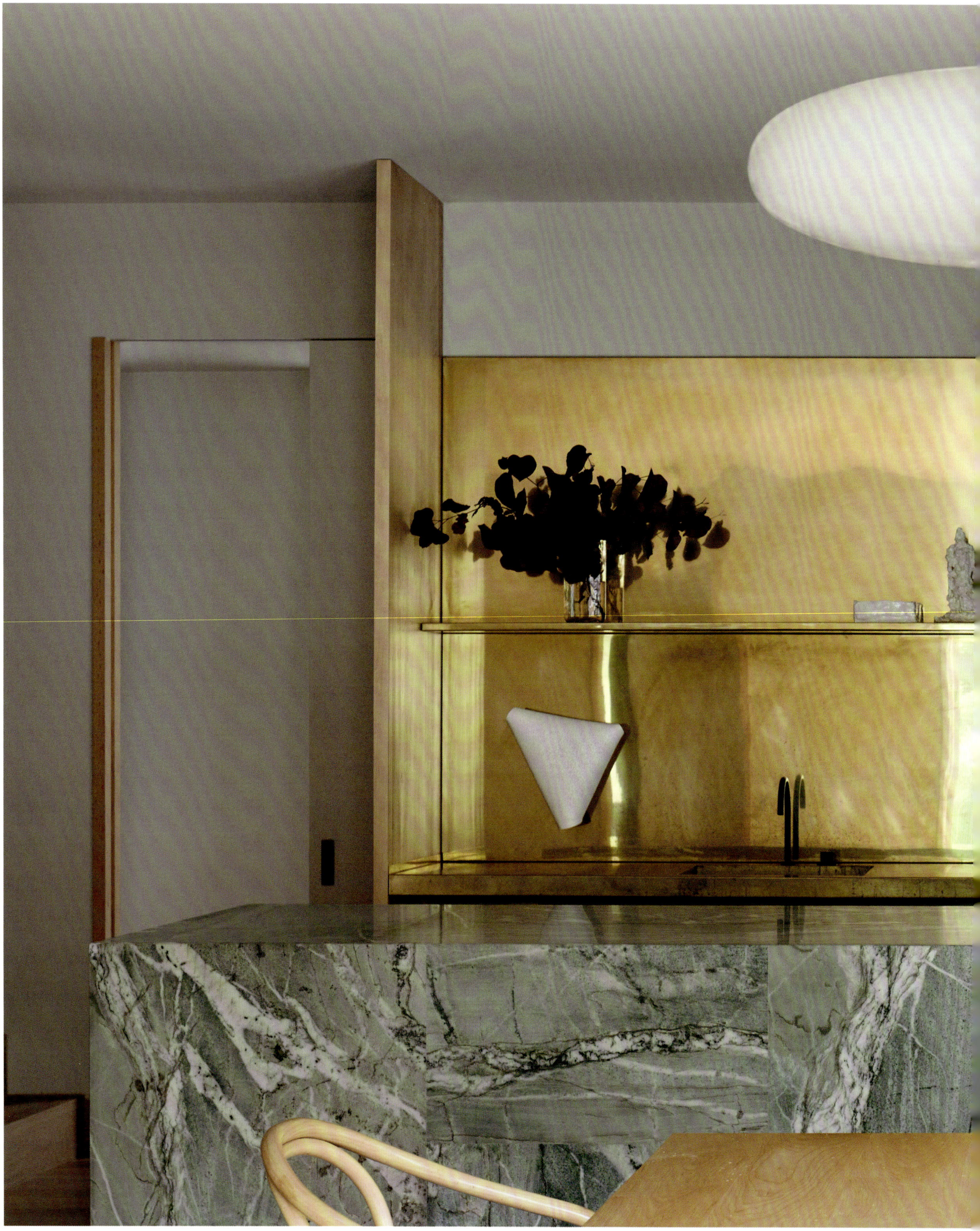

HILL HOUSE.

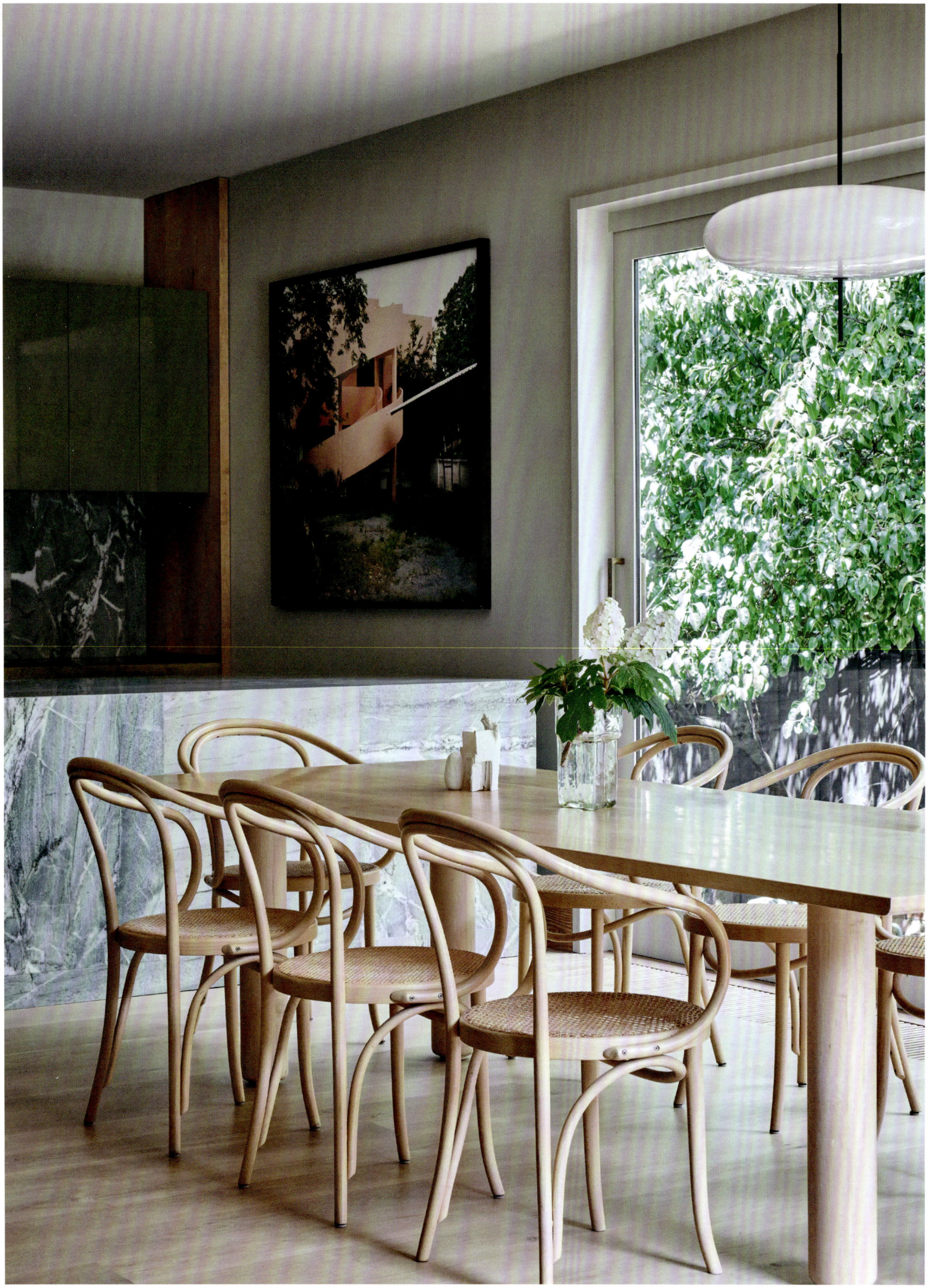

Opposite: Ross Thompson crafted our family table, which I designed, in solid maple. Maple panels also bookend the kitchen bench and cabinetry. Overlooking the space is a dramatic architectural photograph by Chris Pennings from Fini Frames.

This page: A folded brass sheet creates our bench and sink. Above them, is a wall light in painted steel mesh by Spanish designer Arturo Álvarez. Gloss joinery is reminiscent of my kitchen growing up, but here we have beautiful cast bronze handles by Henry Wilson.

HILL HOUSE.

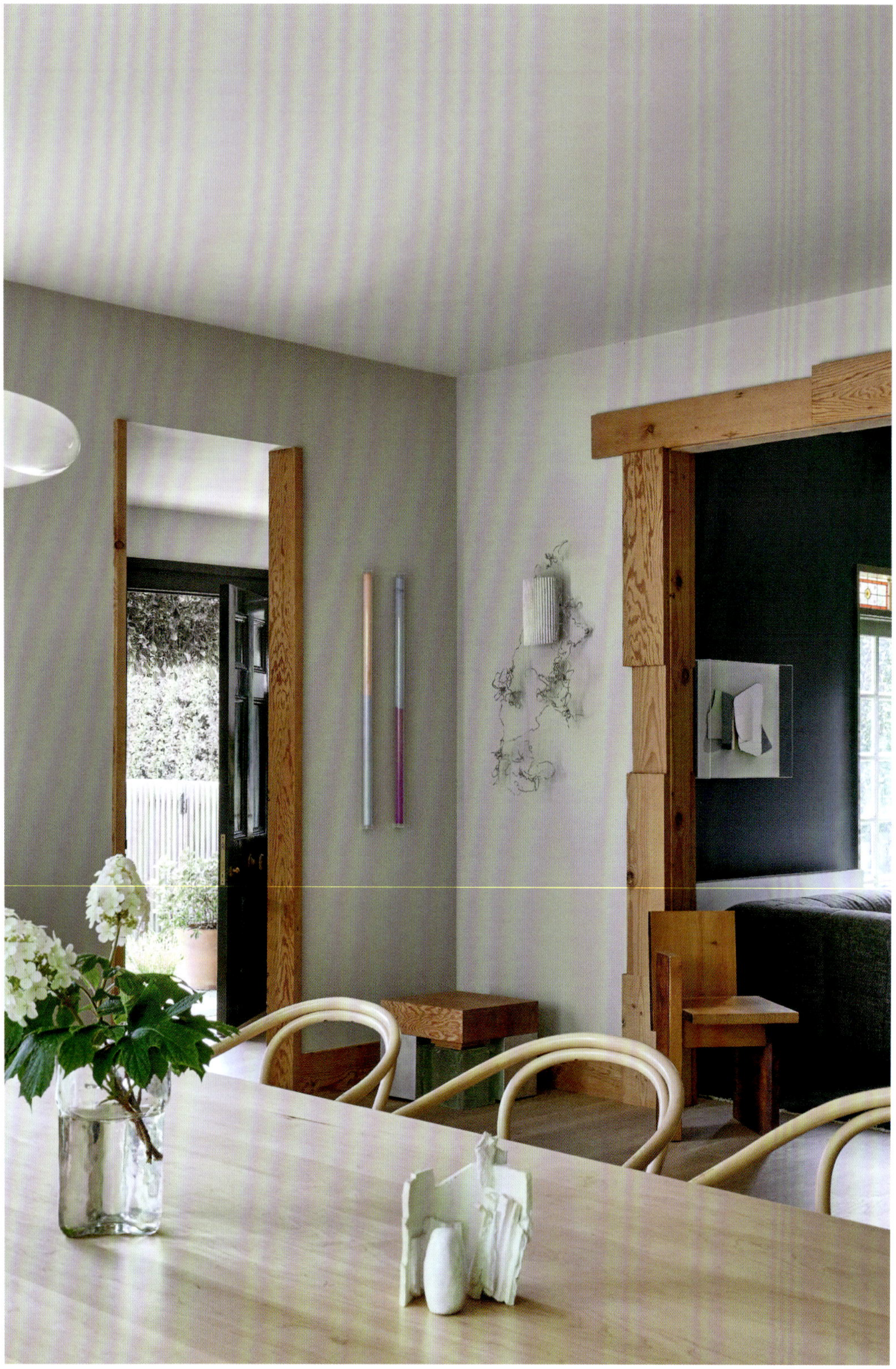

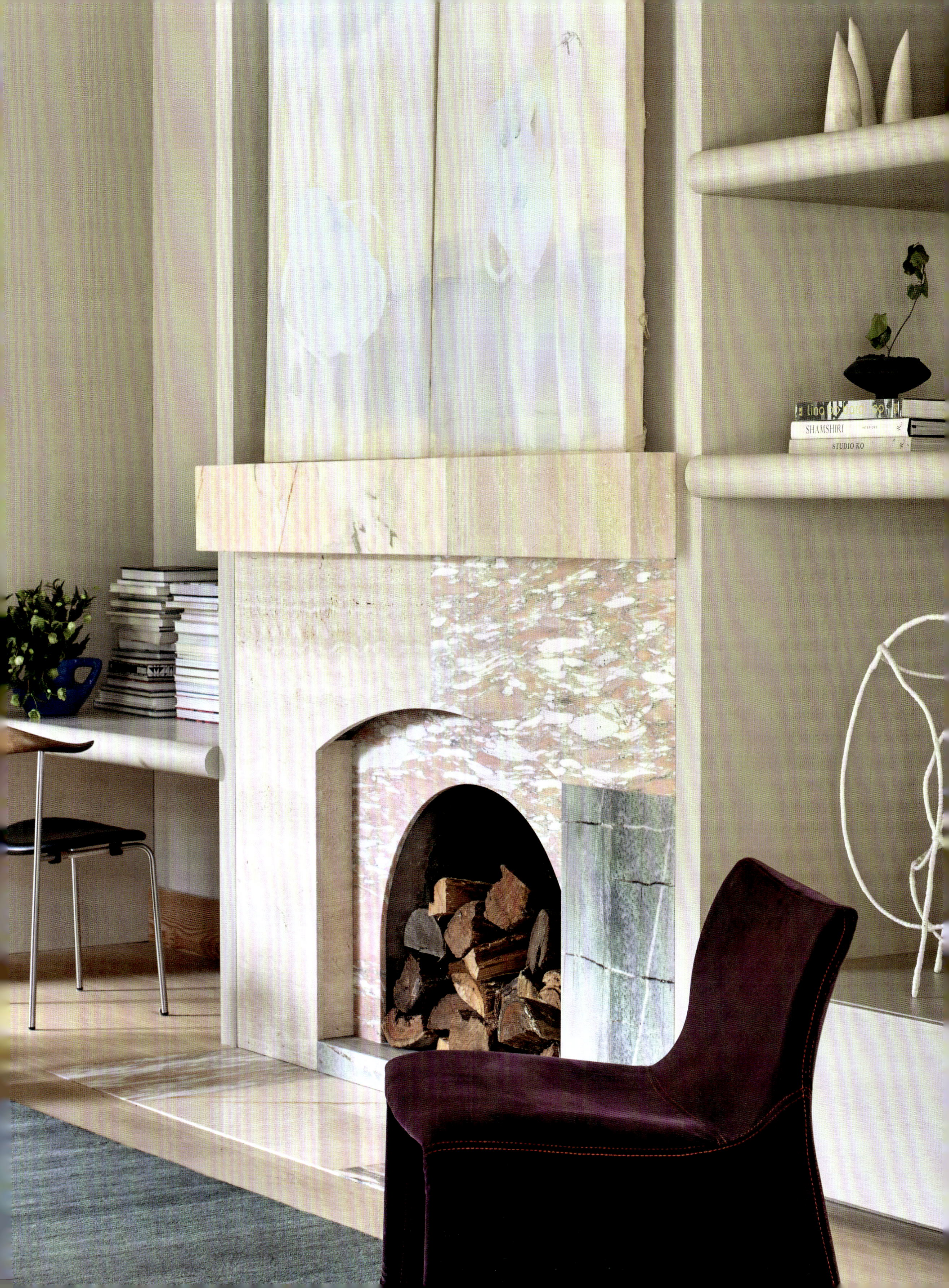
SHAMSHIRI
STUDIO KO

Below: A painting from my student days at RMIT forms our bedhead, alongside an oversized lamp in vintage silk by Fletcher Barns from Oigåll Projects. The colour palette is muted and calming.

Right: Hand-glazed tiles line the walls of our bathroom; I love how every tile is different, with natural light overhead casting shadows across the irregular surface.

HILL HOUSE.

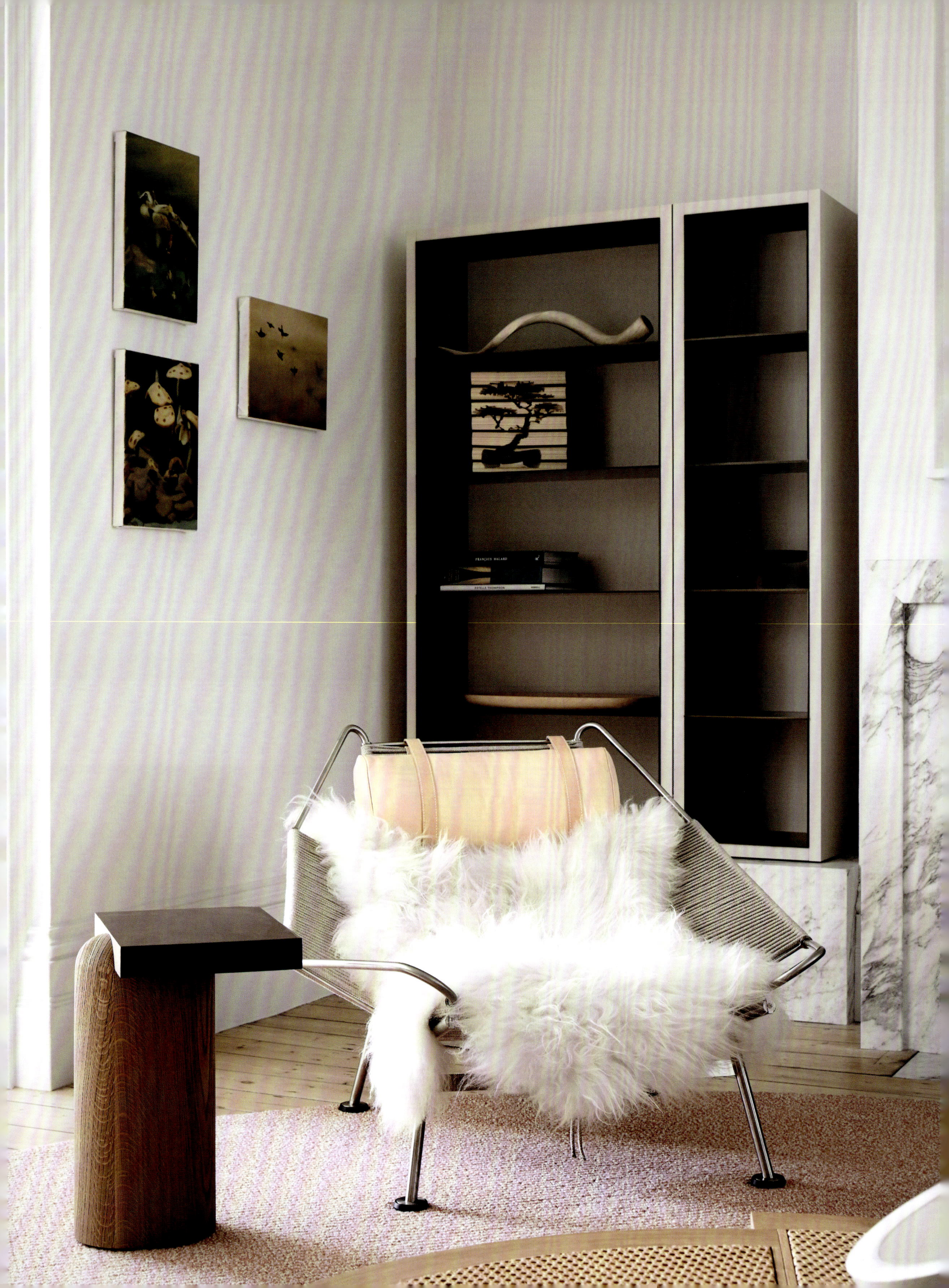

WOOD

South Yarra House.

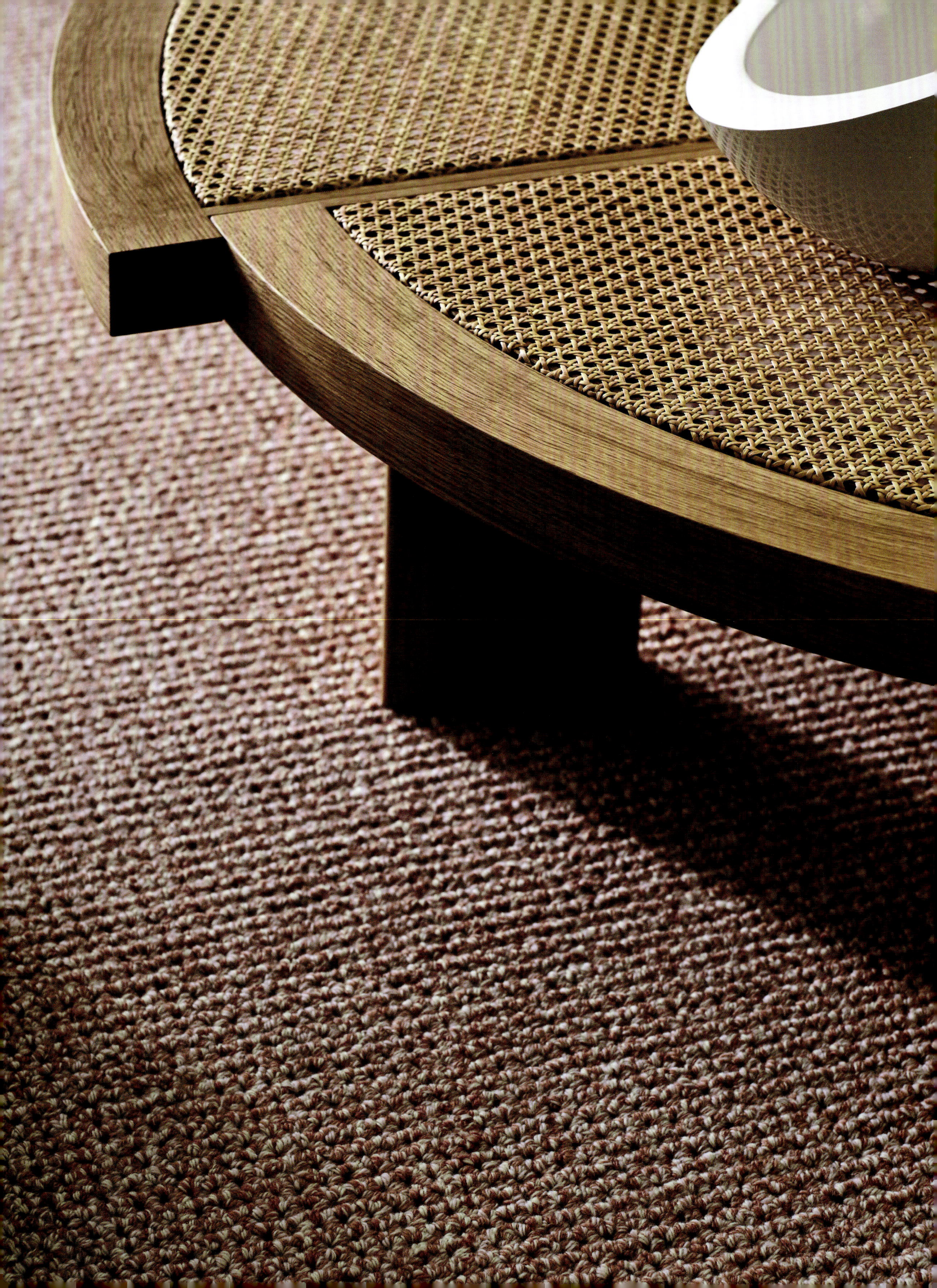

This double-storey Victorian house on a stately tree-lined street had beautifully proportioned spaces; however, they felt dark and unwelcoming, and the furniture was ill-fitting and awkward. Our client wanted to refresh and lighten the formal sitting and dining rooms, creating inviting spaces where they could relax and entertain.

Whitewashing the orange-tinted Baltic pine floors and painting the walls and ceilings a deep-white colour lightened and illuminated the spaces. Then we took our cues from our client's incredible collection of artworks and objects. We wanted to develop a feminine, textural palette that reflected our client's playfulness, and to select collectible furniture that matched the quality of the eclectic art collection.

Painted wood is a feature I use to create mood within a space, while retaining the warmth and softness of timber. For both the sitting and dining rooms, we custom-designed painted oak joinery on Calacatta marble plinths for each side of the fireplaces. We also re-lined the fireplaces with Calacatta marble to match the kitchen island.

In the sitting room, open bookshelves displaying objects and books have painted oak timber veneer frames, with bronze sheet applied to the internal surfaces and shelves. This metal trim is a subtle detail that elevates the bookshelf. In the dining room, the champagne cabinets have painted timber doors with curved solid oak handles. They have an unexpected whimsy to them and were a joy to design. Being a heritage property, the walls aren't plumb, so all the joinery is offset with wide shadow gaps to accommodate the quirks.

We selected furniture with curved and circular forms to transform the sitting room into an inviting space. The Arflex Ben Ben sofa, Charlotte Perriand Rio segmented table in solid oak and rattan, and a pink tweed-like rug anchor the room. The voluptuous Pierre Paulin Pumpkin chair and ottoman provides a cosy corner seat, and the Christophe Delcourt side tables play with geometric forms in different materials. The Roattino Lamp by Eileen Gray has a sinuous S-shaped steel tube, evocative of the dining room cabinet doors. Providing a contrast to the curved and plump forms, the Flag Halyard Chair by Hans Wegner is angular and industrial yet softened with a plush longhaired sheepskin draped over the stainless steel frame and flag-line seat.

Our client wanted a beautiful designer table to be the centrepiece of the dining room. We instantly thought of the YBU Dining Table designed by Jean Pierre Tortil for Christophe Delcourt, which has a playfully organic leg design. It's accompanied by Cassina Cab leather chairs in alternating soft tan and grey, to make the dining room less formal, more relaxed. Overhead, the Circus Pendant lamp by Elise Fouin for Forestier appears like rings of paper but is made of Priplak lampshade offcuts. An Arflex Botolo armchair adds fluffy texture and warmth in the corner.

The rooms are formal while having a quirky playfulness that complements the eclectic art collection. They are also warm and appealing. To the delight of our client, the family now spends much more time in these rooms, which were once rarely used.

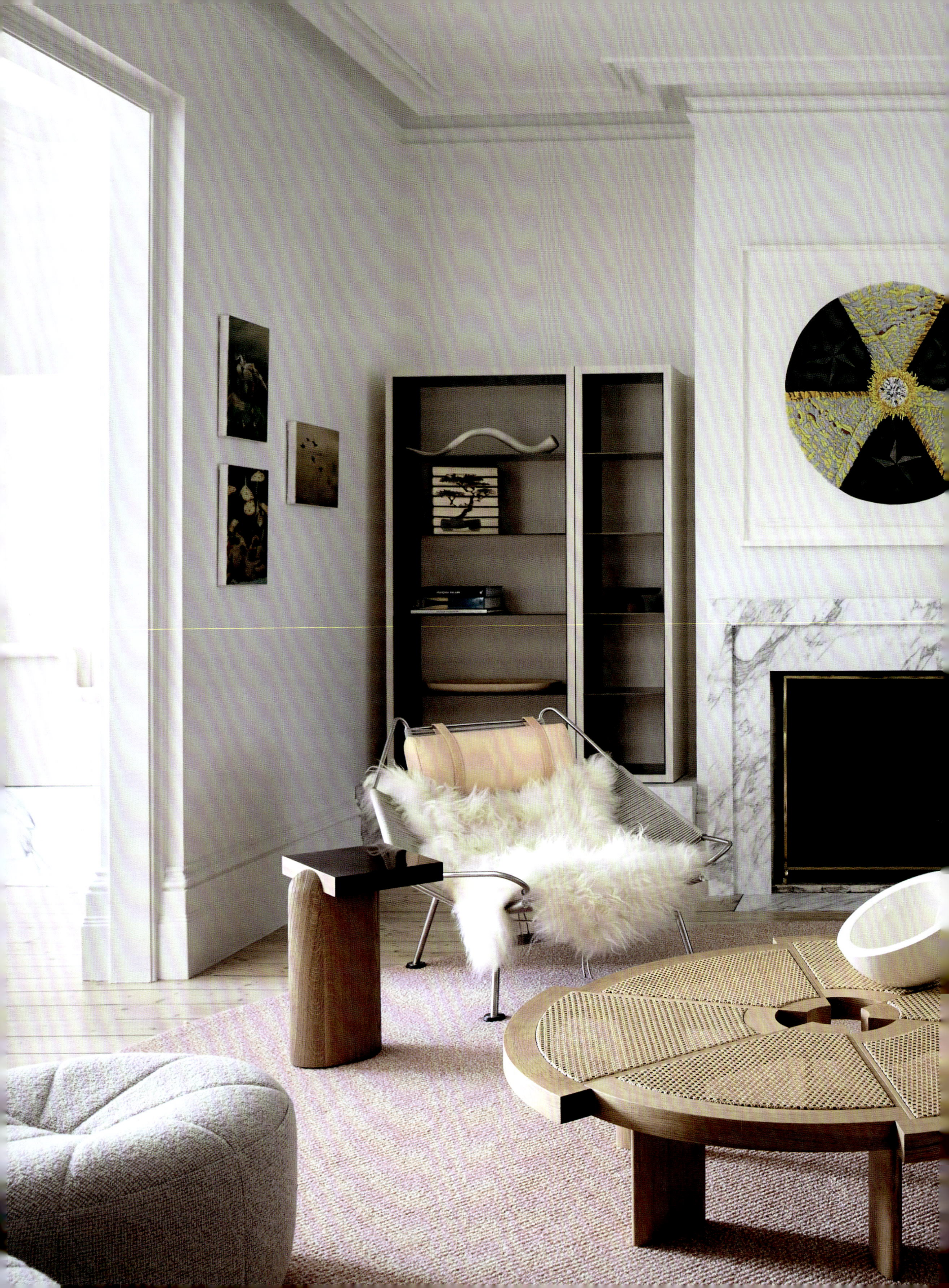

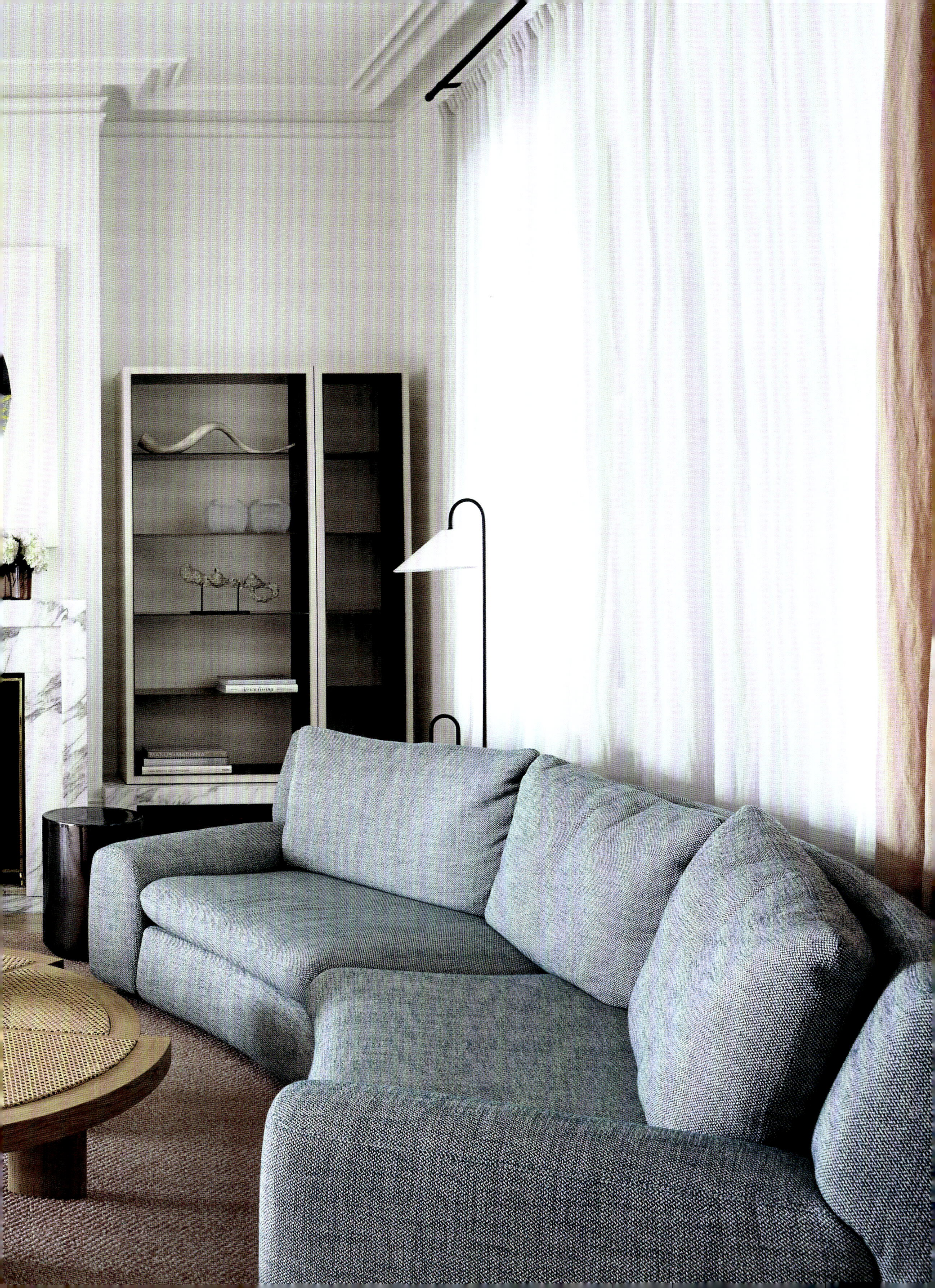

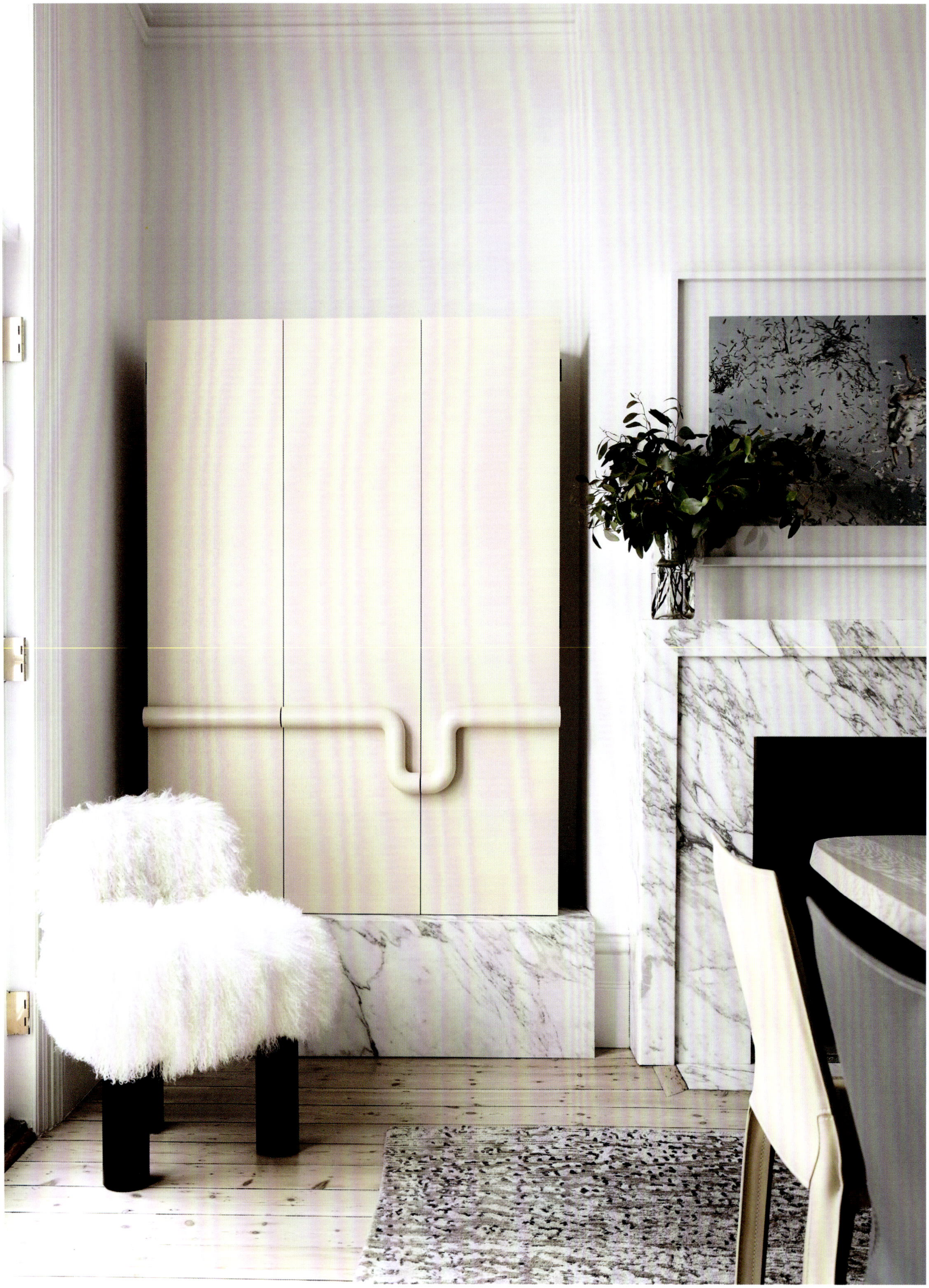

Opposite and above: The painted solid oak handle on the custom champagne cabinet in the dining room is one of my favourite details.

Top: The dining table by Christophe Delcourt, a master of timber finishes, has an innate elegance. The oak has been sandblasted and oiled to give it a warm, tactile finish.

Right: The living room cabinetry is open, with thick brass shelves for displaying the client's objects.

SOUTH YARRA HOUSE.

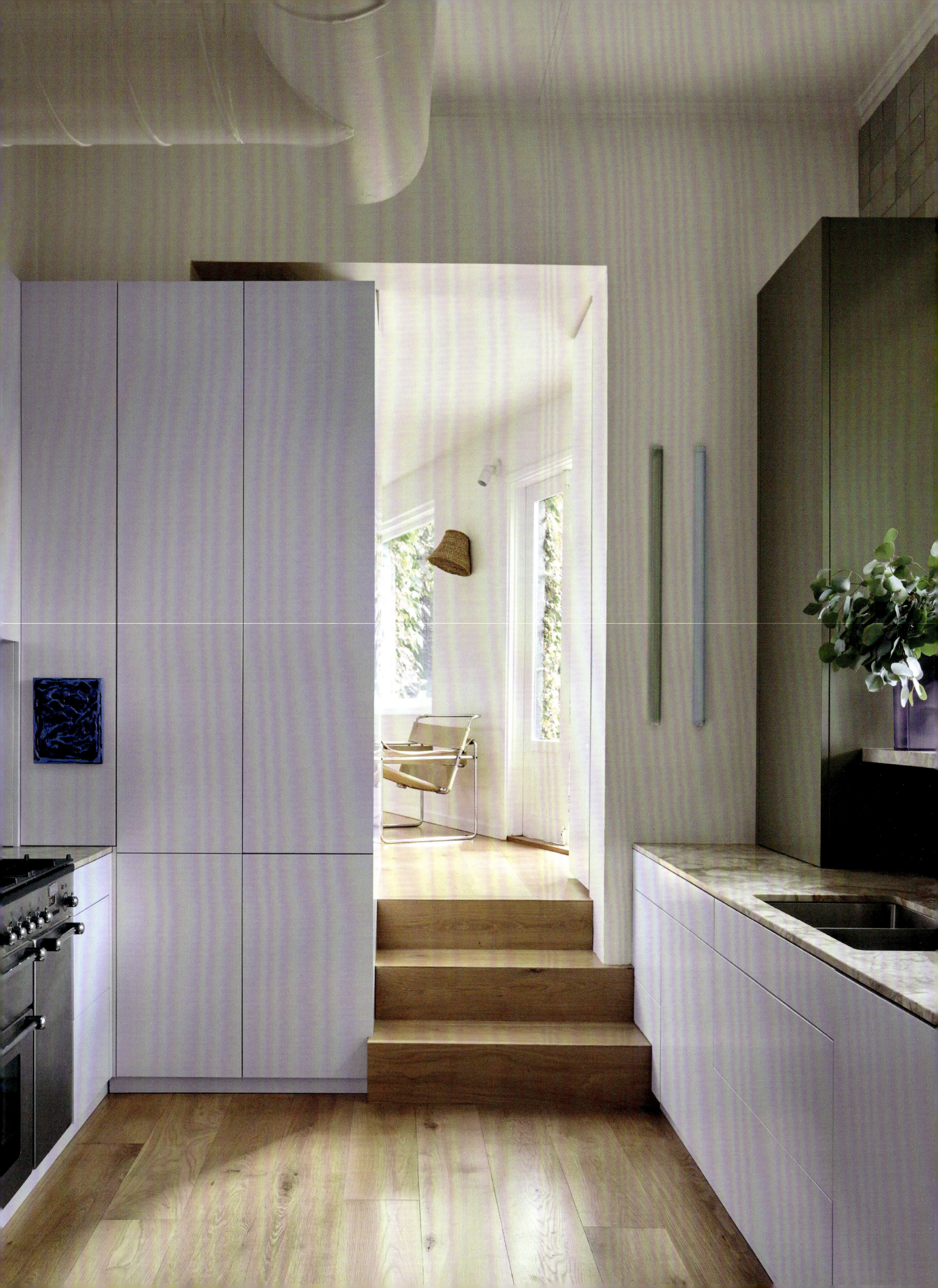

WOOD

Mosaic Garden House.

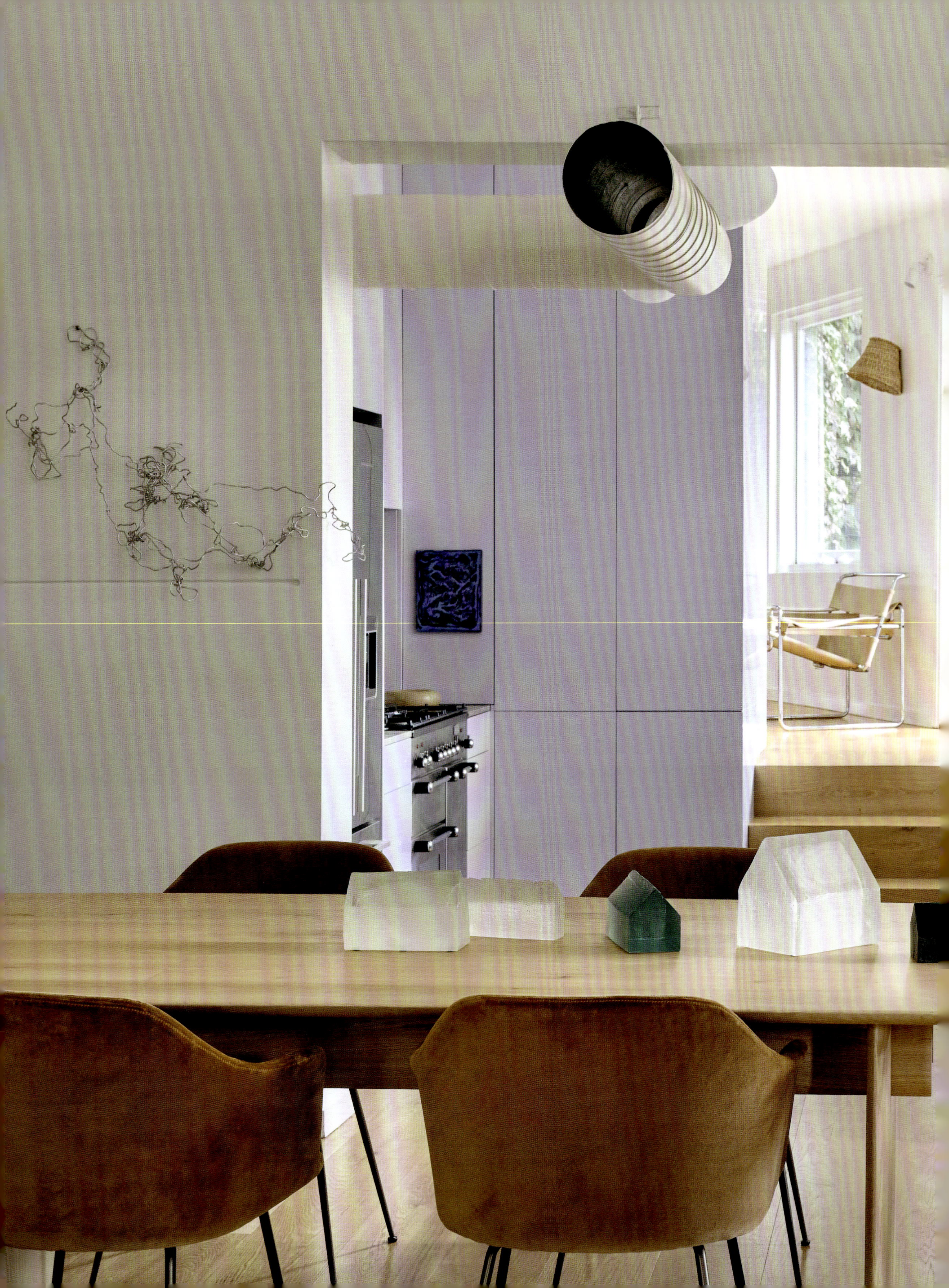

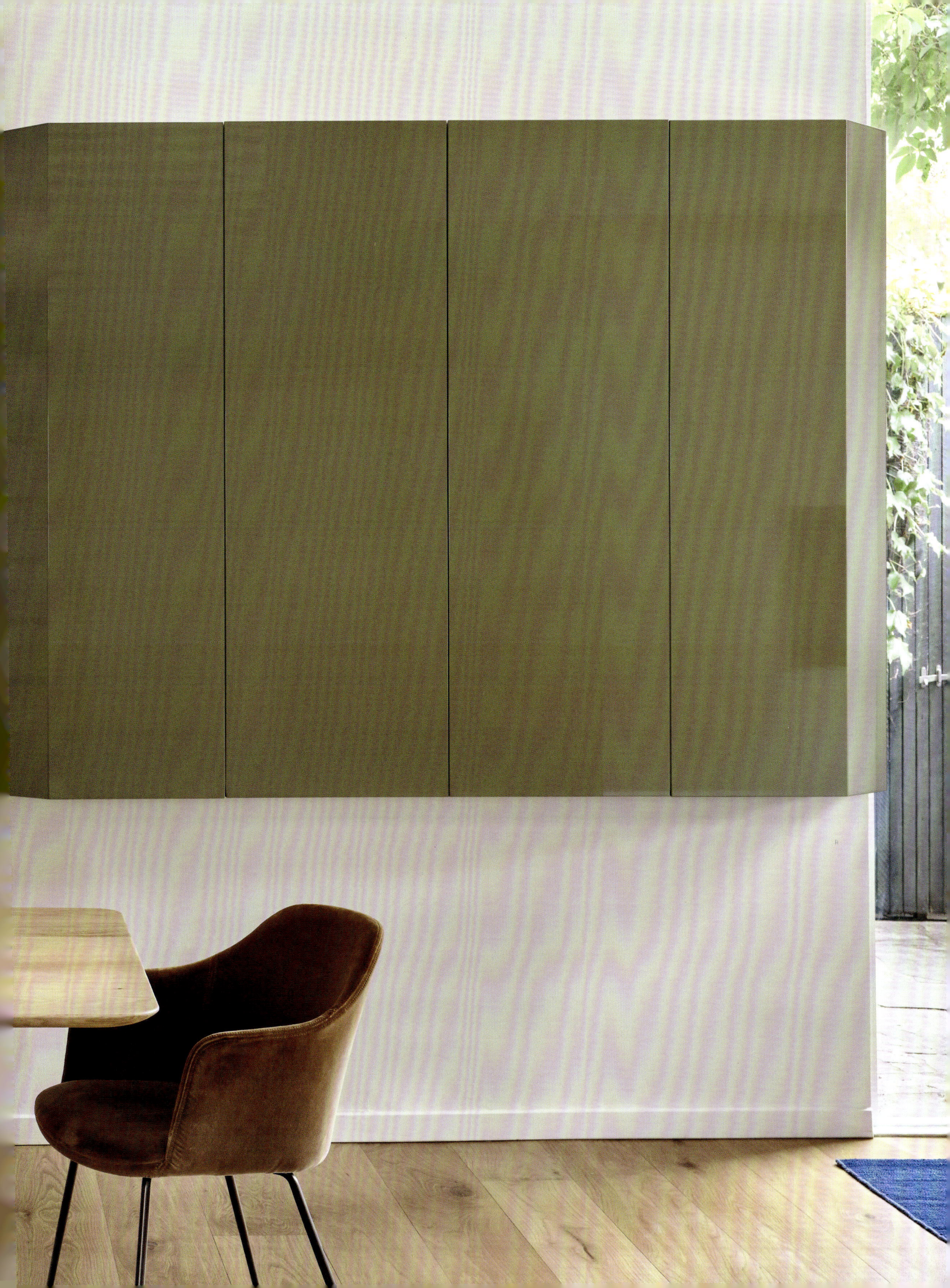

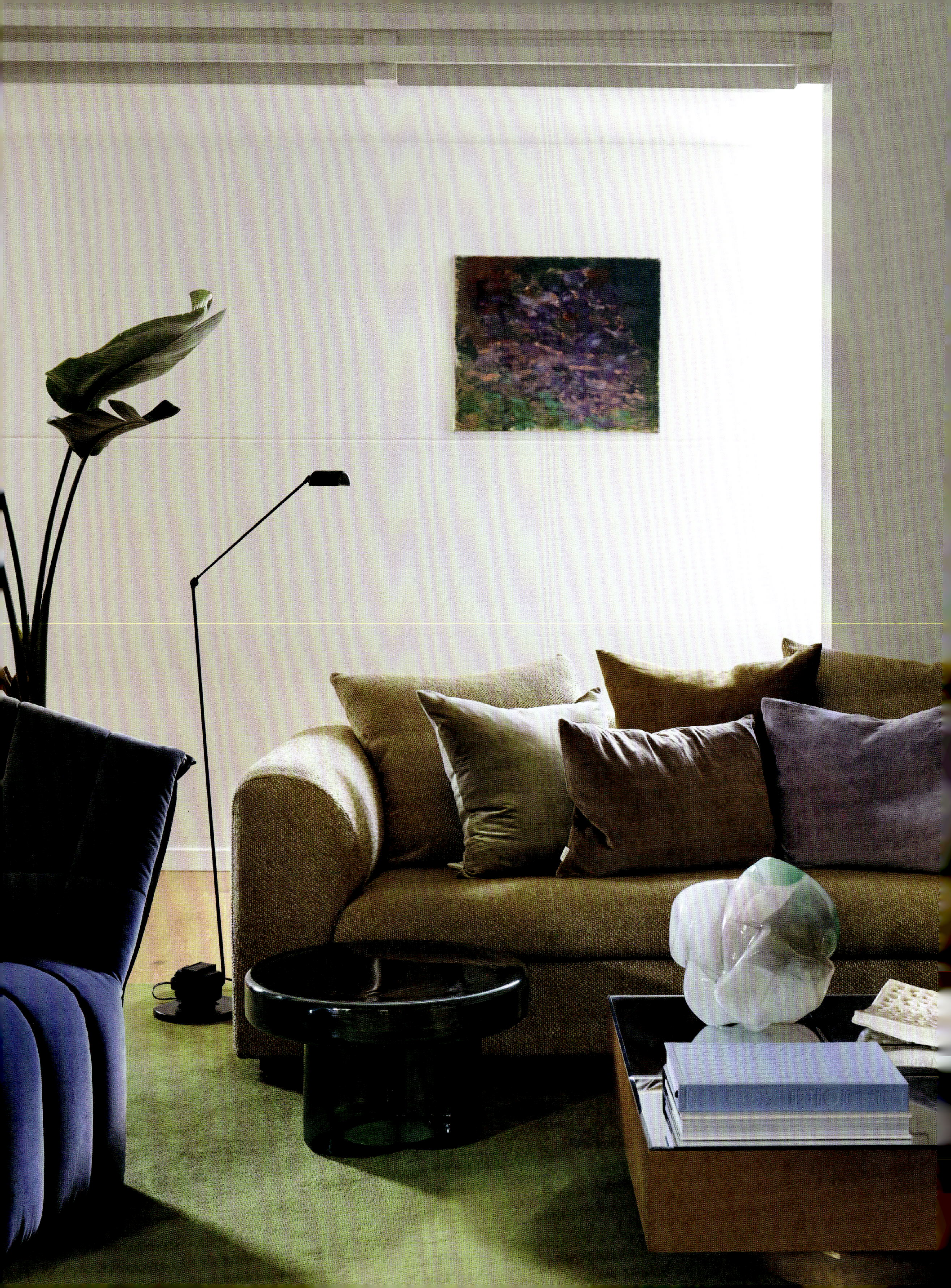

There are not many clients who would be open to a lilac kitchen with contrasting olive-green cabinetry, but the owners of this historical residence have a deep appreciation for bold colour and design.

This Hawthorn East property has a vibrant history of colour. Originally owned by the Methodist Church, it was later home to the award-winning architect and designer Alistair Knox and his wife, the artist Margot Knox. While Alistair was responsible for the redesign of the home, Margot created a renowned mosaic-walled garden that dazzled visitors as part of the Open Garden Scheme in the late 1980s and 1990s.

Many times over the years I have driven past Mosaic House and wondered what was behind the gated wall with its wild garden poking over the fence. In 2024, the owner reached out to see if I would assist with bringing new life to their space. This was a small project for our studio, but it was one that we relished. Our brief was to inject our client's love of colour into the space and provide more opportunity for this family of five to come together. Our client has a deep love of colour and wanted to change the all-white joinery approach from a previous renovation. We used the colours in the mosaic artwork outside the home as the inspiration for the internal colour palette.

The layout of the home is unusual, with the existing kitchen situated in a passage between the living area and bedrooms. It was important that the kitchen felt spacious, while also ensuring that its design elements flowed throughout the adjoining rooms.

There are four bedrooms in this house, cleverly planned to feel protected and private, at one end of the property. The main bedroom looks out onto Margot's mosaic love seat and tropical garden. The aim was for this space to be a magical and calming retreat that still incorporates pops of colour that complement the rich greens of the garden.

The moss green rug and mustard wrap-around sofa – made locally by Jardan – with lilac and brown velvet cushions harmonises with the tones of our client's much-loved Indigenous artworks. A long oak dining table with beautiful glass houses by Luna Ryan and velvet-wrapped chairs by &Tradition tie the space together.

A wine cabinet in gloss olive wraps from the living room into the kitchen. It sits off the floor so as not to overwhelm the space. Existing joinery in the entry was changed to match that in the kitchen and throughout. A blue kilim rug from Halcyon Lake was thrown down to punctuate the entry, with a large monstera plant adjacent.

The study is tucked around the corner by the spiral staircase and is complete with an aubergine-coloured desk and pale green cupboards overhead. On the desk sits a ceramic work by 101 Copenhagen, accompanied by Noguchi's Akari 3X lamp.

It was a joy to create new moments of colour in our client's home that injected new life into the historical space, while also paying homage to Margot Knox's extraordinary mosaic artwork.

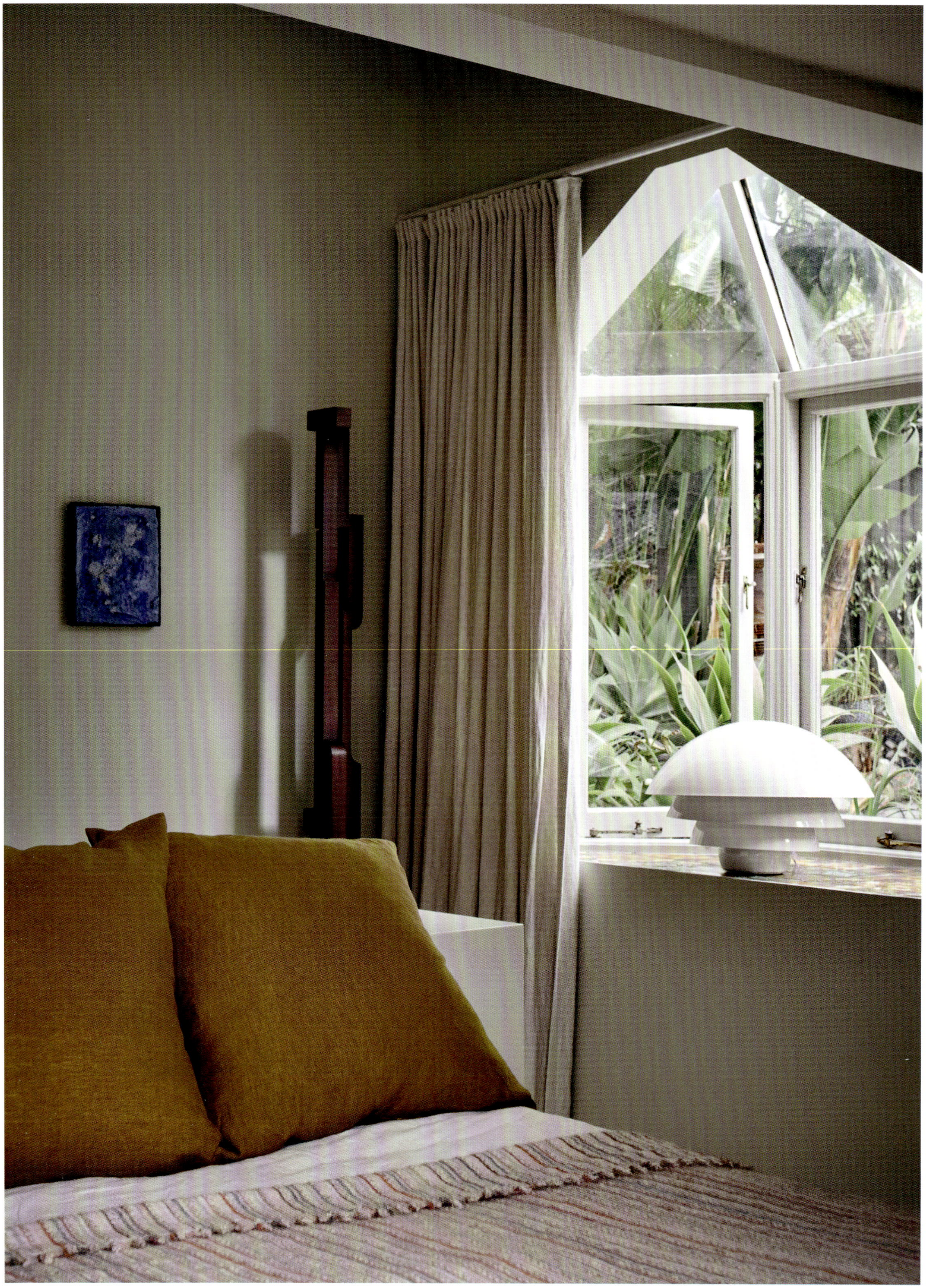

Below: The study sits adjacent to the spiral staircase and the pale green cabinetry and aubergine desk create a calming space. A Noguchi lamp sits beside a vessel from Front Room Gallery.

MOSAIC GARDEN HOUSE.

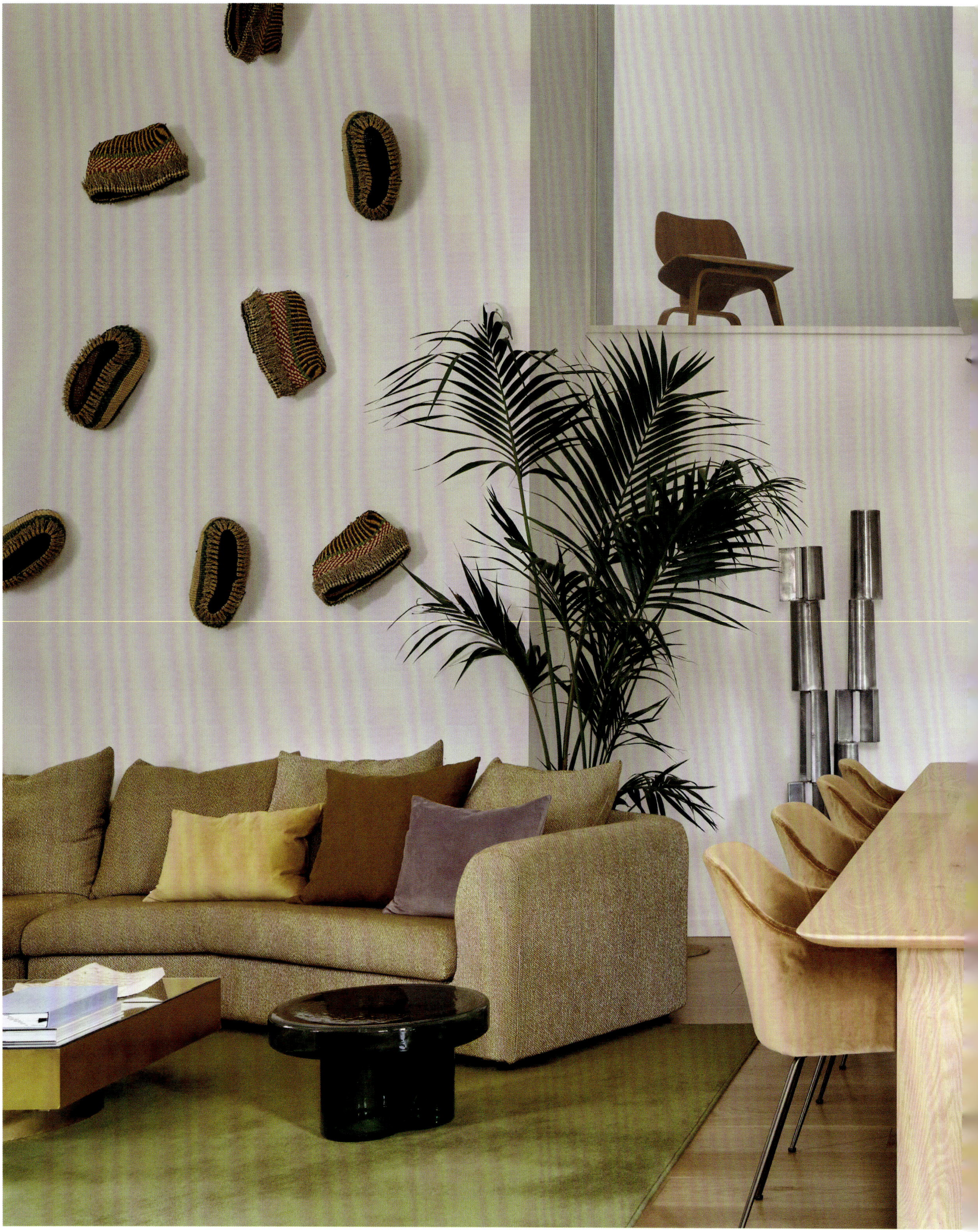

MOSAIC GARDEN HOUSE.

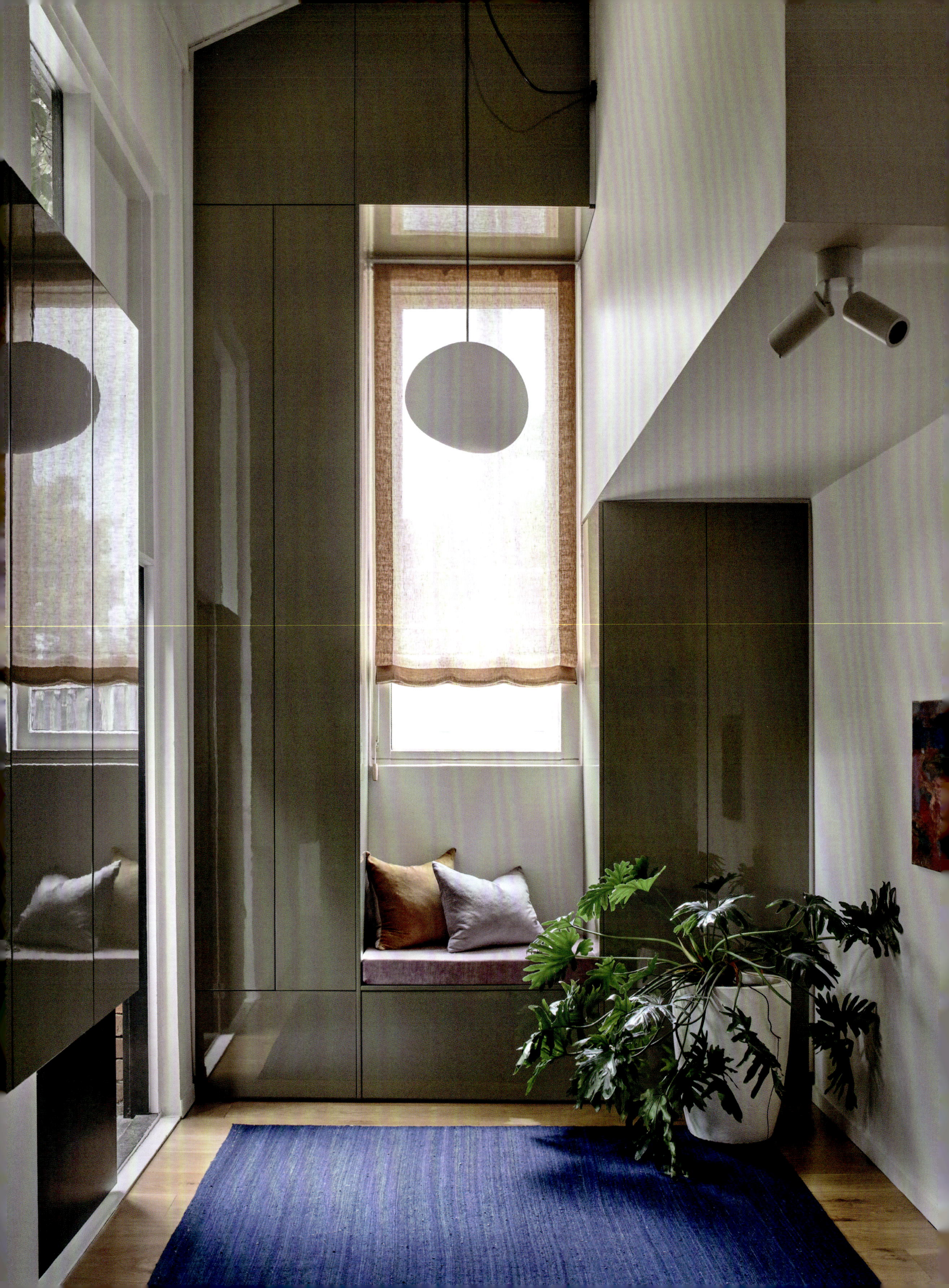

For the design colour palette we took inspiration from some of the colours in the mosaic love seat by previous homeowner Margot Knox that sits proudly in the garden. We were particularly drawn to the mustard, green and blue-lilac tones.

MOSAIC GARDEN HOUSE.

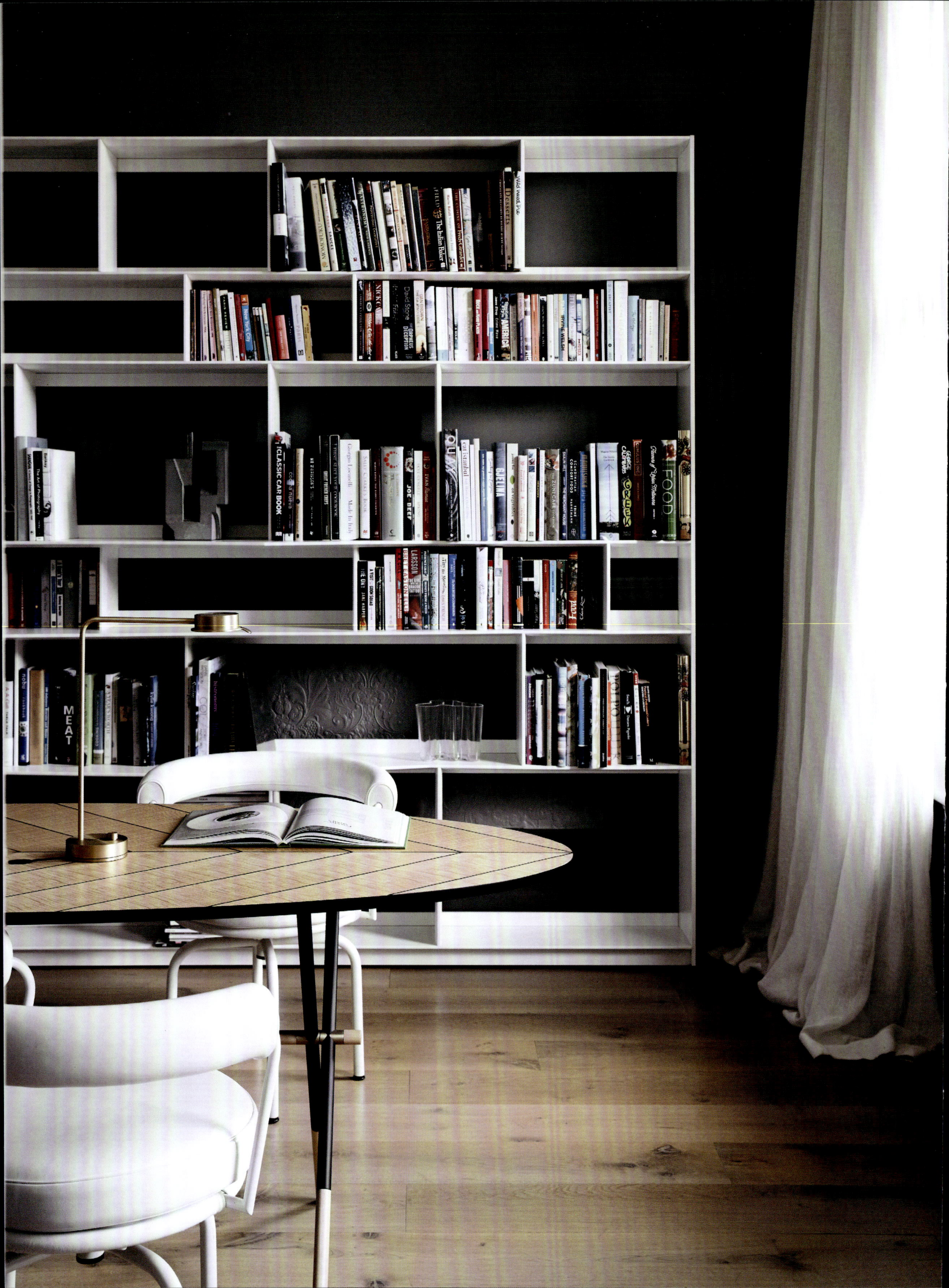

WOOD

Elsternwick House.

WOOD

ELSTERNWICK HOUSE.

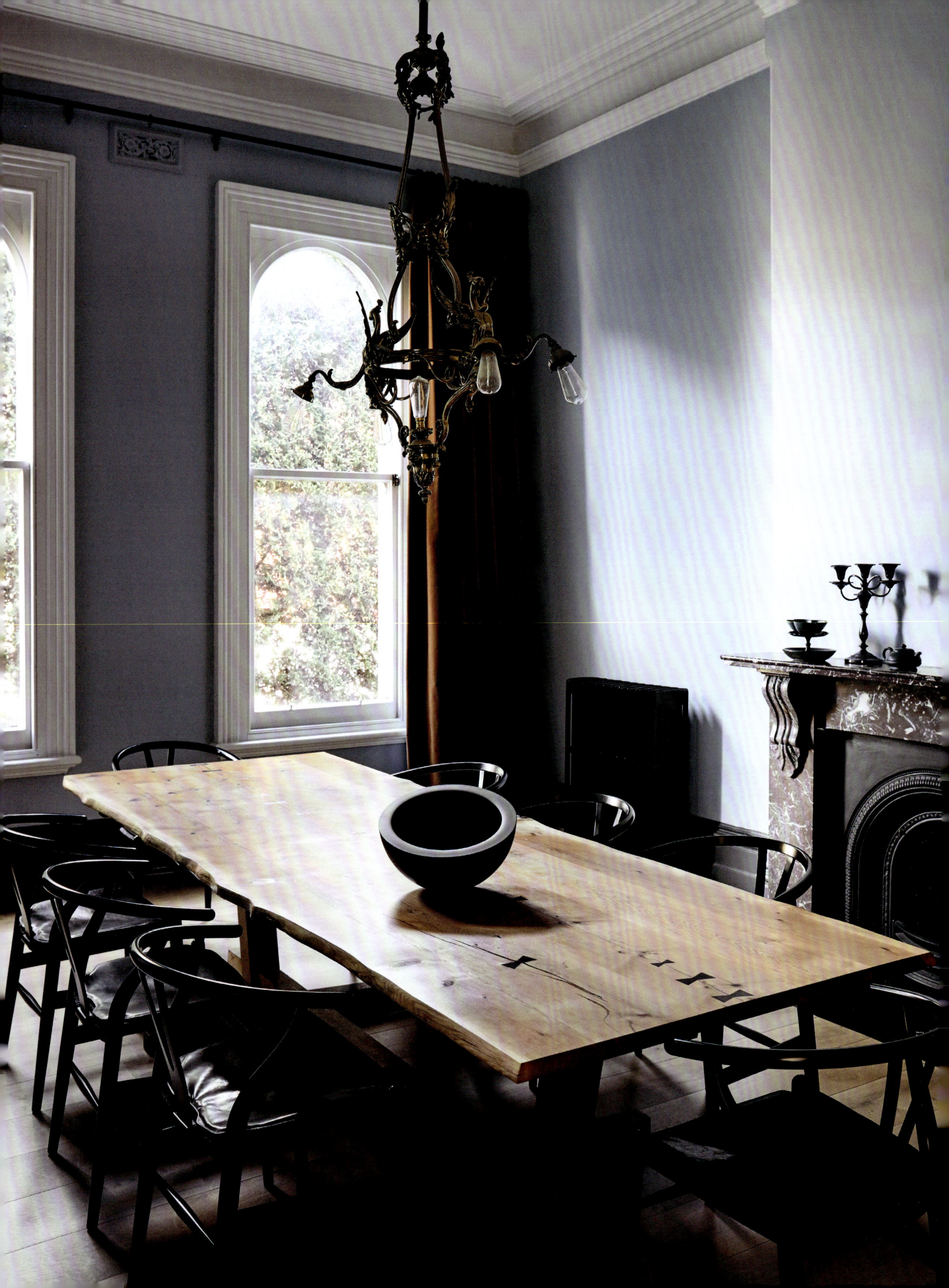

E ach new project offers an element that helps unlock the design process and creates a signature project style. It could be a connection to place, a passion that the client pursues, or the building itself. Our aim at the start of a project is to uncover the design key or focal point.

This magnificent Victorian house in Elsternwick has a celebrated history; it was vital to respect its past as we formed a new vision for the future. Its dignified frame and imposing features became both inspiration and essential ingredients in recrafting a stately home for contemporary living. Magnificent fireplaces and lofty ceilings were a conduit for exploring colour through signature materials. In its way, this too was an echo of the home's origins, with use of colour a hallmark of Victorian decor.

Our client encouraged this foray into colour, which transformed each successive room. A palette of earthy clays in the salon fused into oxide browns in the adjoining study, the brown giving way to a blue-washed dining room. Here, striking blue walls set off the deep russet marble of an original fireplace. Luxurious tobacco-hued velvet curtains fall from near ceiling height to pool on the floor. Deep timber skirting boards and door frames are painted in dark tones of grey and charcoal, forming a demarcation line between timber floors and washed walls. Opulent original features were the cue for a dramatic union of old and new, with a distinctive colour backdrop.

Furniture and art were the other factors central to the home's metamorphosis into a modern sanctuary, and each piece was carefully chosen. The client was passionate about gathering furniture with its own history and significance, and we established a unique narrative for each room, from the sculptural Serge Mouille pendants in the bedroom and living area to the refined Pietro Russo dining table and elegant white leather Charlotte Perriand chairs.

Though drawn from contemporary designers, these exemplars of twentieth-century furniture sit harmoniously within this historic home, mingling to create a unified residence of timeless materiality and elegance.

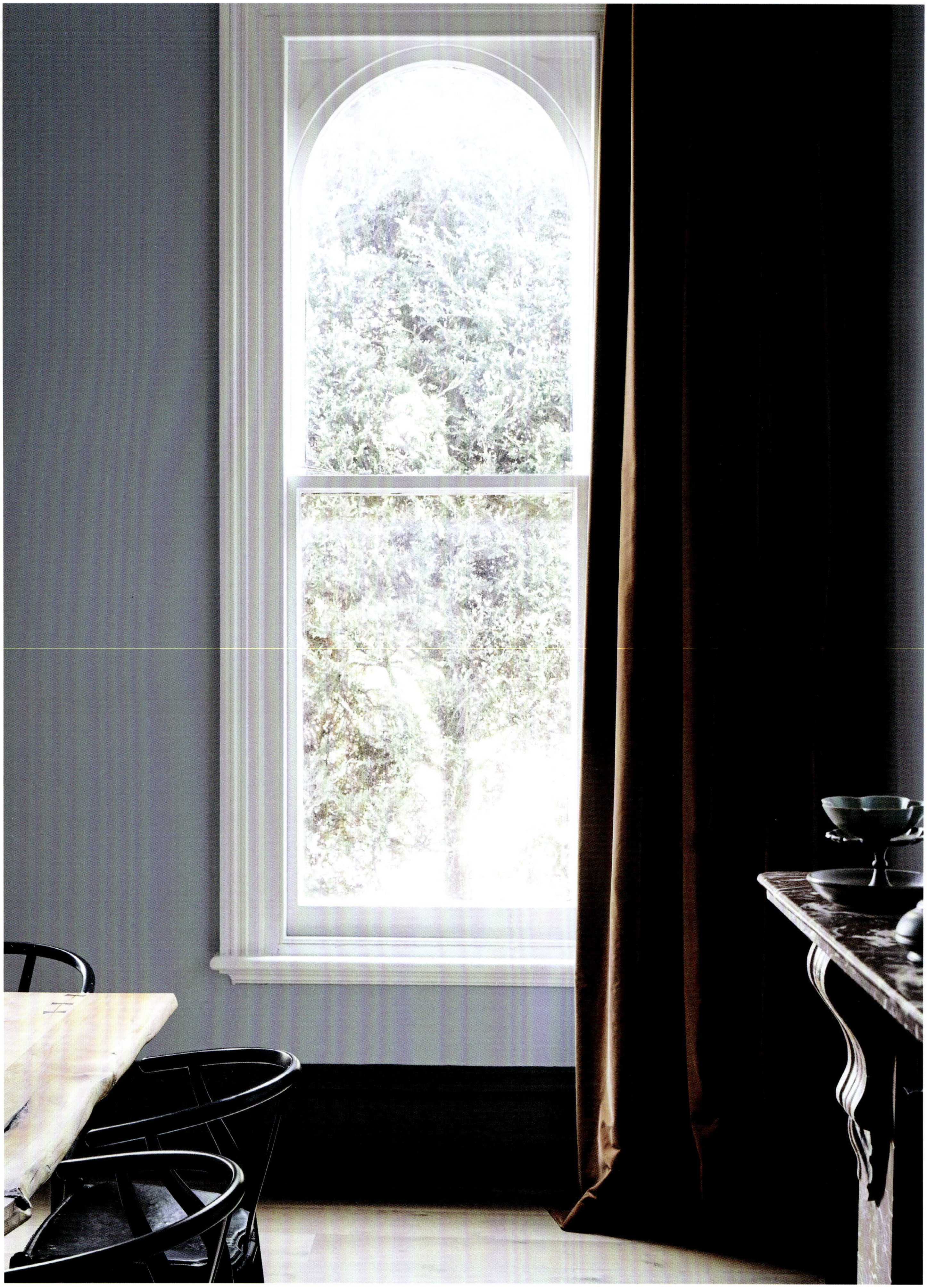

Opposite: In the dining room, the toffee-coloured curtains are offset by the chalky blue walls. While a modern design, the velvet curtains would not have been out of place when this grand Victorian home was built.

WOOD

ST. ALI & THE QUEEN

St. Ali & The Queen is a collaboration between artisanal coffee roaster St. Ali and award-winning mixologist Orlando Marzo. The coffee-meets-cocktails venue is located opposite Melbourne's iconic Queen Victoria Market in the Munro community hub designed by Six Degrees Architects.

Engaged for the fit-out and joinery, our brief was for a casual cafe by day, a sophisticated bar by night. The space has lofty cathedral ceilings and tall, vaulted windows. We wanted to infuse the raw and industrial nature of the building with the warmth and spirit of European hospitality. We embraced the sleek, brutalist feel of the aluminium stalls and stone counters in the market's original food hall, crafting joinery and furniture with clean lines and rectilinear forms. We wanted to bring a social and relaxed ambience, along with the humble, inviting design.

As the centrepiece of the venue, the long counter is crafted from Italian stone, a nod to the owner's heritage. We selected Afrodite marble for its dramatic veining and hues that deepen from green to blue, and softened it with cream-, grey- and silver-veined travertines that break up the length of the bar. Chunky stone plinths and slabs protect the recycled Oregon timber on the face of the bar and define the openings where customers can sit or stand.

We designed the furniture with a European sociability. The low-slung banquettes face outward, embracing the lively atmosphere of the market. The moveable stools provide flexibility – they can be grouped together for a communal feel.

The custom stools, tables and bar seating, crafted by Ross Thompson, are another evolution of our furniture range. They have a strong geometric language, with blocky, elemental shapes and brass detailing that reflects the authenticity of materials and construction. They're humble, understated and not overthought, and the simplicity of their forms shows the beautiful grain of the Oregon pine.

The banquette seats draw on the same design language with straight lines and rectilinear forms. We expressed the panels by rotating the grains and safeguarded the timber with a travertine plinth. A high back creates separation between the seating and providore, providing privacy for both, and integrates storage and display space for products.

Luxurious touches of polished brass, leather and lighting elevate the space from local cafe to stylish neighbourhood bar. People were drawn to the space straight away. It has an attractive, convivial atmosphere, and the natural materials will only get better with age.

190 WOOD

80 COLLINS

80 Collins is a vibrant mixed-use precinct at the Paris end of Collins Street, a city block with corporate towers, a hotel and retail and dining areas. London-based practice Universal Design Studio designed the north and south lobbies of 80 Collins with minimalist architecture and refined materiality, but they wanted a different approach to the furniture and concierge desk to give the space texture and expression. They engaged us to create a sculptural intervention – an antithesis to the formality of the corporate lobby.

The lobbies are elemental in their minimalist design and materials. We sought to bring another perspective into the space with the introduction of nature and a sense of ritual. We had recently held an exhibition, *Work Shop*, showcasing artist Makiko Ryujin's timber vessels. Makiko's work is raw, tactile and quite poetic in the way it expresses the imperfections of the timber. Collaborating with Makiko, we set out to enlarge her vessels to human scale to create seating arrangements and totemic artworks that reshape the typical lobby experience.

We designed the assemblage of stacked wooden vessels and seats using solid Monterey cypress timber reclaimed from Victorian farms. These impressive trees were originally planted on farms as windbreaks. Woodturner Charles Sandford and his team turned the vessels, which Makiko then torched to achieve the charred, blackened effect. *Shou Sugi Ban* is a traditional Japanese wood-preserving technique also known as *yakisugi* – *yaki* meaning to heat with fire, *sugi* referring to cypress. Firing the wood creates a protective layer that gives the timber a textured, ebony finish, accentuating the grain and folds and knots in the wood.

The stacked vessels rise to 4 metres high. They have a grace and weightlessness to them, despite being solid wood. Delicately resting or balancing upon one another, they seem to defy gravity. I say seem to, because this was a highly technical and engineered project. Each piece is very heavy and needed to be secured. The organic arrangement is considered, providing a natural pathway and comfortable areas to sit, encouraging visitors to pause and take a closer look.

As a contrast to the blackened timber, the concierge desks within both lobbies are formed with hand-finished recycled aluminium. Inviting and engaging, the desks are more subtle than the corporate reception counter. The geometric plinth-like forms of the desks and counter are stacked and cantilevered, with Makiko's vessels exhibited upon both.

We titled the installation *MATTER*, and it's one of the few major works by a female artist in the Melbourne CBD. It's a privilege to have worked on this project and with Makiko to create such a significant and beautiful work.

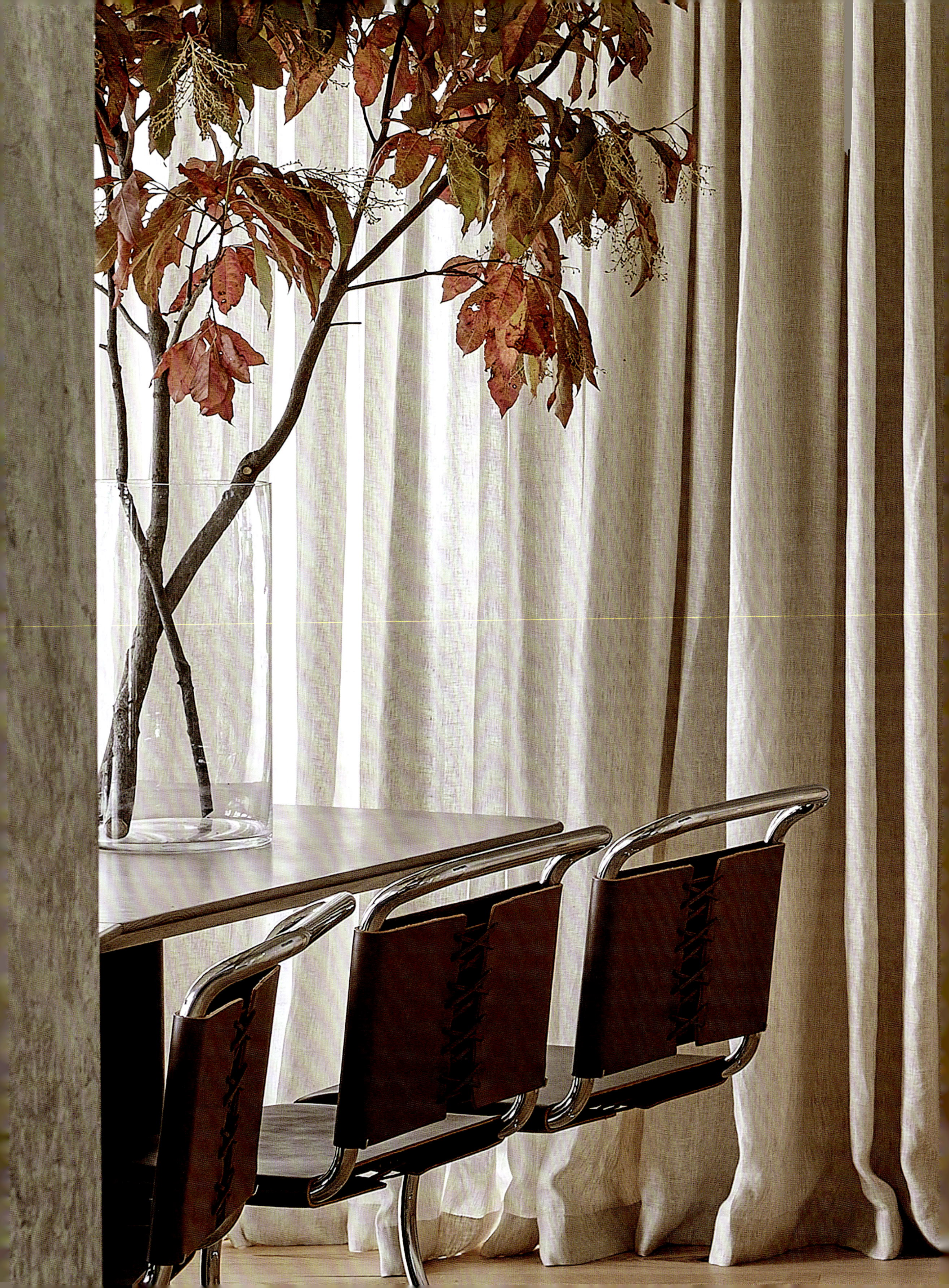

TEXTILE

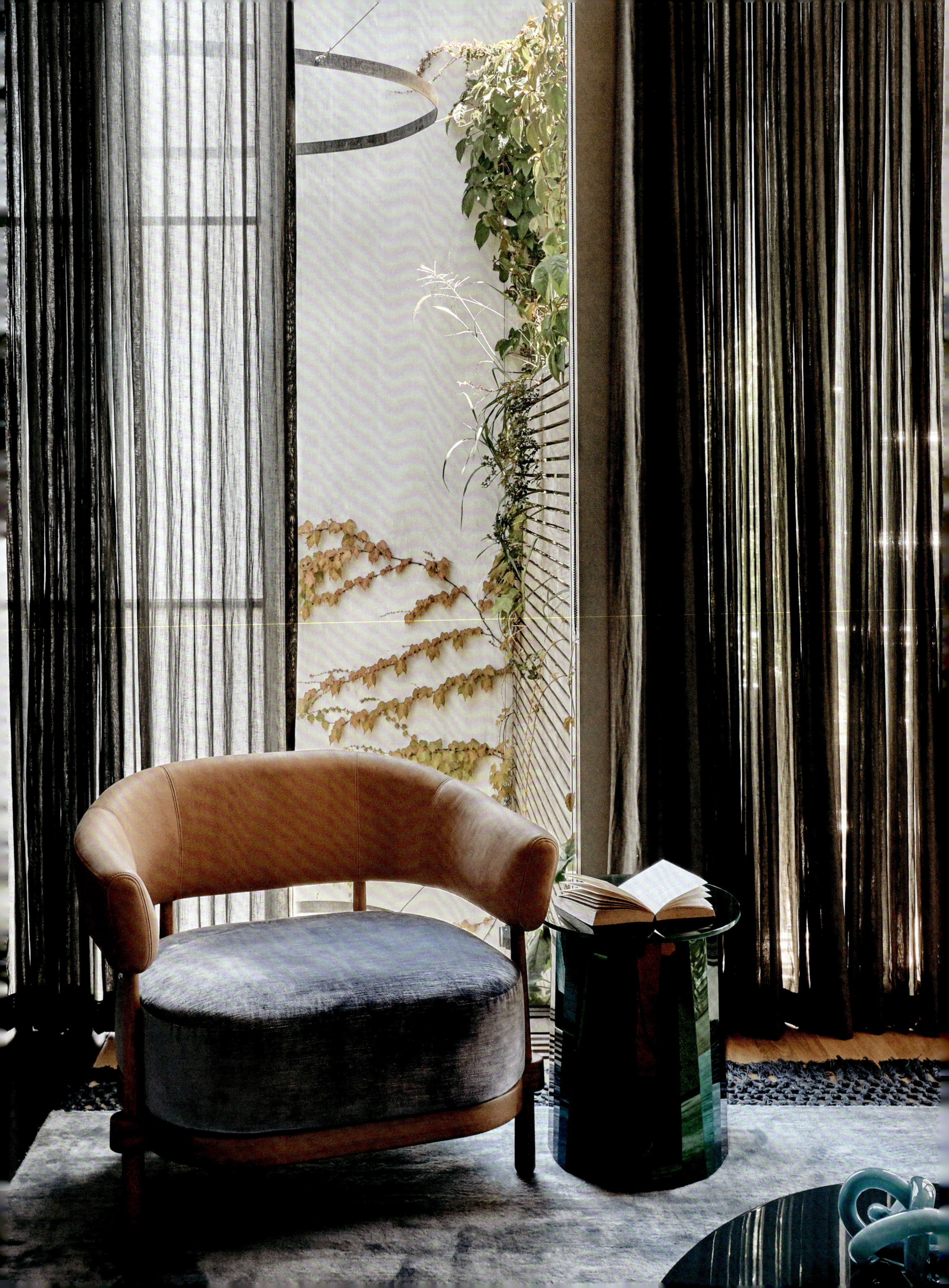

When I think of textiles, I think of materials that flow and are composed of fibres. Not just fabrics, but other materials that are pliable and can be moulded to give an appearance of motion and movement, like plaster, leather or fibreglass.

In 2020, I saw Rei Kawakubo's Commes des Garçons exhibition at The Met in New York. The techniques she uses to fold and construct garments, her experimentation with forms that are both sculptural and detailed, and her use of non-traditional materials are inspiring.

Textiles can achieve a distinctive and unique aesthetic, and the projects that employ textiles alongside more traditional materials can often yield more expressive, unconventional or daring settings. At Grace Park, we wrapped a pale, ruched swathe of leather around a travertine plinth, creating a luxurious, theatrical mood within the kitchen. An insertion of softly sculptural curved fibreglass, illuminated by a neon light within, forms an ethereal backdrop for the rounded dining table in Burnley House. In other projects, fabrics are vessels for colour and tactility, and raw finishes can introduce an unanticipated ambience. And using wicker in Sorrento House enhanced the relaxed, earthy mood of this beachside home.

Textiles can also speak to the past. My great-aunts were seamstresses who grew up a block away from the Ace Hotel, one of our projects in Sydney. When I learned the building had been a garment factory, I was inspired to link some of its history to the new interior. The fabric adorning the window surrounds on the terraces is raw linen with pigment that we loosely tacked to the wall, giving it softness and movement.

I dedicate this chapter to my aunts, who also loved textiles.

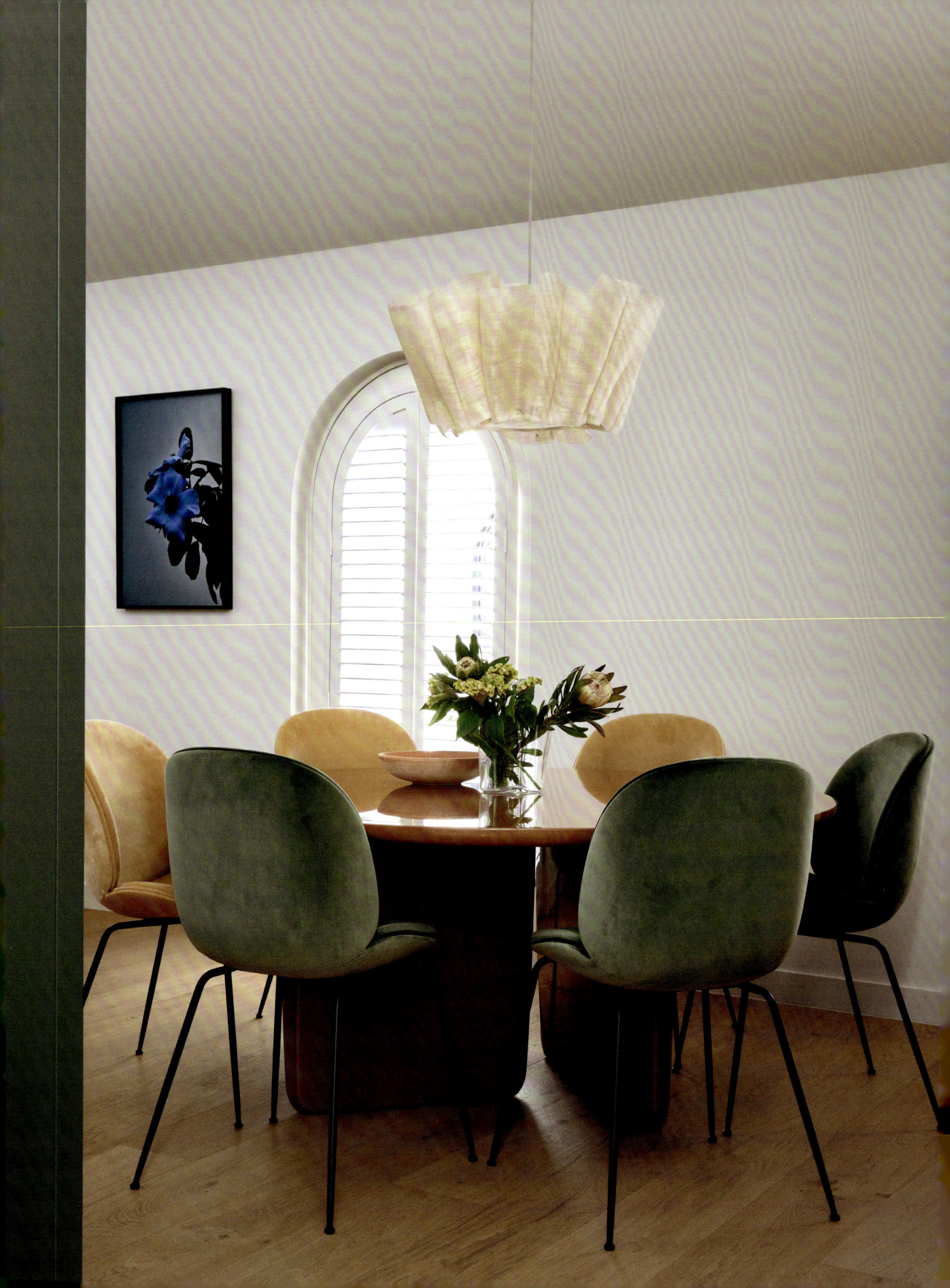

TEXTILE

Grace Park Residence.

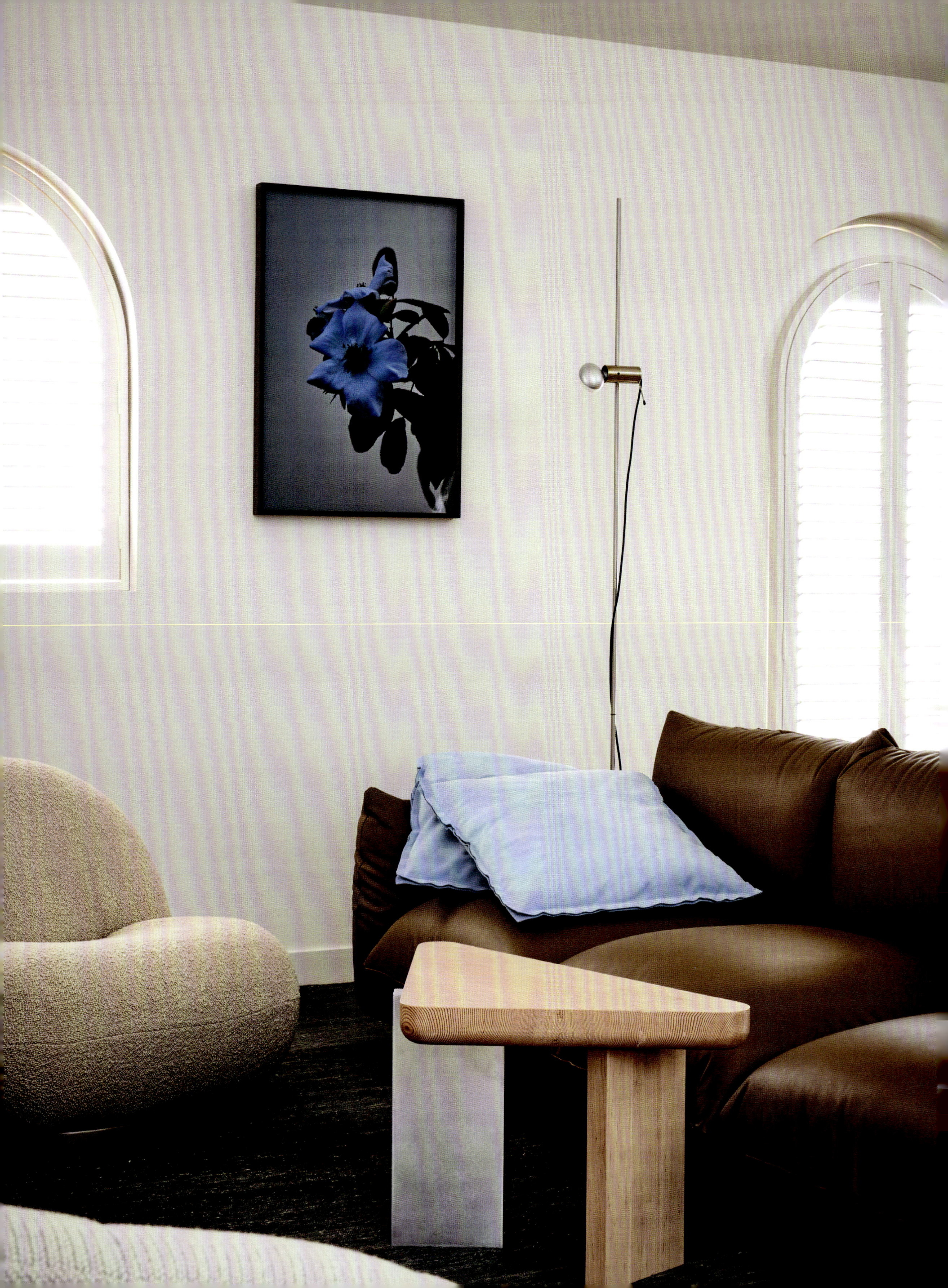

Inspiration for a design can come from many different places – the materials, craft, setting, clients and other sources. For this residence, we drew inspiration from its 1970s Spanish Revival architecture to create a fresh and modern interior that played off the era and features of the building. Evocative of Los Angeles, the townhouse complex has towering palm trees at the gate, terracotta-tiled roofs, arched doorways and windows, and oversized Juliet balconies above the central driveway.

Our client had lived in her townhouse for quite a few years before deciding to renovate. High pitched ceilings and clerestory windows brought beautiful light into the kitchen, dining and living area, but the planning was awkward, with a large, central piece of joinery segmenting the space. We removed this to enhance the openness and effortless flow of movement. Then we brought in curves and colours inspired by the architecture, and textiles to add another layer of warmth and texture.

Like many of our projects, the palette began with the marble for the kitchen benchtop and splashback. We sourced a rich green Vaticano marble from Italy that has a swirling pattern, like the ocean being stirred. Beneath the smooth honed slab of the island benchtop, the curved travertine base is enveloped with pumice-coloured leather that softens and relaxes the space. I was inspired by Le Corbusier's iconic Palace of Assembly in Chandigarh on which the hyperbolic roof sweeps upward. Our client is very interested in art and loved this idea. The leather is like a piece of sculpture billowing around the sides and front with a deliberately ruched effect, and its undulating folds catch the light and descend into shadow.

The travertine base and textile-covered joinery continue in the dining room, where the cupboards are covered with a natural-coloured handwoven raffia grasscloth. Two of the doors retract to reveal an opulent cocktail bar, like a hidden jewel. Trimmed with brass, the luminous Cristallo Rosa onyx has an almost translucent pale-pink background with expressive white and glistening gold veining.

We also took our cues from the architecture for the furniture, selecting pieces with voluptuous curved forms or that reference the building's 1970s origins. Our client entertains frequently and wanted a beautiful table for hosting dinners. We chose B&B Italia's large, circular Tobi-Ishi table with glossy tobacco-coloured lacquer. The Gubi Beetle dining chairs are upholstered in olive-green and camel-coloured velvet. Overhead, the Anders pendant from PINCH is ruched and folded, sculpted from layers of fibre derived from the banana plant.

In the living area, the furniture is relaxed, comfortable and low to the ground. Designed in 1970, the Arflex Marenco sofa has inviting, pillowy forms that we upholstered in a handsome brown leather. The two chairs, both by Pierre Paulin, are also low-lying and organic in shape, and the 1963 vintage USM sideboard has a metallic goldy-brown finish.

Grace Park Residence is quite a feminine home, but with robust elements too. Each space has its own character, while being tied together through forms, materials, textures and colours inspired by the architecture.

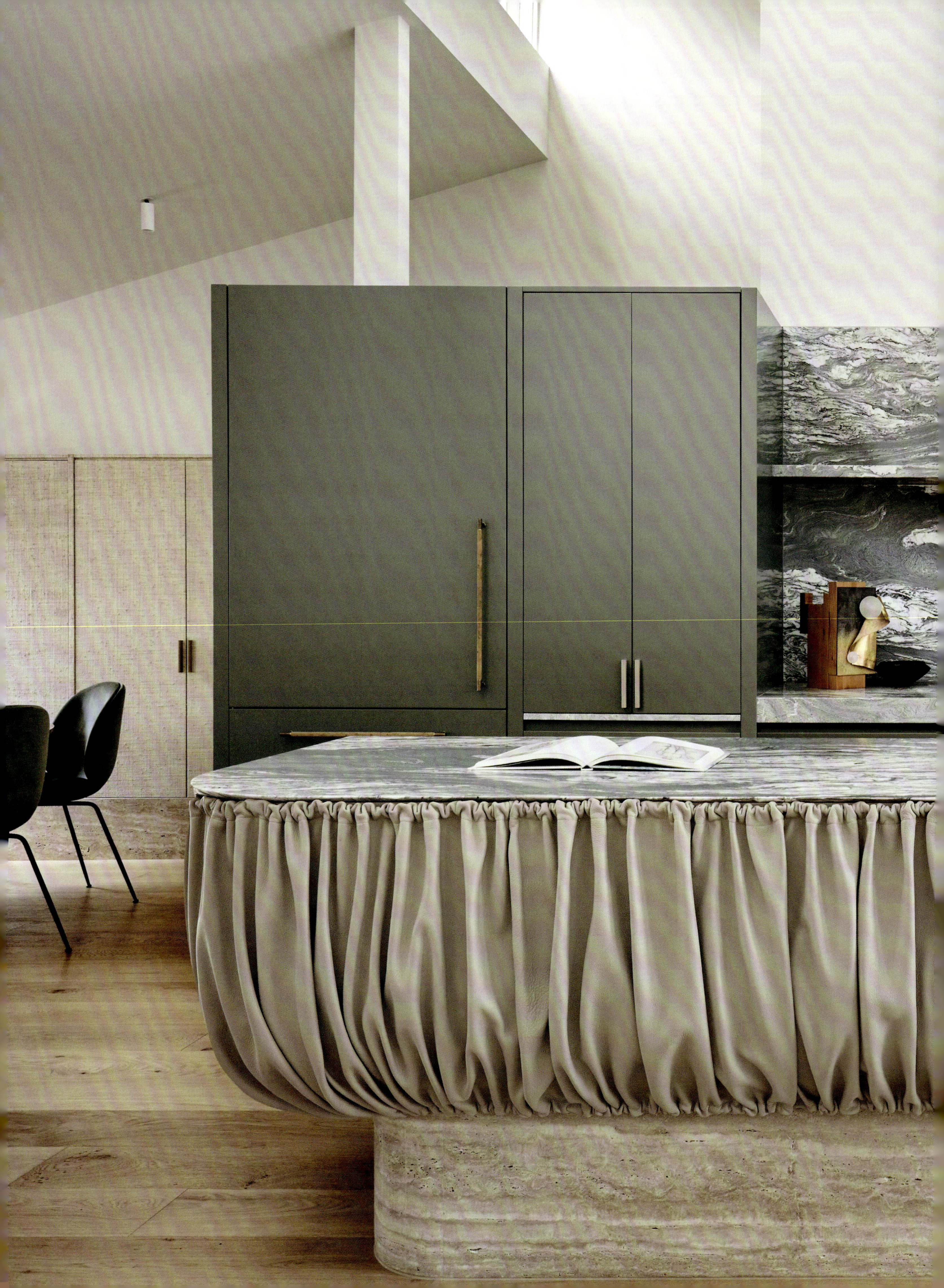

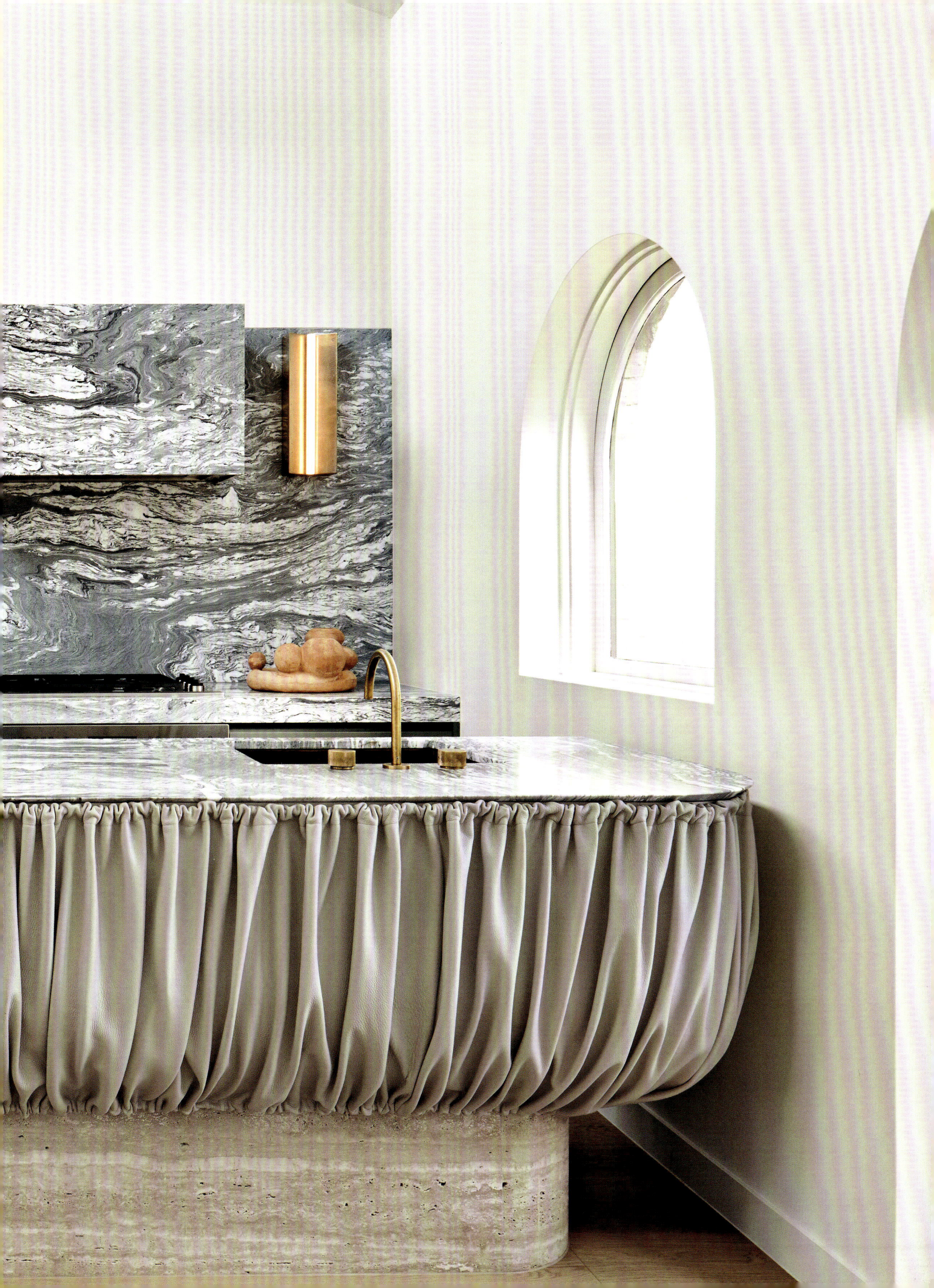

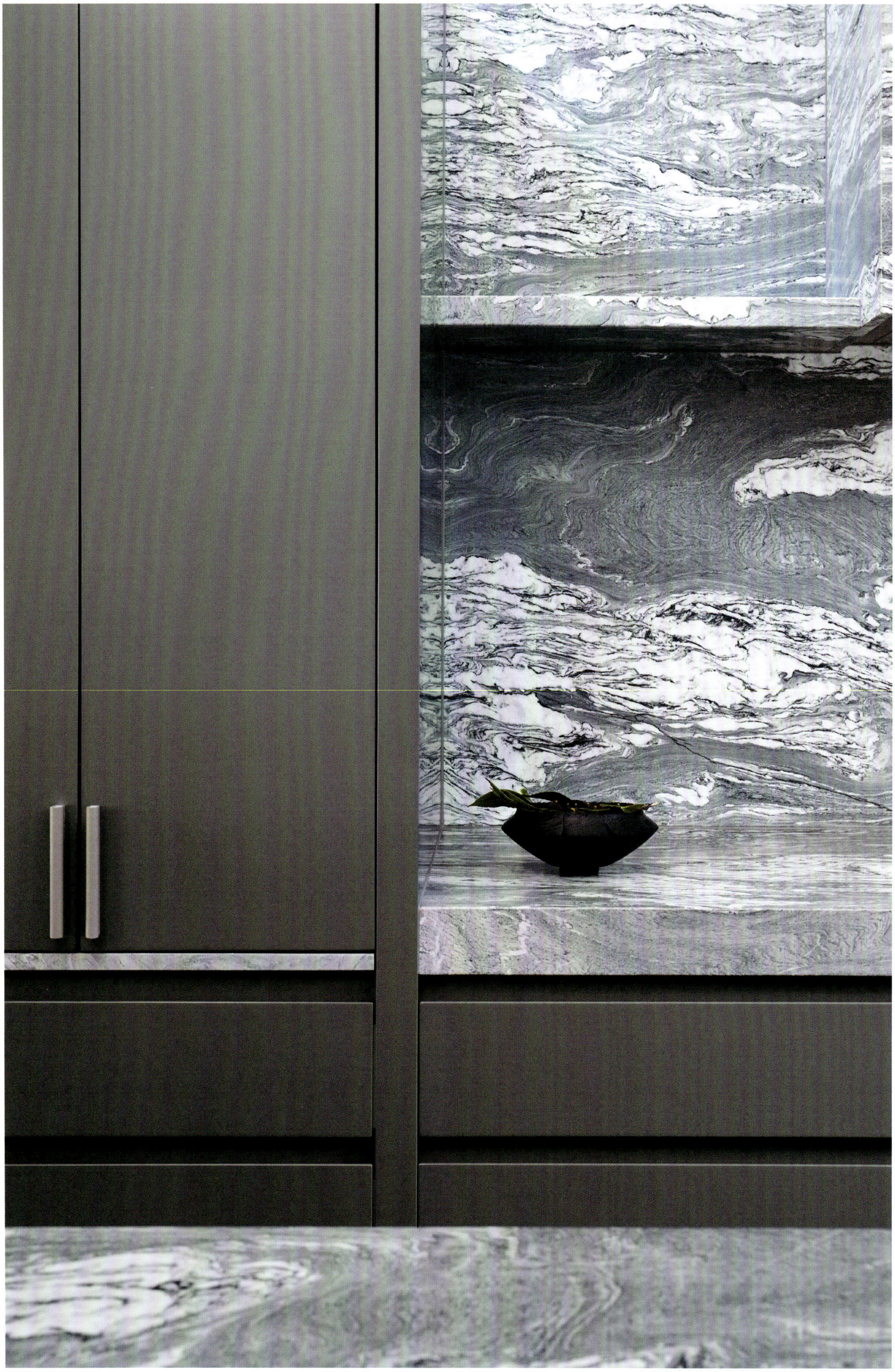

GRACE PARK RESIDENCE.

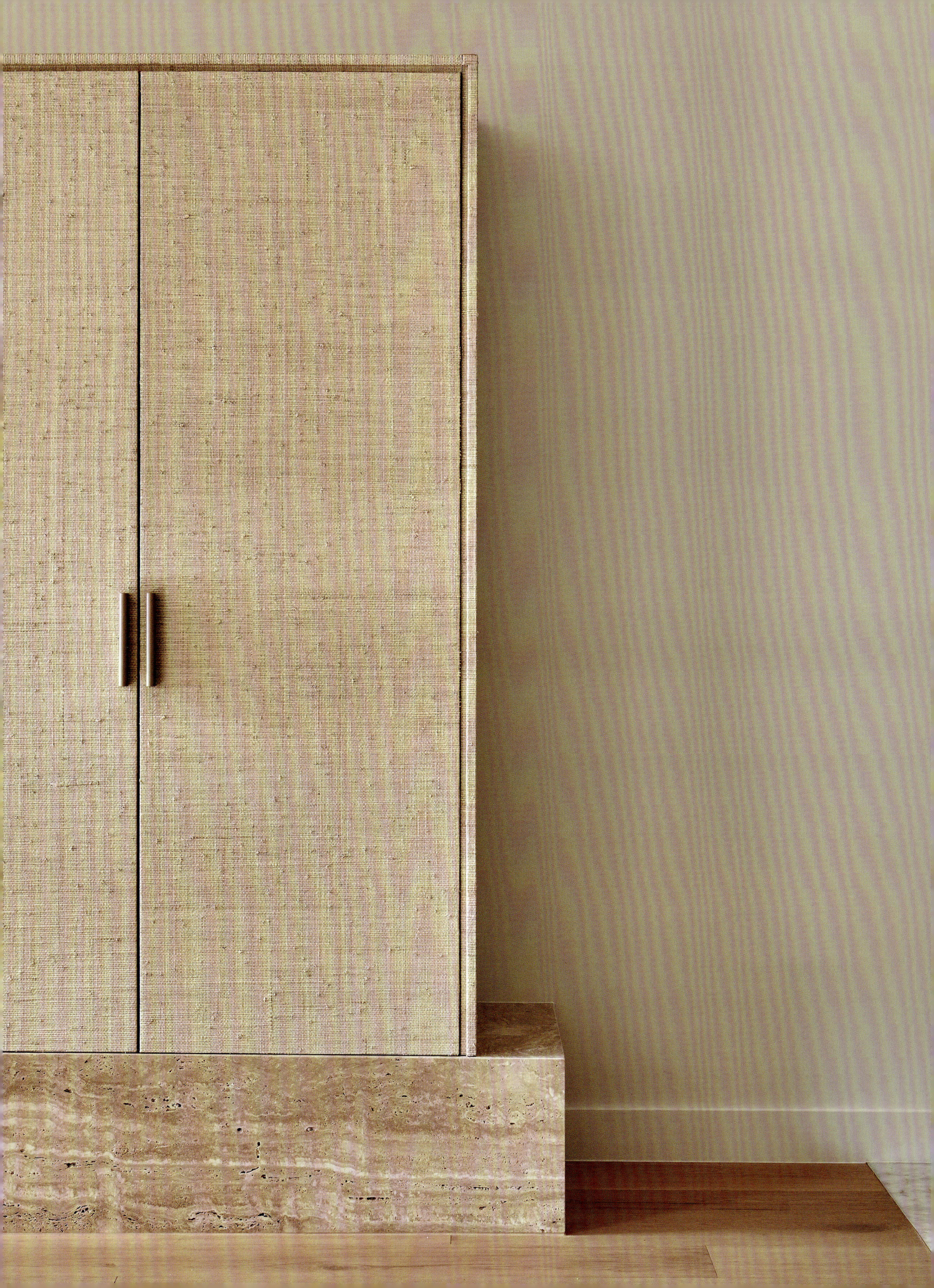

Opposite: The bespoke drinks cabinet is cloaked with grass cloth paper and stands on a travertine plinth.

This page: The living room houses a striking collection of pieces: the Arflex Marenco sofa by Mario Marenco, the Pacha lounge chair and Alpha Club chair by Pierre Paulin; and our studio's triangle table in maple and aluminium, and Toni light designed in collaboration with Volker Haug. The USM sideboard, in both the living room and study, is one of our favourite pieces.

GRACE PARK RESIDENCE.

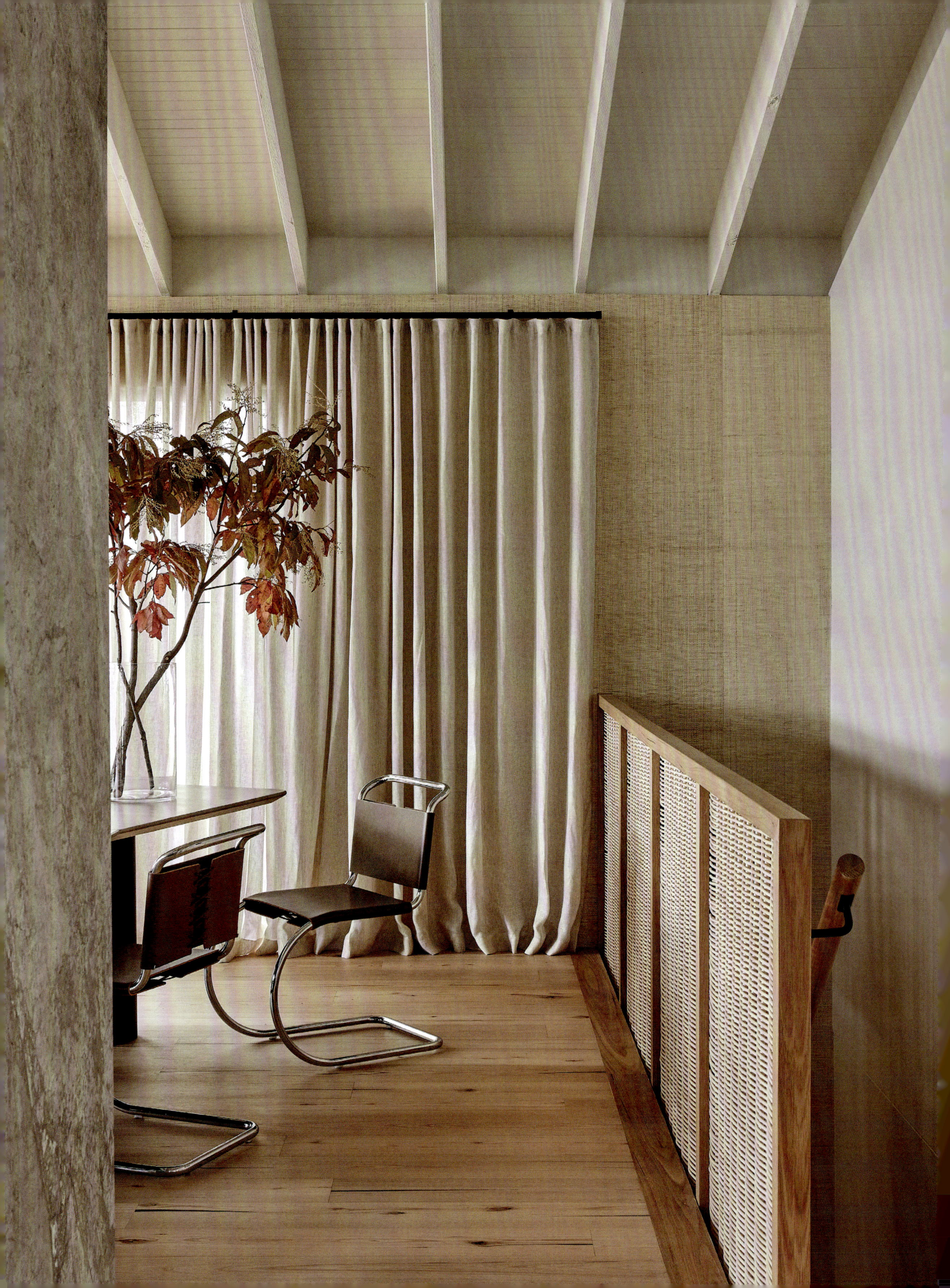

TEXTILE

Sorrento
House.

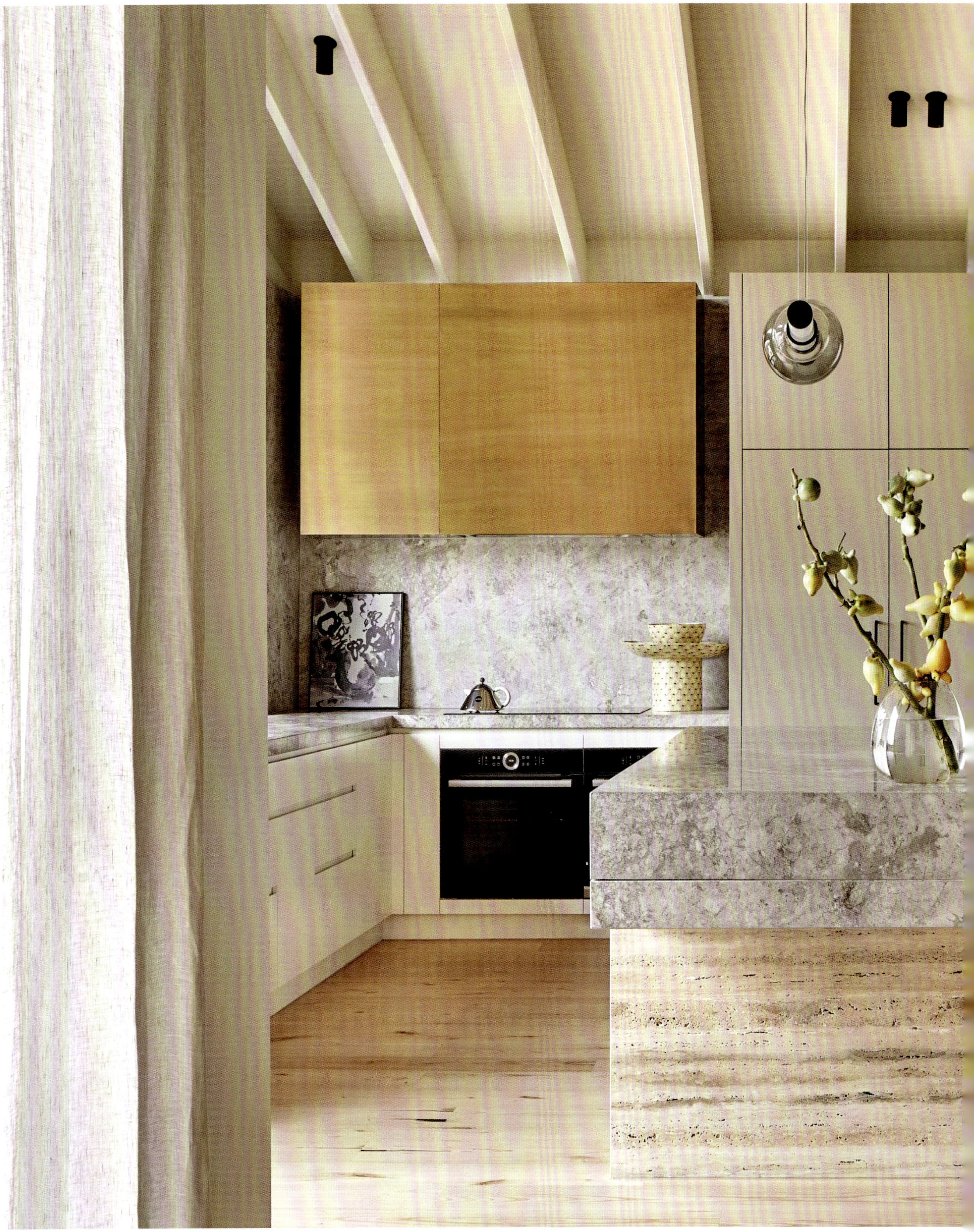

SORRENTO HOUSE.

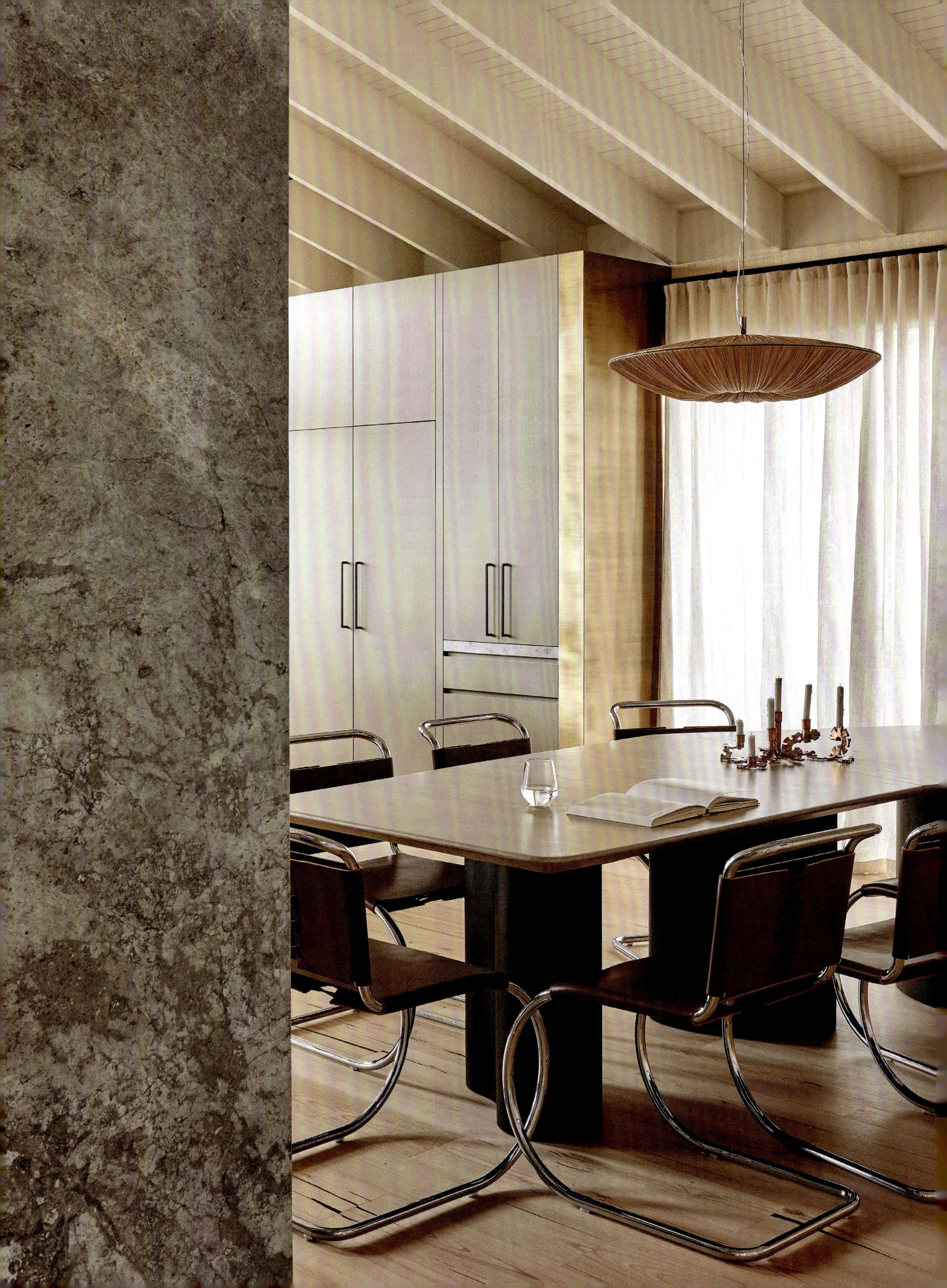

It's always a joy to work with a client again and build on an established design relationship. That trust and knowledge enables us to explore new opportunities and push the boundaries. We had worked with this client previously to design their family home in Williamstown, Melbourne. We developed a polished and sophisticated inner-city home with strong, simple materials and bold colours to contrast with the predominantly black and white interior.

We took a very different approach to the family's beach house in Sorrento on the Mornington Peninsula. They had bought a 1970s house originally designed by project house-building company Merchant Builders and recently altered with an unsympathetic renovation. We were engaged to do a full renovation of the two-storey house, including the furniture, to create a relaxed and layered retreat.

Our client's Italian heritage – as well as the Italian namesake of the location – inspired our Positano palette, with a mix of earthy textures, beachy hues and bleached pastels. Woven and crafted elements, such as linen curtains, raffia wallcoverings and handmade wicker screens, infuse the home with texture. The clarity and simplicity of Italian Rationalism is embodied in the symmetry and minimalism of the joinery.

We began by reducing the size of the main bedroom to widen the narrow hallway and elevate the sense of arrival and entry into the home. A curved wall around the bedroom eliminates any jarring angles in both the bedroom and hallway, where sage-green polished plaster catches and reflects the sunlight and gives the walls a crushed velvet sheen. In the bedroom, wheat-toned raffia wallcovering wraps around the curves to create a cosy, textured cocoon.

European oak floorboards lead into the living, dining and kitchen area, where linen curtains and glazed doors slide open to the terrace and magnificent views of the bay. In true 1970s fashion, the soaring ceiling has raked beams, and a double-sided brick fireplace serves as a room divider between the dining area and living room. We painted the ceiling and walls a warm white and covered the fireplace with polished plaster and limestone.

Transforming the kitchen into the social hub of the home is the monolithic island bench, comprising stacked, chunky planes of limestone atop a honeycomb-like travertine base. The offset slabs provide a tiered benchtop for cooking and sitting. Polished brass cladding the rangehood and joinery returns infuses the kitchen with a subtle shimmer.

Our client loves to invest in distinctive, high-quality furniture and understands that the right combination of pieces can enhance the mood and enjoyment of a space. This is showcased in the dining area, where the gentle angles of the Australian-designed Prince dining table from Grazia & Co contrast with the sleek curves of the MR Side Chairs by Mies van der Rohe. The steel chairs are upholstered in brown leather, laced at the back. Aqua Creations' Stand By pendant light is enveloped with gathered, crushed silk, creating a sculptural diffusion of light. These textile elements play beautifully with the custom wicker screen that serves as a banister. Handmade by third-generation Melbourne weavers Camberwell Cane, the screen descends to the lower level and filters natural light to the staircase.

Downstairs, we transformed the storage area into a large informal lounge and bar area, opening some of the walls and creating flow to outside. A drawn curtain fosters a more intimate atmosphere in the wine-tasting area, where the custom table has a softly curved limestone tabletop, and the timber shelving is a refined rendition of vernacular speed rails.

Our client is passionate about their Italian heritage, manifest in their deep love for cooking and enjoying life. Their beach house is now a place for the family to do that. It's a relaxing, hospitable retreat where they can spend time together, sharing good food and wine.

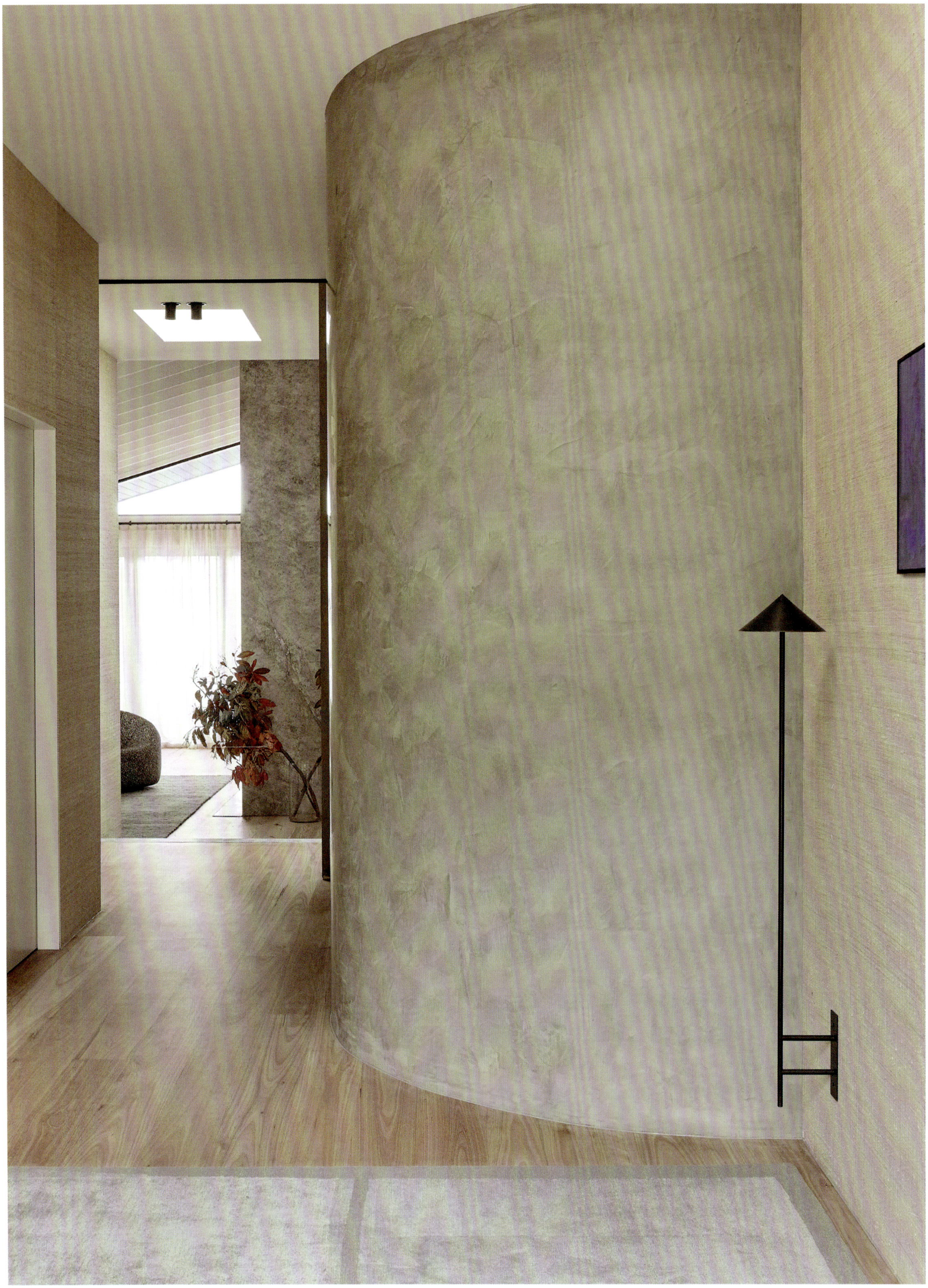

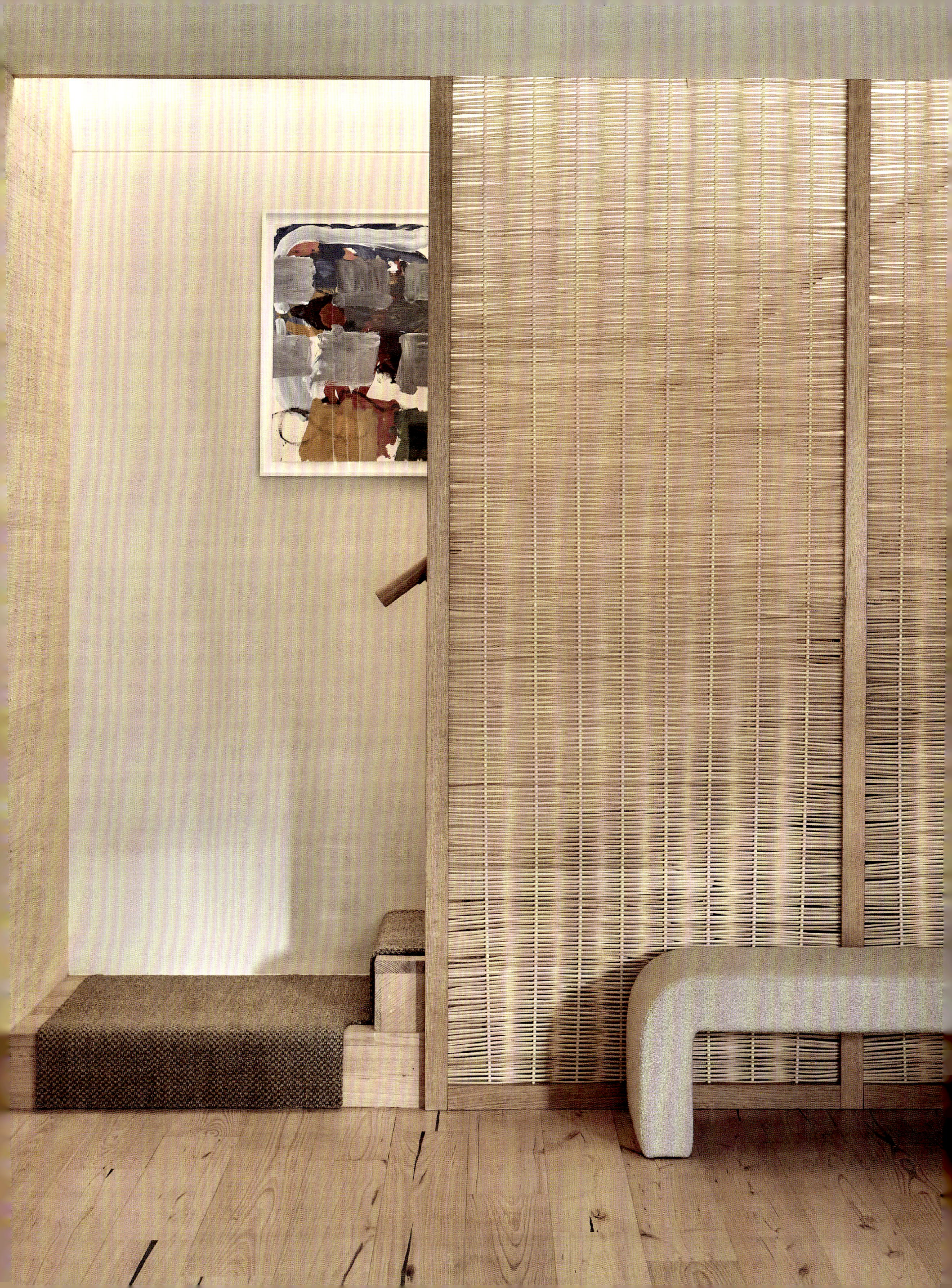

TEXTILE

SORRENTO HOUSE.

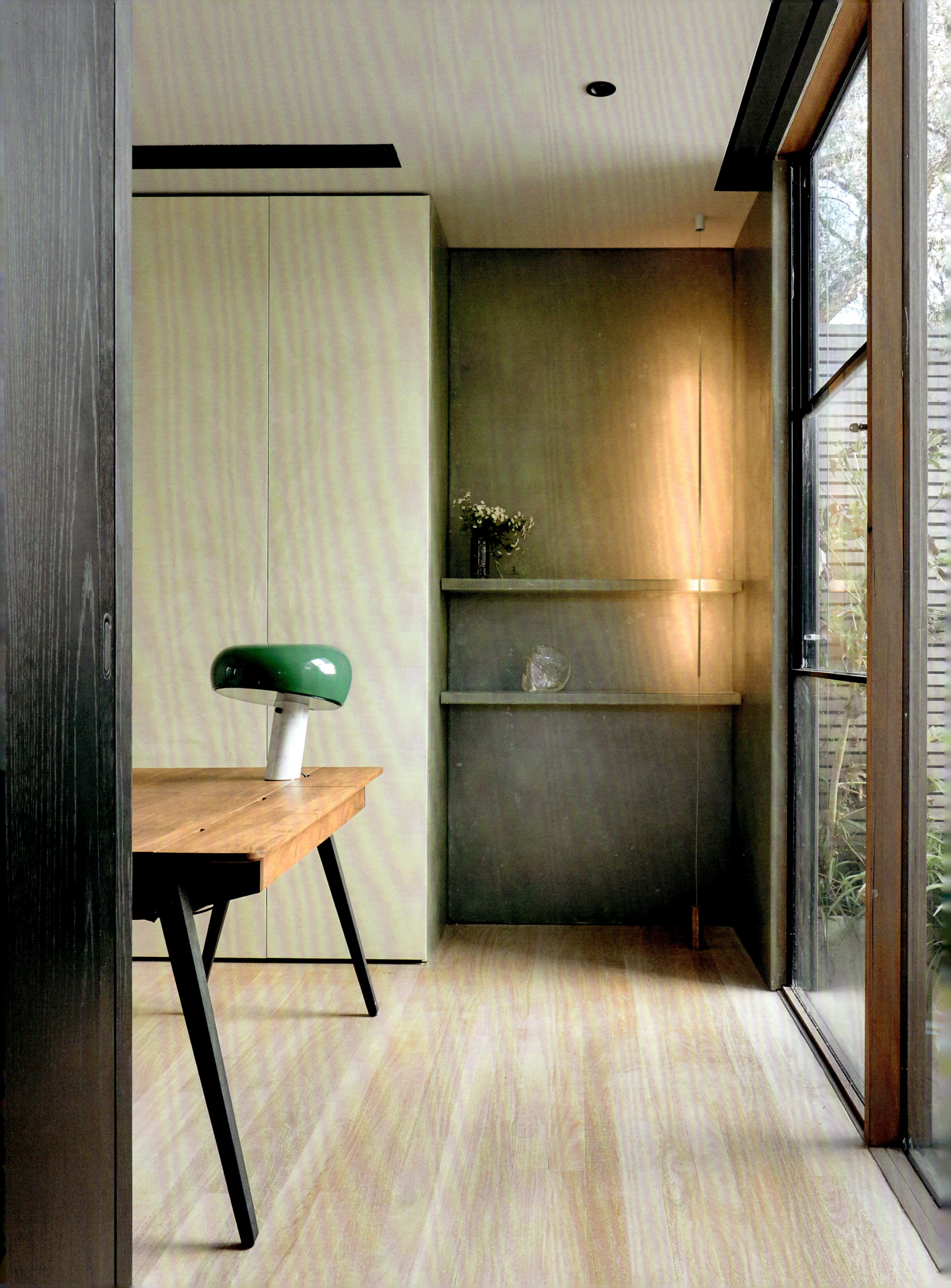

TEXTILE

Burnley House.

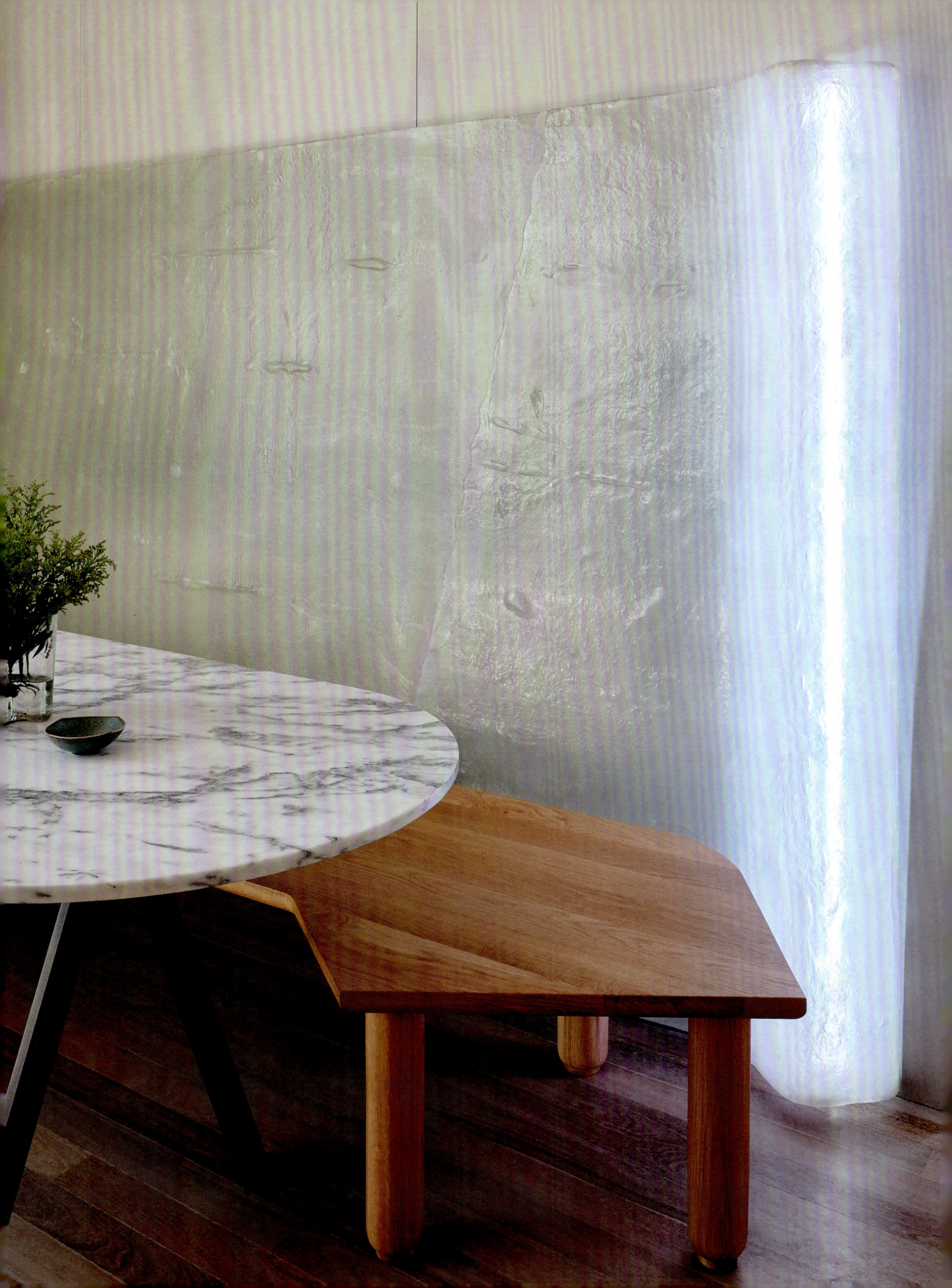

Our client had admired our work for some time and was inspired by our Fitzroy House project. When he bought a three-storey townhouse in Burnley, Melbourne, he gave us freedom to use artisanal, out-of-the-ordinary materials. I had long been interested in using fibreglass and saw this project as a wonderful opportunity to explore the material, as well as commissioning significant pieces from artists.

The existing interior felt cold, dark and oppressive, with grey rendered panels on the walls. We wanted to unify and brighten rooms and create a softly luminous sanctuary. Fibreglass is a product I've always prized. German-born American sculptor Eva Hesse did pioneering work in fibreglass and plastic in the 1960s, including *Repetition Nineteen III*, a series of nineteen vessels made of polyester and fibreglass resin. British artist Rachel Whiteread also used fibreglass, but on a much larger scale. Inspired by the beauty of their work, we commissioned Melbourne-based artist Brenton Angel, a jewellery maker who also crafts large objects in handcast fibreglass and neon. He made a series of handcast fibreglass interventions that imbue the townhouse with subtle shifts in colour and materiality and link spaces together.

In the dining area, a fibreglass panel along the back wall gently curves to coil around a neon tube at one end. The imperfectness of the fibreglass is what makes it so lovely. It has a duality of softness and thickness, appearing bubbled in places. We designed the solid oak seat with an angle at one end to mimic the panel and curve around the table. To create more interest and light through the space, we took out a bank of cupboards dividing the kitchen and living area and replaced it with perforated aluminium shelves overhead.

In the living room, a gently folded fibreglass panel is more delicate, translucent and lithe. Its textured surface catches the light, as does the velvety sheen of the polished plaster above the fireplace. The glacial, milky soft green of the panels and polished plaster draw in the hues of the terrace garden designed by Eckersley Garden Architecture. Luxurious oceanic blue tones in the Maralunga sofa from Cassina, GUM armchair by Christophe Delcourt and rug from Baxter add another layer and depth.

Upstairs, we exploited the magic of feature lighting for the fibreglass joinery in the study. An elongated neon tube on a thread-like brass fixture tethered to the floor and ceiling casts a brilliant golden glow on the fibreglass and the plaster wall.

Previously a rumpus room, the ground floor opens to a sanctuary-like courtyard that is also a three-storey lightwell. It was the perfect space to create a private and relaxing retreat for the main bedroom, with ensuite and walk-in robe, as well as a wine bar and media room. We developed a muted, moody and textural palette for the carpet and furnishings, and the densely mottled fibre cement sheet walls usher a sense of quietness. In contrast to the subdued nature of the room, an artwork by Canberra-based artist Hannah Quinlivan brings together LED light and wire in an organic, free-flowing form. We suggested our client visit one of her exhibitions and he fell in love with that work.

There's alchemy at work when the design process sparks curiosity for both us and our clients. It's a joy when this leads to new artistic approaches to interior design. Experimenting with fibreglass added elements of intrigue to this townhouse while creating a beautiful, luminous sanctuary.

This page: Sculptor Brenton Angel crafted the handmade panel that forms a backdrop to our custom oak bench – the two elements gently folding in parallel at the end.

Opposite: Polished plaster draws in the hues of the terrace garden, while the GUM armchair by Christophe Delcourt and rug from Baxter feature immersive oceanic blue tones.

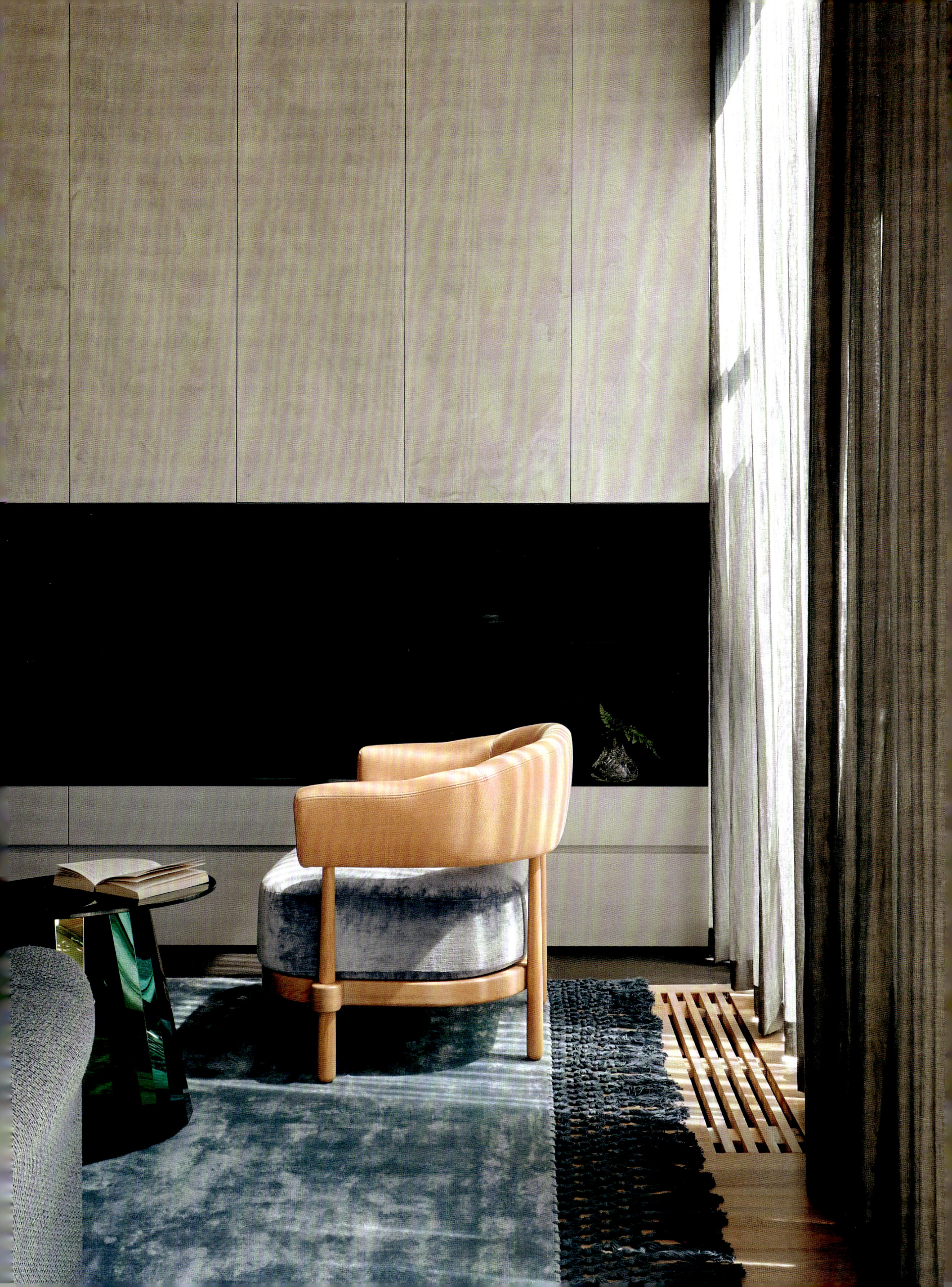

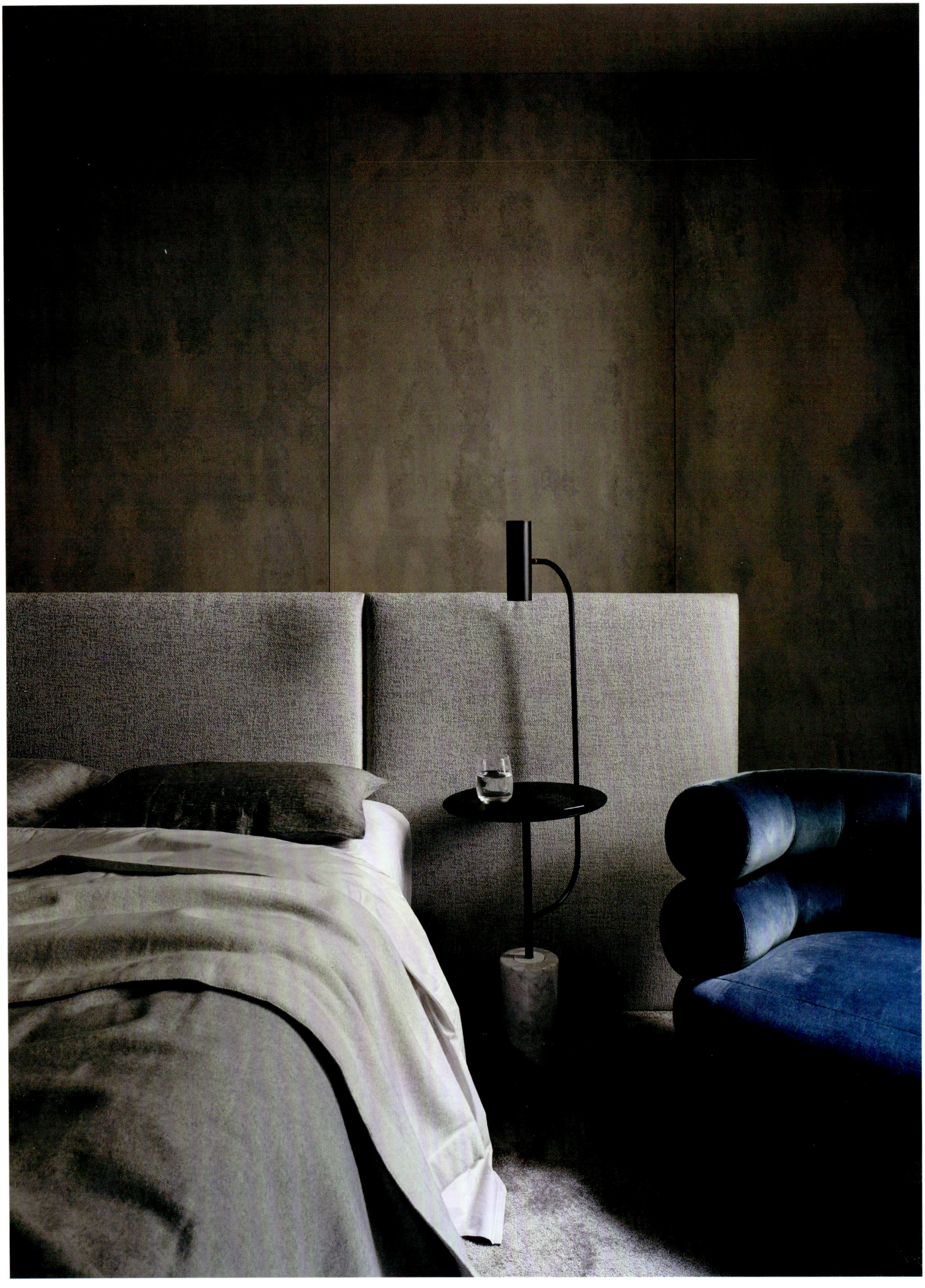

BURNLEY HOUSE.

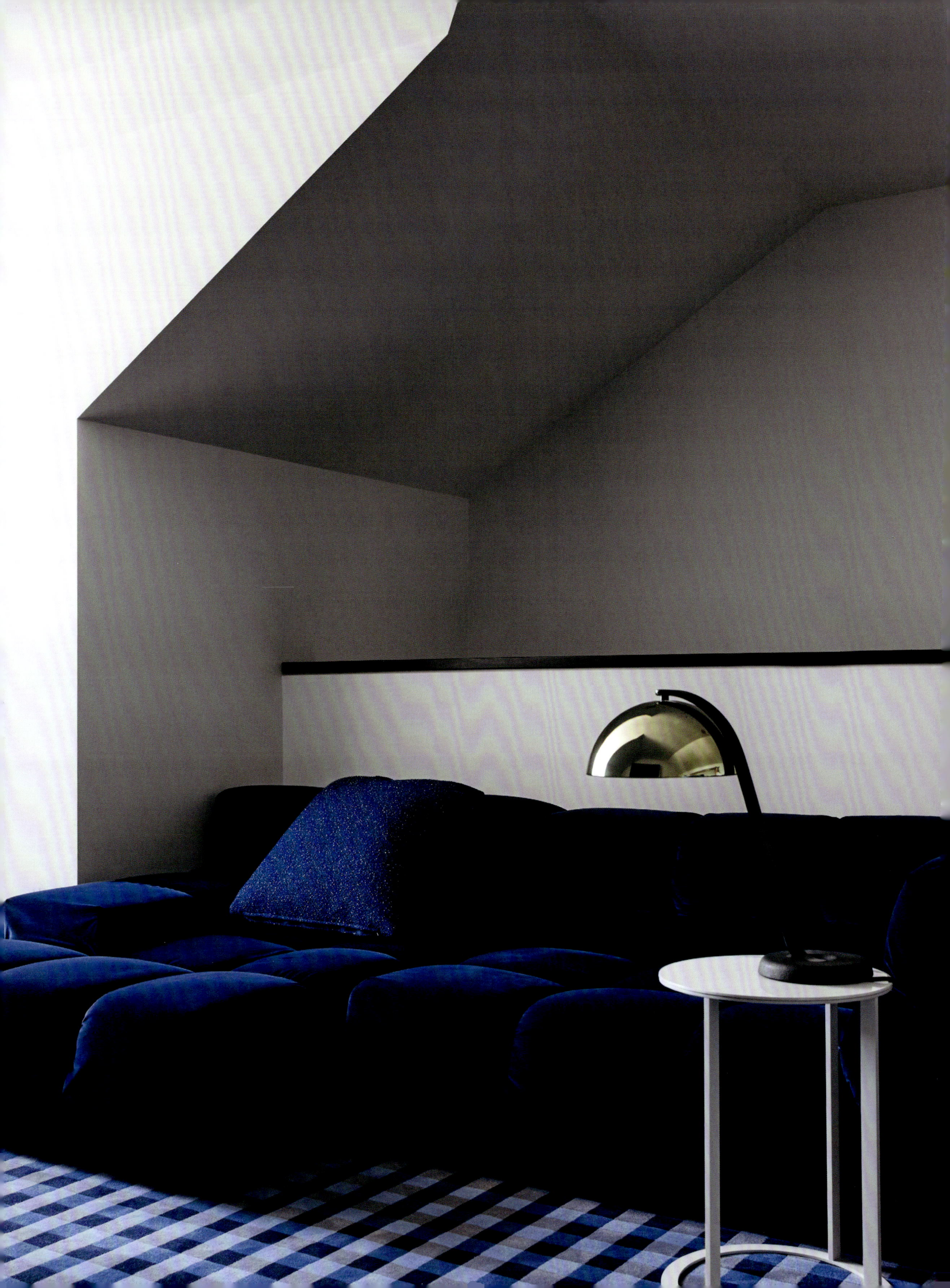

TEXTILE

Paddington
Terrace.

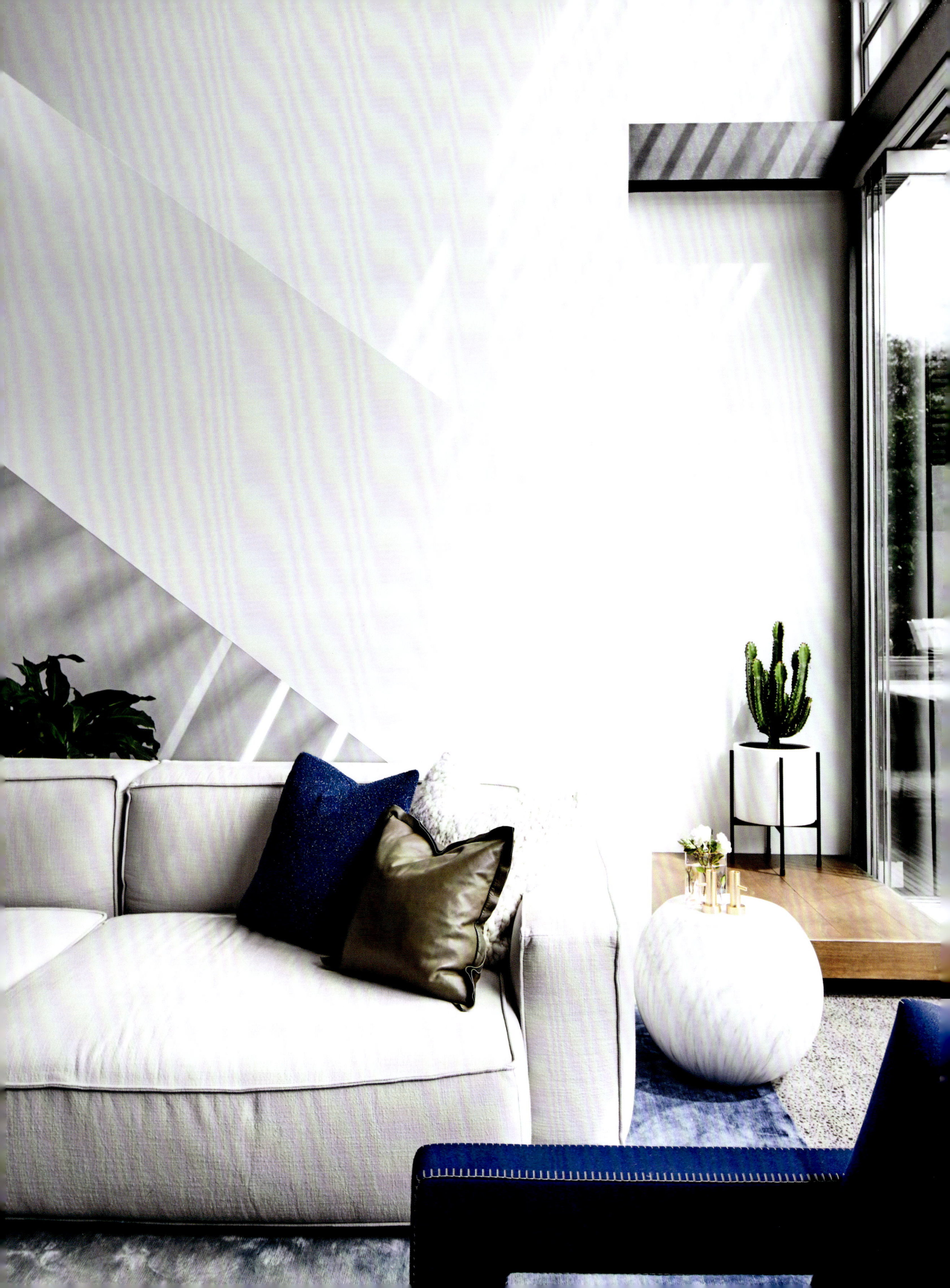

The owners of this grand Victorian terrace are young professionals with a vibrant and eclectic taste for modern design. Their home, which rambles over four levels, is a hub for generous hospitality, with a rear extension designed to create a welcoming space for convivial gatherings. This project offered a unique chance to showcase the owners' modern aesthetic and love of entertaining. It is a home of contrasts, respecting the original but amping up the mood with a fizzing, contemporary vibe.

The traditional rooms at the front of the house have been opened to create an airy yet cosy formal living room; the bend of the window arch repeats in the soft curve of the furniture. Open shelves either side of the marble-lined fireplace create a stylish library that is home to a curated collection of graphic novels. From here, the floorplan flows into the main living and entertaining area at the rear, where a finely wrought steel balustrade emphasises the sense of scale in the double-height space, maintaining the expansive feeling of light and brightness.

To counter the effect of a formerly restrained, somewhat masculine palette, the existing joinery was reworked, in keeping with our aim of sustainability and re-use of available materials. Cabinetry was re-lined and overlaid with new finishes to bring a warmer aesthetic. Natural materials were selected for their texture, with an emphasis on light tones and bursts of colour, introducing individuality and a playful energy at the core of the home.

A considered material palette of brass, blackened steel, painted oak and natural stone has created a lively, tactile interior with patterns and finishes that are disparate yet congenial. This is an intentional contrast with the conservative character of the original house. Richly coloured velvets and storytelling rugs draw the eye; saddle stitched chairs, knotted cushions and faux fur add a sense of exuberance to an elegant setting. Though each space within the home platforms its own quirks and eccentricities, there is a deliberate and consistent design narrative throughout, creating a delightful feeling of fun and relaxation.

Driving the sense of fun in this sociable abode is the clients' love of colour and covetable furniture from the 1960s. There is confidence and boldness in the selection of iconic pieces of furniture, upholstered in bright colours and daring fabrics. There is playfulness in over-scaled elements, and whimsy in the sculptural light fittings, a humorous nod to the home's original elaborate pendant lights. The result is a distinctive and welcoming residence that reflects the style, warmth and personality of its creative occupants.

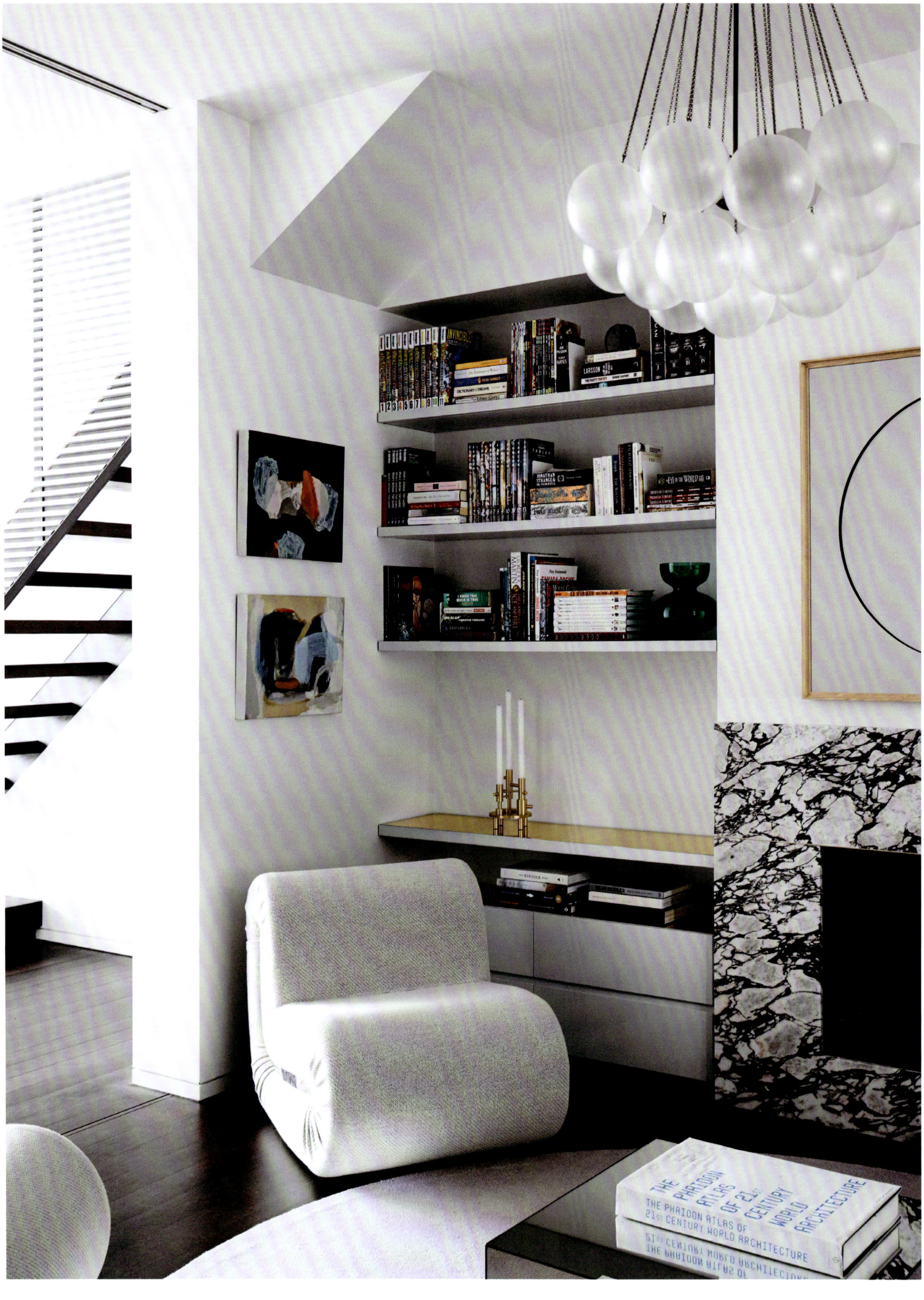
THE PHAIDON ATLAS OF 21st CENTURY WORLD ARCHITECTURE

PADDINGTON TERRACE.

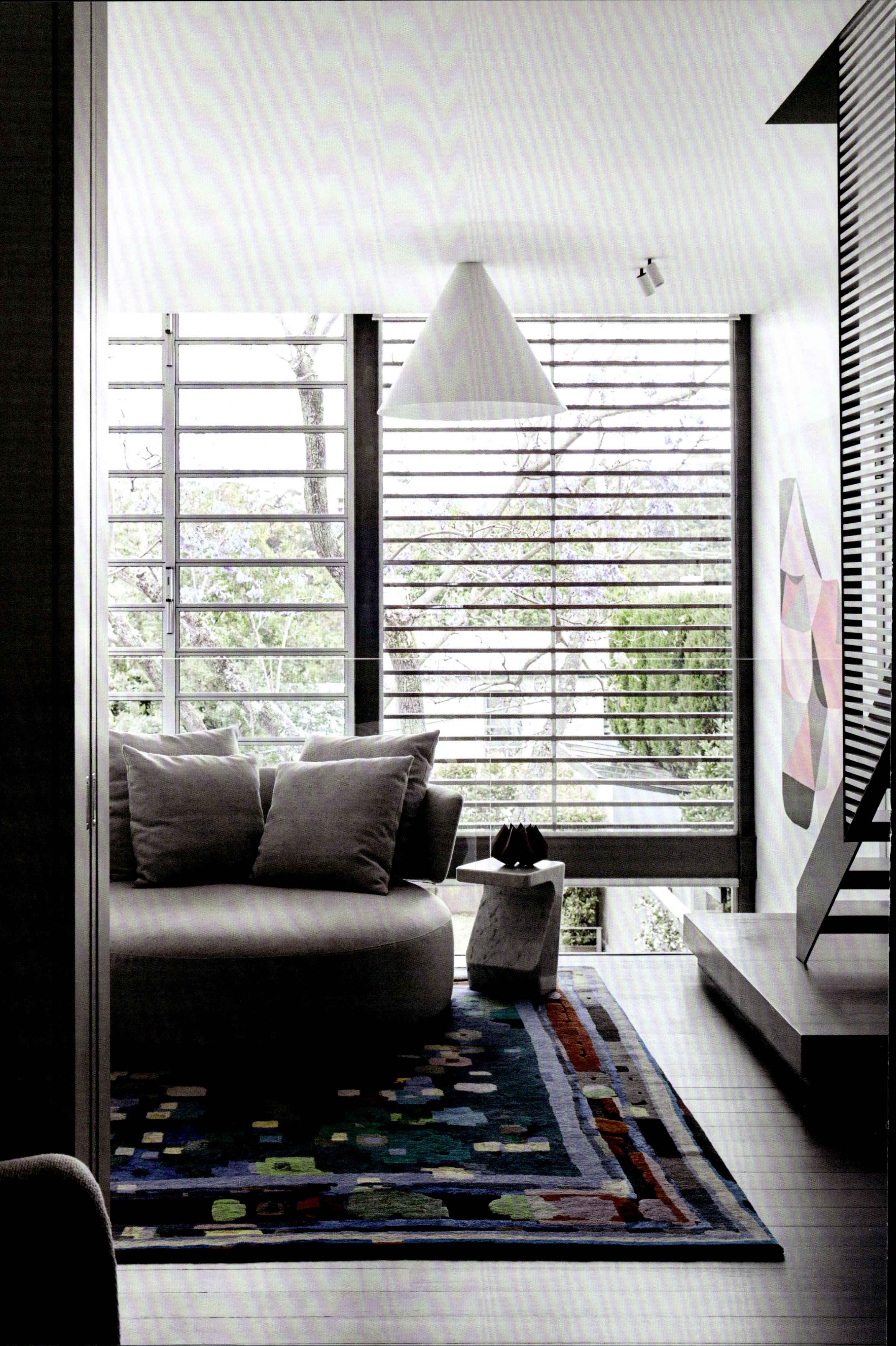

Opposite: The landing at the top of the stairs is cosy, furnished with a Robyn Cosgrove rug, Maxalto love seat, marble side table and cone light by Claesson Koivisto Rune. Beyond the stairs is David Band's painting *Dancing* (2008).

This page: The Baxter Nepal armchair, designed by Paola Navone, sits in the corner of the main bedroom, which looks out to a large jacaranda tree.

TEXTILE

KILN, ACE HOTEL SYDNEY

Perched on the 18th floor of Ace Hotel Sydney, Kiln is a unique and evocative expression of Australia, brought to life through a patchwork of influences and alchemy of materials.

Our brief for the rooftop restaurant was to create an Australian version of Ace Hotel, as this would be the first in the Southern Hemisphere. In response, we stitched together a narrative of place by layering different influences and materials. Textiles, metal, bricks and ceramics reflect the history of Surry Hills and the site – first as a former warehouse that housed one of Australia's oldest known kilns, and later as a garment factory. Colours and textures capture the Sydney landscape, and a palette of Australian materials celebrates our local environment. There are also subtle influences that nod to Ace Hotel's American origins, including the rich history of patchwork, inspired by the incredible exhibition *Fabric of a Nation: American Quilt Stories* that I witnessed at the Museum of Contemporary Art in Los Angeles.

I pictured the entry to Kiln as a dramatic reveal. From the lift lobby, a cavernous passageway with off-form concrete walls, evocative of rammed earth and inspired by the sandstone cliffs at Bondi, draws guests toward the restaurant. The khaki green of the polished plaster ceiling harks back to the 1970s, while the beautiful Australian stones underfoot form a collage of colours and textures. As the restaurant and bar unfolds, timber-framed windows offer panoramic views of Sydney and retractable glass ceilings showcase the colour of the sky.

To pay homage to the seamstresses who once worked in the building, we developed a bespoke textile that wraps around the walls of the terrace. During construction, the builder salvaged metal and brick from the site; this was then crushed and made into pigments. We worked with Spacecraft Studio to create the textiles, splattering them with coloured waste pigments. It has a relaxed, imperfect quality, like a drop sheet that might have been found on the studio floor of American expressionist painter Joan Mitchell.

We introduced metal throughout Kiln as a nod to the notorious razor gangs that once dominated the area. Aluminium joinery has a soft reflectiveness behind the bars, and aluminium panels sprayed with brass filings screen the glass-washing area and enclose the private dining room. Chunky brass countertops on the main bar nod to the tradition of brass in Australian pubs and sit alongside Australian stone, including Harlequin Granite with its sprays of green, red and gold.

As part of my research for Kiln, I spent time in the United States on a study tour of American design. I visited the Noguchi Museum in New York, and Frank Lloyd Wright's Hollyhock House and Rudolph Schindler's eponymous house in Los Angeles. I was taken with the forms and honesty of materials and wanted to bring these American influences into the timber furniture. The chunky, geometric and asymmetric forms take their cues from Noguchi, Wright and Schindler, as well as Donald Judd. The patchwork fabrics tie back to the garment industry and the memorable *Fabric of a Nation* exhibition. We left the edges raw and unfinished, with the trailing threads slightly undone as an expression of the making.

An Yves Klein Blue wall breaks up the tonality of the space and is a saturated take on the blue Sydney sky. It introduces a vivid punch of colour, as it does in Melbourne Penthouse. We worked on several projects at the same time as Kiln – the Penthouse, Ottawa House, Hill House and St. Ali & The Queen. Though each is different, one project often influences another, creating a thread that weaves through our work as we explore materials and their meaning.

MATERIALS LIBRARY

1 Dulux 'Russet Tan' lacquer panel
2 Patinated copper
3 Polished plaster
4 Travertine Rosso
5 Beauford sandstone
6 Breccia Pernice marble
7 Brushed bronze
8 Classic Tumbled travertine
9 Balmoral Green granite
10 Tugela Apple Green marble
11 Polished plaster
12 Light Classic travertine

1   Blackened Monterey Cypress
2   Calacatta Viola marble
3   Extra Light Classic travertine
4   Aubergine leather
5   Verde Bardini granite
6   Venetian glass brick
7   Magente stone
8   Oak Solid timber
9   Travertine Litzo
10   Brushed brass
11   Vert D'estours marble
12   Polished plaster

MATERIALS LIBRARY

1	Flamed bluestone
2	Travertine Zena
3	Balmoral Green granite
4	'Everglade' lacquer panel
5	Calacatta Vagli marble
6	Amber opal resin
7	'Tamed Texan' lacquer panel
8	Aluminum and brass
9	Glazed lava stone
10	Blue Opal resin
11	Hand-worked aluminum
12	Ocean Blue travertine
13	Mint Opal resin

1   Polished brass
2   Aquarzo Quartzite
3   Norwegian Rose stone
4   Reclaimed Oregon Pine
5   Travertine Zina
6   Cast bronze joinery handle
7   'Amazon Depths' high gloss lacquer panel
8   'Seafoam' glazed wall tiles

MATERIALS LIBRARY

1   Pearl grey lacquer panel
2   Azure Blue Fringes rug
3   Calacatta Vagli marble
4   Venetian glass brick
5   Oak timber
6   Fiberglass sheet
7   Grey pebble lacquer panel

MATERIALS LIBRARY

1	Balmoral Green granite	9	Amber Opal resin
2	Harlequin granite	10	Custom Belgian linen hand-painted with salvaged waste material pigment
3	Australian Blackbutt timber		
4	Australian Oak timber	11	Australian Stringybark timber
5	Austral Coffee granite	12	Australian Huon pine
6	Polished plaster	13	Austral Juniper granite
7	Blue Opal granite	14	Calca Red granite
8	Aluminum and brass	15	Cork cladding

MATERIALS LIBRARY

PROJECT CREDITS

p. 1
Project: Sorrento House
Photography: Dave Kulesza

pp. 4–5
Project: River House
Photography: Sharyn Cairns
Artwork: (left, on coffee table) sculpture by Michael Staniak, (above fireplace) *Fortunes Can Change* (2022) by Seth Birchall

pp. 8–9
Project: Melbourne Penthouse
Photography: Sharyn Cairns
Artwork: (top shelf) woven basket from Pan After; (middle shelf, left to right) *013 vessel* by Jade Paton from Pan After, *172* (2021) artwork by Jake Walker from Station; (bottom shelf) Hexx table lamp by Diesel with Foscarni Living, organic gourd basket, cork candle from Tom Dixon and organic gourd basket from Pan After.

INTRODUCTION

p. 10
Photography: Sharyn Cairns
Artwork: Kate Tucker from Daine Singer

pp. 12–13
Sketches and photo by Fiona Lynch

pp. 14–15
Photography: Sean Fennessy

pp. 16–17
Photography: Tom Ross
Artwork: Floral photographic artwork by Jacopo Moschin

pp. 19
Photography: Pablo Veiga
Artwork: (left to right, top to bottom) *Dolly on Country* (2022) by Kaylene Whiskey; *Australian Shawl* (2017) by The Huxleys; *YOU'LL NEVER find another WOMAN Like ME* (2018) by Nell; *Carol Jerrems, Mozart St* by Rennie Ellis (1970); *I made a camera* (2003) by Tracey Moffatt; *No Title 1 (Series with 2 lithographs)* (2023) by Mithu Sen; *The Siblings (Kumbakarna)* by Val Wens; *Kylie Arranged: Posing Birthday Version* by Kathy Temin; *Moana Lisa (after da Vinci)* by Yuki Kihara (2021); *Shaken up* by Destiny Deacon; *Passage* (2017) by Tracey Moffatt.

STONE

Somerville House
Architect: Pandolfini Architects
Builder: IDB Developments
Photography: Pablo Veiga

River House
Architect: Marcus Martin (original, 1930); Fiona Lynch Office (renovation and extension)
Builder: Macrobuild
Photography: Sharyn Cairns
Artwork: (adjacent to staircase) painting by Angus White (p. 36); wooden charred Eucalyptus vessel by Makiko Ryujin from Sophie Gannon Gallery (p. 41); (on island bench) metal sculpture *Wazon Aluminiowy* by Brud Studio from Oigall Projects, (back bench vase) *Table Slip Vase* by Anna Varendorff from Oigall Projects (pp. 42–3); (on top shelf) sculpture by Angus White, (on second, third and bottom shelves) sculptures all by Kenya Peterson, (painting on third shelf) Kate Tucker from Daine Singer (p. 45).

Auburn Residence
Architect: Alistair Knox (original), Carr
Builder: Beaton Projects
Photography: Sharyn Cairns
Artwork: (on kitchen bench) Hehe Stool 002 from Pan After (pp. 50–1 & 52–3); (top left) sculpture by Angus White, (middle shelf, left) sculpture by Mark Douglass, (bottom right) *Red Moon* sculpture by Hiromi Tango, (on floor) *Actual Virtual 18* sculpture by Alex Seton from Sullivan + Strumpf (p. 55).

Ottawa House
Architect: Fiona Lynch Office
Photography: Sean Fennessy
Artwork: painting by Sean Bailey from Daine Singer (p. 60); *Untitled 2020* by Consuelo Cavaniglia from Station Gallery (p. 70).

Rose Bay House
Photography: Pablo Veiga
Artwork: painting by Steve Tyerman (p. 81).

St Kilda Apartment
Architect: Fiona Lynch Office
Photography: Tom Ross

GIANT STEPS
Architect: Fiona Lynch Office
Builder: EMAC Constructions
Photography: Sharyn Cairns
Artwork: (bottom left) wooden charred vessel by Makiko Ryujin from Sophie Gannon Gallery (p. 94).

METAL

Melbourne Penthouse
Architect: Fiona Lynch Office
Builder: COMB Construction
Photography: Sharyn Cairns
Artwork: (second shelf from top and on back bench) glass objects by Mark Douglass, (third shelf from top) *Vessel 020* by Jade Paton from Pan After (p. 100); *Telephone Wire Bowl* from Pan After (p. 103); (tall vase on left) *Keyhole Vase* (2022) by Jake Walker from Station Gallery, (far right) *171* (2021) by Jake Walker (p. 104); (on wall) *Underland* (2020) by Adam Lee, DC1514 Bookshelf (cast-bronze) by Vincenzo De Cotiis, (bottom left) Pli side table high by Classi Con, (bottom right) custom floor sculpture by Brodie Neill, (p. 106–7); (centre on bench) *The Loafers* (2018) by Patricia Piccinini (pp. 108–9).

Fitzroy House
Photography: Sharyn Cairns
Artwork: (bottom image) artist of work unknown, She Chair by Tracey Deep (p. 123); *When One Direction Becomes All Directions (Green over grey)* by David Thomas (p. 124); photograph by Tim Hillier (p. 125).

Surry Hills House
Photography: Sean Fennessy

LEE MATHEWS
Photography: Cieran Murphy

WOOD

Hill House
Architect: Fiona Lynch Office
Photography: Sharyn Cairns (pp. 144, 150, 152–3, p. 155, 157, two right images on 158, 159); Pablo Veiga (pp. 146, 154, 156, left image on 158).
Artwork: painting by Sally Ross (p. 146); (left) *Dreaming in Purple Pyjamas* (diptych) (2022) by Rhett D'Costa, (right, top and bottom) paintings by Seth Birchall (p. 148–9); (centre) white sculpture by Kenya Peterson (p. 152–3); artwork by Chris Pennings from Fini Frames, (on table) ceramic sculpture by Fiona Lynch Office (p. 154); Block custom-designed corner side table by Fiona Lynch Office for Melbourne Design Week 2022 (p. 156); (far left) blue vase by Jade Paton Ceramics from Pan After (p. 157); (bottom left) painting by Fiona Lynch, (bottom right) brass vessel by Michael Gittings (p. 158); (top shelf) work by unknown artist, (second shelf) scorched timber vessel by Makiko Ryujin; (bottom shelf left) Huseyin Sami wire sculpture, (bottom shelf right) artwork by Anie Nheu (p. 159).

South Yarra House
Architect: Fiona Lynch Office
Builder: COMB Construction
Photography: Sharyn Cairns
Artwork: three artworks on wall and one on shelf by unknown artists (p. 160); (above fireplace) artwork by eX de Medici (pp. 164–5), photograph on wall by Rosemary Laing (p. 166).

Mosaic Garden House
Architect: Alistair Knox (original architect), Carr
Builder: Russell Haythorne
Photography: Tess Kelly
Artwork: (on cabinet door) artwork by Sean Bailey (p. 168); glass houses by Luna Ryan (pp. 170–1); (on wall) *Green Study* by Angus White, (on table) sculpture by Mark Douglass (p. 172); artwork by Sean Bailey (p. 174); object on desk by 101 Copenhagen (p. 175); (far left wall) basket works by Paula Savage, (centre) artwork by Seth Birchall, (far right) wire sculpture by Fiona Lynch Office (pp. 176–7); mosaic chair by Margot Knox (p. 179).

Elsternwick House
Photography: Sharyn Cairns
Artwork: *Divided by strychnine* (2015) by Mike Parr from Anna Schwartz Gallery (pp. 182–3)

ST. ALI & THE QUEEN
Architect: Fiona Lynch Office
Builder: EMAC Constructions
Photography: Tom Blachford

80 COLLINS
Architect: Universal Design Studio
Photography: Sean Fennessy
Artwork: bowls shaped by Charles Sandford and charred by Shou Sugi Ban artist Makiko

TEXTILE

Grace Park Residence
Photography: Tess Kelly (pp. 196, 198, 202, 205); Dave Kulesza (pp. 200–1, 203, 204).
Artwork: Floral photographic artwork by Jacopo Moschin (pp. 196 & 198); (left to right on bench) Barbican lamp by Fiona Lynch Office x Ross Thompson & Volker Haug, scorched timber vessel by Makiko Ryujin, *Sol* sculptural vase by New Volumes (pp. 200–1).

Sorrento House
Architect: Fiona Lynch Office
Photography: Dave Kulesza
Artwork: (far left) artwork by unknown artist (p. 208); *Untitled* (2019) by Jake Walker (p. 213).

Burnley House
Builder: RAD Construction
Landscaping: Eckersley Garden Architecture
Photography: Amelia Stanwix
Artwork: *Holding Pattern* (2017) by Hannah Quinlivan from Flinders Lane Gallery (p. 223).

Paddington Terrace
Builder: Scott Howard
Photography: Sharyn Cairns
Artwork: (left, top and bottom) artworks by Michael Cusack (p. 228); (on wall) *Dancing* (2008) by David Band (p. 230).

KILN, ACE HOTEL SYDNEY
Architect: Bates Smart
Builder: Hickory
Photography: Pablo Veiga

MATERIALS LIBRARY

pp. 234–39
Photography: Sharyn Cairns

ENDMATTER

pp. 242–3
Photography: Pablo Veiga
Artwork: see p. 19 credit

pp. 246–7
Photography: Sharyn Cairns
Artwork: (far left) artwork by Jo Davenport

G'day from W.A.
Kings Park
YOU'LL NEVER find another WoMAN Like ME...

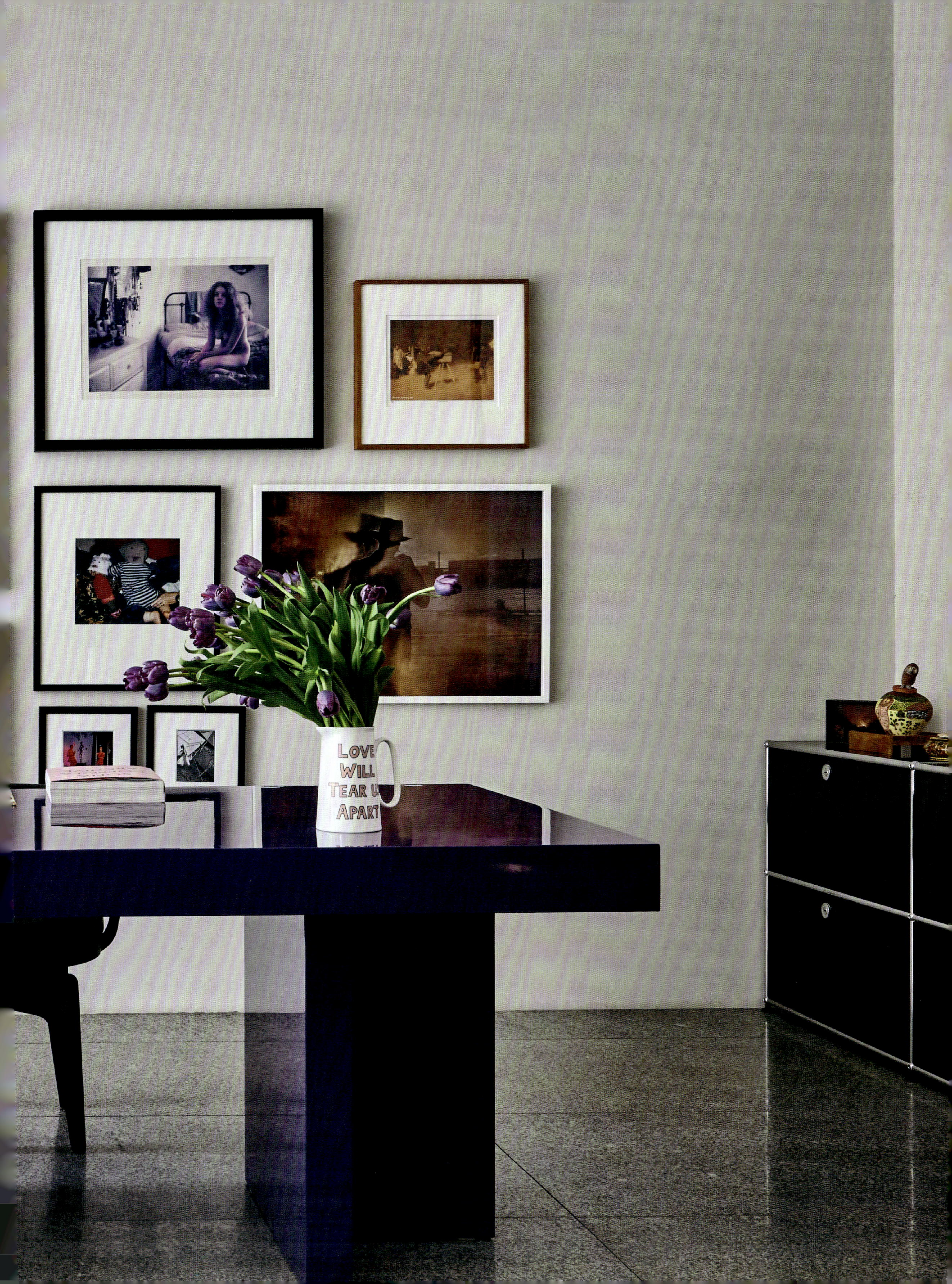
LOVE
WILL
TEAR U
APART

ACKNOWLEDGEMENTS

Sharing my love of materials and the way we have used them across our projects has been a wonderful way to review our studio's work and approach to design. My early childhood memories of following Dad around the farm have very much influenced my passion to experiment. It was those friendships and the conversations that my dad had with local tradespeople that I listened to and learned so much from.

From the earliest days of starting my studio I have understood the importance of forming good relationships. Building is complex, and many times I have called one of our talented craftspeople to discuss how to solve a problem. I would like to thank Vic Adamo, Terry Martin and Scott Burchill.

To my wonderful clients, I have enjoyed every moment of working with you. Your patronage has enabled my studio to grow and supported young designers entering the industry. Thank you for allowing us to photograph your home and to feature it in this book. Sharyn Carins and Pablo Veiga, I'm grateful to you for so beautifully capturing our work.

Thank you to my talented team. Your passion, diligence and love of design have contributed so much to the success of our finished projects and growth of our studio. Will Hogg, you are the heart of the studio – thank you for your ongoing support.

Special thanks to Natalie King for suggesting I write this book and for introducing me to Kirsten Abbott of Thames & Hudson. Deepest thanks to Rebecca Gross for her assistance in writing the project narratives and capturing our studios' work; Emily O'Neill for creating a design that showcases and celebrates our work; and Kirsten, Lisa Schuurman, Shannon Grey and the team at Thames & Hudson.

Many people have supported me with sound advice and friendship. Thank you, Dan Buultjens, Joe Toscano, Megan Morton, Felicity Rulikowski, Tania Birks, William Smart, William Dangar, Hannah Tribe, Christopher Boots, Simone Le Amon and John Wardle.

To my beautiful family, and especially Steve, I'm grateful to have you by my side. My children Conor, Patrick and Emma, thank you for being wonderful. To my dear brother, Hamish MacKinnon, my gratitude.

To my mum, Margaret, you have always been there for me.

Dad, you were gone too soon, and I wish you could have been here with me on this journey.

BIOGRAPHY

Fiona Lynch studied fine art and trained as an artist before turning to interior design. Her capacity for boundless creativity and her pragmatic preoccupation with constructing space in her canvases inspired a seamless segue between the two disciplines. These practices and characteristics continue to manifest in her built environments today, embodied in a distinct style of spirited minimalism that prioritises bespoke elements and ecological responsibility.

Previously Fiona has worked for various esteemed design practices, including MGT Architects, Bates Smart and John Wardle Architects before co-founding an interior design business, then eventually branching out on her own with Fiona Lynch Office in 2013. The office, comprised of a multidisciplinary team, works across residential, commercial, institutional and hospitality projects.

Fiona's artistic insight guides the studio's aesthetic, combining natural materials and sculptural elements, harmonisation of the raw and refined, and tactical and inventive uses of space. From urban to coastal settings, place strongly informs the design schemes, with material expression and innovation fuelling the process. The result is striking yet inviting interiors punctuated by unique art and objects that exude tactile comfort and warmth.

Named as Interior Designer of the Year 2024 by *Vogue Living*, and hailed as one of the 'true design influencers in the world' in Germany's *Architectural Digest* list of top 200 design influencers, Fiona is also a recipient of multiple design accolades, including the designer of the year at both the IDEA and Belle Coco Republic Interior Design Awards. She is a regular panel participant, podcast guest and industry-awards judge, and her work is widely published in Australia, Europe, North America and beyond.

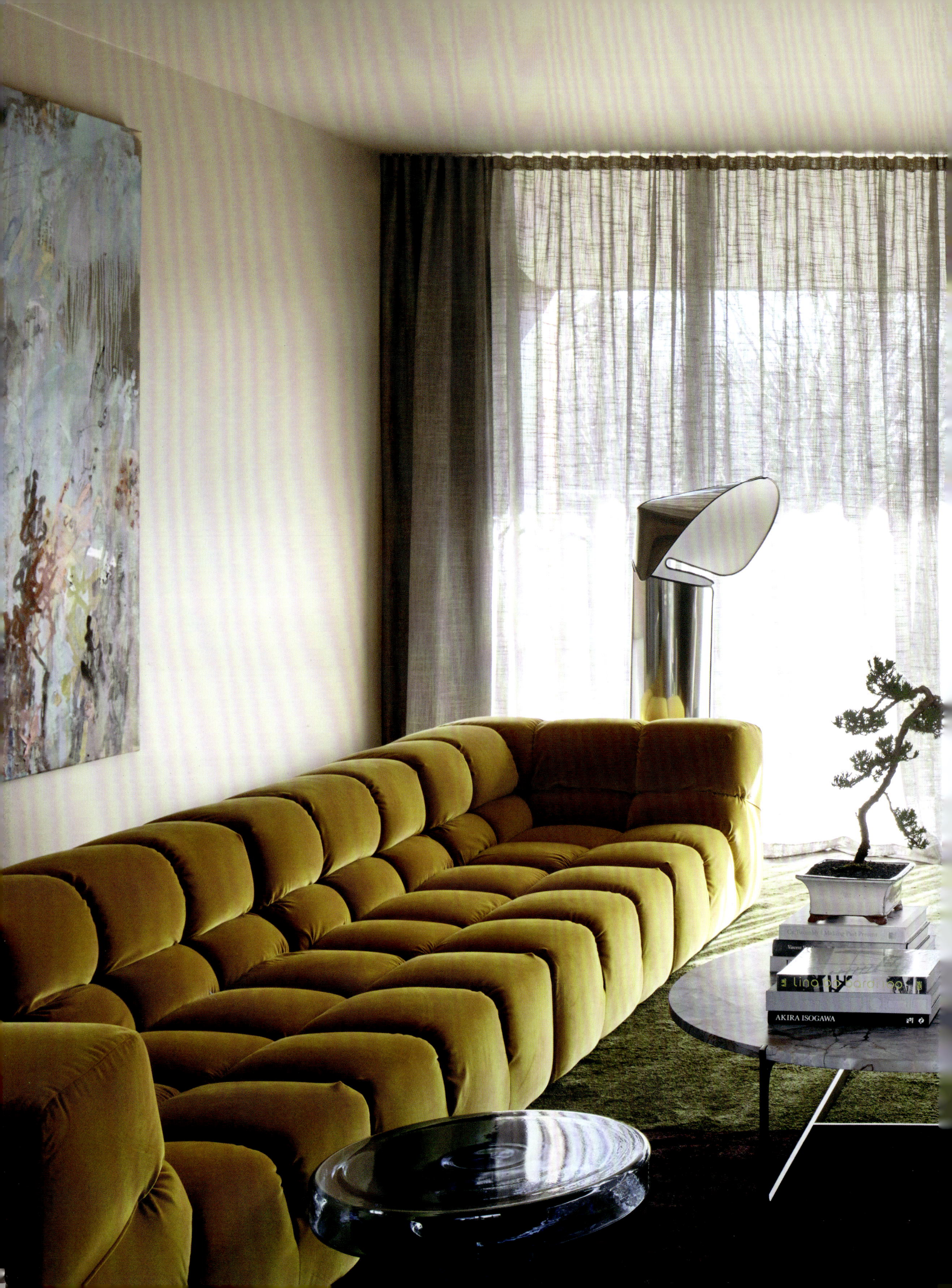
lina
AKIRA ISOGAWA

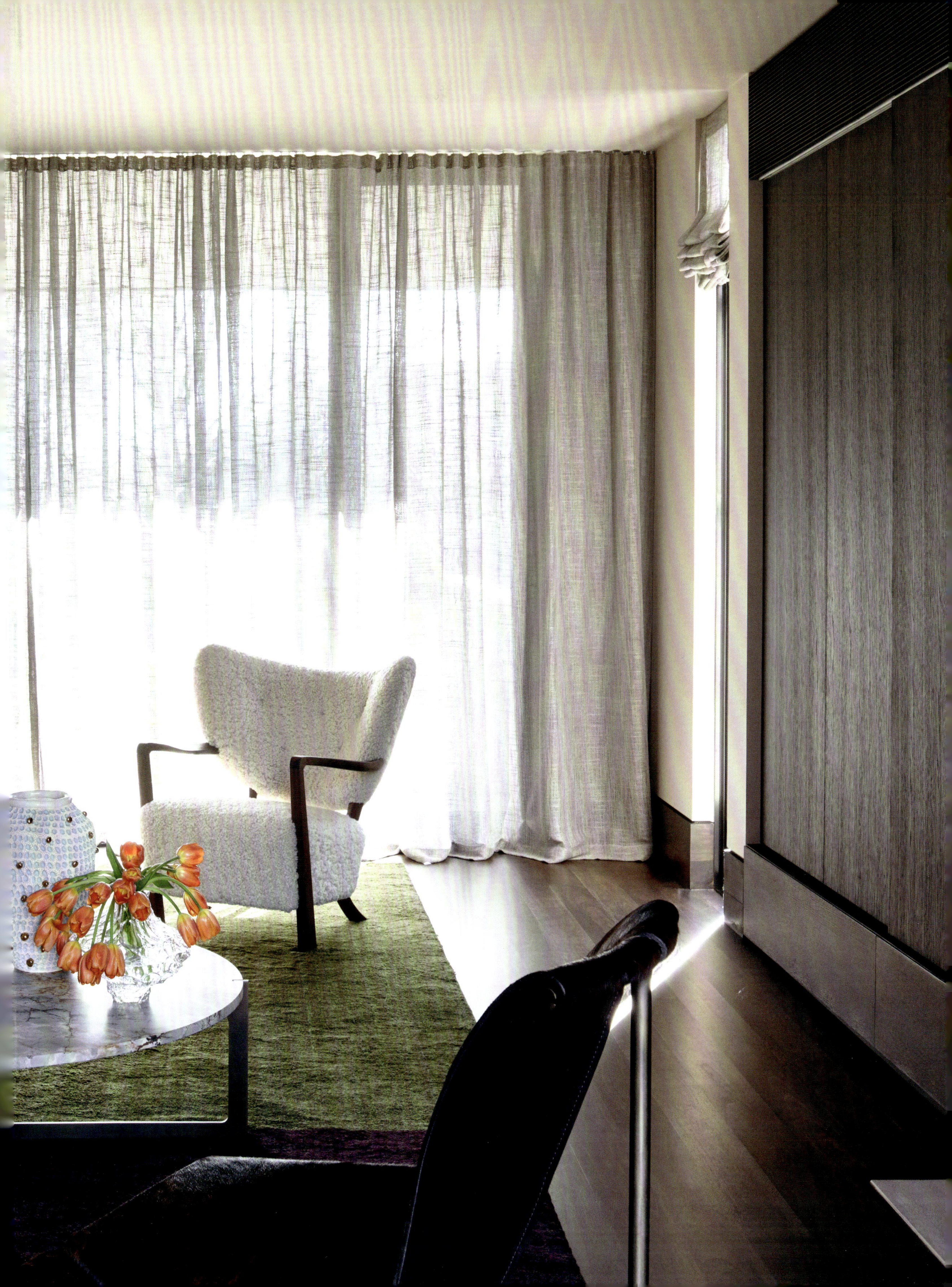

First published in Australia in 2025
by Thames & Hudson Australia
Wurundjeri Country, 132A Gwynne Street
Cremorne, Victoria 3121

First published in the United States of America in 2025
by Thames & Hudson Inc.
500 Fifth Avenue
New York, New York 10110

Material Wonder © Thames & Hudson Australia 2025

Text © 2025 Fiona Lynch Pty Ltd

Copyright in all texts, artworks and images is held by the creators or their representatives, unless otherwise stated.

28 27 26 25   5 4 3 2 1

The moral right of the author has been asserted.

All rights reserved. No part of this publication may be reproduced or transmitted in any form or by any means, electronic or mechanical, including photocopy, recording or any other information storage or retrieval system, without prior permission in writing from the publisher.

ISBN 978-1-760-76483-8
ISBN 978-1-760-76522-4 (U.S. edition)

A catalogue record for this book is available from the National Library of Australia

Library of Congress Control Number 2024953043

Every effort has been made to trace accurate ownership of copyrighted text and visual materials used in this book. Errors or omissions will be corrected in subsequent editions, provided notification is sent to the publisher.

Front and back cover: Somerville House
Photos: Pablo Veiga

Design: Emily O'Neill
Editing: Sally Holdsworth
Printed and bound in China by C&C Offset Printing Co., Ltd

MIX
Paper | Supporting responsible forestry
FSC® C008047

Thames & Hudson Australia wishes to acknowledge that Aboriginal and Torres Strait Islander peoples are the first storytellers of this nation and the Traditional Custodians of the land on which we live and work. We acknowledge their continuing culture and pay respect to Elders past and present.

Be the first to know about our new releases, exclusive content and author events by visiting

thamesandhudson.com.au
thamesandhudson.com
thamesandhudsonusa.com